JOHN PAYNTER

*Sound
&
Structure*

CAMBRIDGE
UNIVERSITY PRESS

Published by the Press Syndicate of the University of Cambridge
The Pitt Building, Trumpington Street, Cambridge CB2 1RP
40 West 20th Street, New York, NY 10011–4211, USA
10 Stamford Road, Oakleigh, Victoria 3166, Australia

First published 1992

Printed in Great Britain at the University Press, Cambridge

British Library cataloguing in publication data
Paynter, John 1931–
   Sound & Structure.
   1. England. Schools. Curriculum. Music
   I. Title
   780.71242

Library of Congress cataloguing in publication data
Paynter, John.
   Sound & Structure / John Paynter.
      p.   cm.
   Includes bibliographical references and index.
   ISBN 0 521 35581 8.–ISBN 0 521 35676 8 (pbk)
   1. School music–Instruction and study. 2. Composition (Music)
I. Title. II. Title: Sound and structure.
MT1.P319   1992
372.87–dc20   91–9650   CIP

ISBN 0 521 35581 8 hardback
ISBN 0 521 35676 8 paperback

∾ indicates item on the cassette (ISBN 0 521 35677 6) which accompanies this book. The
cassette may be ordered through a bookshop or, in cases of difficulty, direct from the
Schoolbooks Marketing Department, Cambridge University Press.

Illustrations on pages 97, 99 (bottom) and 157 by Oxford Illustrators. Those on pages 23,
25, 99 (top), 141 and 160 by Gillian Riley.

Cover design: Gillian Riley
Cover illustration: Tralsi Tralno, Giacomo Balla (1871–1958). By kind permission of
Collection Balla, Rome.

The music in this book was typeset by Henry Brown, Florence, Italy.

Contents

Publisher's acknowledgements

Every effort has been made to reach the holders of copyright material in this book. The publishers would be glad to hear from anyone whose rights they have unknowingly infringed.

p. 37: extract from *Stripsody* by Cathy Berberian © 1966 by C.F. Peters Corporation, New York, reproduced by permission of Peters Edition Ltd. *p. 49:* 'Stones', from Christian Wolff's *Prose collection*, with thanks to Christian Wolff. *p. 56:* the short quotation from Bartók's String Quartet No. 3, reproduced by permission of Universal Edition (London) Ltd. *p. 61:* the short quotation from Stravinsky's *Petrushka* © Copyright 1912 by Edition Russe de Musique. Copyright assigned 1947 to Boosey & Hawkes Inc. for all countries. Revised version © Copyright 1948 by Boosey & Hawkes Inc. *pp. 75–6:* 'Happy birthday to you', words and music by Patty and Mildred Hill © 1935 Summy Birchard Inc. *p. 77:* 'I never saw a purple cow' by Gelett Burgess from *The Burgess nonsense book*, reprinted by permission of Dover Publications, Inc. *p. 77:* 'The camel' and 'Nine miles to the railroad' ('The country is a funny place') by Ogden Nash © 1936 Ogden Nash, reprinted by permission of Curtis Brown Ltd. *pp. 77–8:* Woody Guthrie's words of 'Wild aminul' © 1963 TRO-Essex Music Ltd and © 1962 Ludlow Music Inc. New York, and 'Race you down the mountain' © 1963 Kensington Music Ltd, Suite 207, Plaza, 535 Kings Road, London SW10 0SZ and Folkways Music Publishers, Inc., New York. International Copyright Secured. All Rights Reserved. Used by Permission (Ed. Mus. MARIO AROMANDO S.r.l. – 40, Via Quintiliano / 20138 MILAN, Italy – controls the Sub-Publishing Rights for Italy. © Copyright TRO-Essex Music Ltd.). *p. 88:* 'Siesta of a Hungarian Snake' and 'Chinese Cat', both by Edwin Morgan from his *Collected poems* (1990 edn), reprinted by permission of Carcanet Press Limited. *p. 94:* 1 bar of Stravinsky's *Symphony of Psalms* © Copyright 1931 by Edition Russe de Musique. Copyright assigned 1947 to Boosey & Hawkes Inc. for all countries. Revised version © Copyright 1948 by Boosey & Hawkes Inc. *pp. 101 & 103:* five haiku from *An Introduction to Haiku* by Harold G. Hendersen. Copyright © 1958 by Harold G. Hendersen. Used by permission of Doubleday, a division of Bantam Doubleday Dell Publishing Group, Inc. *p. 103:* 'Rain drums on the pane' © by J.W. Hackett from *The Zen Haiku and Other Zen Poems of J.W. Hackett*. Tokyo: Japan Publications, Inc., 1938. Distributed by Kodansha International, 114 5th Avenue, New York, NY 10011. *p. 110:* 'Grasshopper and snail', from *24 canonic studies* by Yehezkel Braun, edited by Ephraim Marcus, with thanks to Yehezkel Braun. *p. 121:* 'Streepjes' by Guus Janssen, reproduced by permission of Donemus (Amsterdam). *pp. 139 & 140:* the two extracts from Bartók's *For children*, Vol. I, no. 26 and Vol. II, no. 34, © Copyright 1946 by Boosey & Hawkes Inc. By permission of Editio Musica Budapest. *p. 201:* 'Over the rainbow', music by Harold Arlen and words by E.Y. Harburg. Copyright © 1938, 1939 (Renewed 1966, 1967). Metro-Goldwyn-Mayer Inc. All Rights Controlled by Leo Feist, Inc. All Rights of Leo Feist, Inc. Assigned to EMI Catalog Partnership. All Rights Administered by EMI Feist Catalog. International Copyright Secured. Made in USA. All Rights Reserved. *p. 201:* music only of 'As time goes by' (words/music Herman Hupfield) © Redwood Music Ltd. *p. 201:* melody of 'Summertime', words by DuBose Heyward, music by George Gershwin © 1935 Chappell & Co. (Renewed) All Rights Reserved. Used By Permission.

The publishers would like to thank the following for permission to reproduce photographs and illustrations: *p. 47:* The University of York (Javanese gamelan). *p. 50:* F. Baschet (sound-sculptures). *p. 51:* Randi Haukeland ('Ode til lyset'). *p. 98:* Dr John S. Shelton (folded strata). *p. 100:* Aerofilms (delta). *p. 150:* Vera Vasarhelyi (graphic design). *p. 167:* The Horniman Museum, London (aeolian harp). *p. 197:* Mick Sharp (Lundin Links standing stones at Largo Bay, Fife, Scotland).

Preface

This world of imagination is Infinite & Eternal . . .

WILLIAM BLAKE

In 1967–68 Peter Aston and I wrote *Sound and silence*. That book reflected our work in schools and Colleges of Education during the preceding decade, as well as ideas and methods independently developed but later synthesized through our teaching at the Department of Music in the University of York.

On the basis of our experiences and the results we had obtained, we set out to show why we believed creativity was important in the school music curriculum, and why musical composition was as viable for the majority of school students as any of the other imaginative and expressive activities that were so widely and so readily accepted in education.

The techniques we developed paralleled those that had already been successfully demonstrated by visual arts teachers; that is to say, showing that it was possible to offer children a view of artistic endeavour from the inside, valuable for its own sake as well as for the way in which it enhanced understanding of other artists' work. Experience had suggested to us that a creative approach to the study of music could similarly provide a useful basis for appreciating the work of composers in any period of history, not least our own.

The influence of contemporary music was important. The composer Henri Pousseur has since pointed out that it was the avant-garde musical styles of the 1950s and 1960s which made possible developments in school music at that time; developments which so often came directly from composers themselves, as so much of the subsequent literature has revealed. The very 'difficulty' of the (then) New Music prompted questions about the hitherto accepted directions of music in education which, in turn, encouraged teachers to explore new possibilities.

Sound and silence was published in 1970. It seemed that the view of music education it promoted was welcomed, particularly by those teachers who, like us, had been seeking fresh solutions to old problems. At courses and conferences they added the weight of their experience to a call for reappraisal and redefinition of music's place in the curriculum.

In the intervening years a great deal has happened to music education and, indeed, to the education services generally. Looking back we see how often the underlying philosophies have come under scrutiny. In the mid 1970s Charles Carter drew attention to the inevitability of demographic waves in education; cycles which have implications for everything from buildings to curriculum style and content.[1] Now, once again, the 'swings for the schools', as Carter called them, have brought important changes. Yet there remains a marked lack of unanimity in the popular view of what education is about and what it should be achieving.

[1] Sir Charles Frederick Carter and others, *Swings for the schools: an essay on demographic waves in education* (London, Policy Studies Institute, 1979).

The most clearly discernible trend is towards greater formality; to defined standards and criterion-referenced assessment of pupils' achievements. Such thinking may be right at this time, but it could also have a tendency to depress the position of the arts in education, if only because artistic activity is not so obviously susceptible to that kind of evaluation.

Yet, in spite of everything, the impetus given to music education by the new directions of the late 1960s and early 1970s has been maintained. The current prospects for music in schools may not be all that we would wish them to be, and there are still large areas of disagreement (could it ever be otherwise?); but there can be no doubt that in the last twenty-five years music has been brought closer to the centre of the educational debate, and, as a result, there have been some significant and memorable achievements.

Three major Schools Council Projects in the 1970s – *The arts and the adolescent, The musical education of young children,* and *Music in the secondary school curriculum* – highlighted the need to ensure that active involvement with music and other arts would be available for the majority of pupils, regardless of their previous experience and training; and this without compromising commitment to advanced and talented students. That philosophy has been worked upon and refined, and is evident now in much of what we see in schools.

Emphasis both upon greater pupil involvement and the inventive aspects of musical activity have also figured prominently in the unusually large number of books and articles on music education appearing world-wide over the last ten years, among them the small but highly influential document, *Music from 5 to 16* produced by the Department of Education and Science in the HMI series *Curriculum matters.*[2]

[2] DES, *Music from 5 to 16: Curriculum matters 4* (London, HMSO, 1985).

All this thought and effort has done much to strengthen moves towards examination reform, leading us through the various modes of CSE to the agreed criteria for the GCSE and now to the defining of the key stages for music in the National Curriculum. One obvious characteristic of the new view has been the 'compose, perform and listen' ethic; a change of direction stimulating for some teachers, but for others perhaps rather daunting. Because of the powerful influence of some long-established views in music education, composition teaching had, for many, never been a major consideration. It is, though, in the composition element specifically that we now see a need for more detailed help, particularly in matters of musical structure and the ways in which students can be encouraged to generate and develop musical ideas. These are the questions I address in *Sound and structure*.

In the earlier book our first concern was to demonstrate that children could work imaginatively with sounds to create their own music in much the same way as they had been seen to work and produce using other arts materials. In *Sound and structure* my object is to build upon that principle, following the project format of *Sound and silence* but examining more closely the structuring processes: the techniques we evolve in musical composition to help us make something of our first thoughts and to hone and refine ideas in order to obtain the utmost clarity and coherence in the finished piece of music. These are now important issues for music education.

Sound and silence remained in print for nearly twenty years. It was translated into German, Italian and Japanese, and sections of it appeared in Swedish, Dutch, Spanish and Portuguese. It also provided the background for various educational series on radio and television. Peter Aston and I would be gratified if it were felt that *Sound and silence* had stimulated people's thoughts about the place of music in the school curriculum and had given some help with the development of classroom practice. Likewise, if the present book can answer at least some of the questions that have arisen over the years in which composition teaching has been developing in schools; if it can assist teachers with meeting the expectations of the National Curriculum; and if it can make a modest contribution towards the future of music in education, I shall be very pleased.

John Paynter
York, December 1989

Author's acknowledgements

It is usual – and quite properly so – for an author to share responsibility for the work (though not, of course, blame for its shortcomings) with friends and colleagues who have helped a book on its way. For the invaluable inspiration they have given me in this present work I thank most particularly Wilfrid Mellers, Richard Orton, Murray Schafer, Austin Wright, Arne Nordheim, Graham Vulliamy, Piers Spencer, Brian Loane and two very special people who, sadly, we can now only remember: Morton Feldman and Harry Rée. I also owe no small debt of gratitude to those who have worked with me over many years, and who, in so doing, have revealed more and more exciting new pathways into the world of musical imagination: former students of the University of York, especially Deborah and Henry Brown; Valerie Mills and Andrew Wood; the teachers associated with the Schools Council's Secondary Music project 1973–82; and my friends in Fiesole and Bolzano – particularly Fiorella Cappelli and Mario Sperenzi.

My thanks must also go to Dr Susan Kendall for drawing my attention to some particularly apposite words of Debussy; to Nye Parry for composing a work specially for this book; and to Neil Sorrell and the players of Gamelan Sekar Petak, Guus Janssen, Bernard Rands and Trevor Wishart for generously allowing me to quote so extensively from, and to comment upon, their work.

As to the book itself – the writing of it and the editorial 'brainstorming', advice and encouragement without which it simply would not have happened – I thank most sincerely Annie Cave, Peter Nickol, and my wife Elizabeth: they know, I am sure, how much their help has meant to me.

JOHN PAYNTER

Introduction

Challenge and commitment: the arts and the curriculum

Change in education is a slow process. Old convictions die hard, and teachers whose work points in new directions often find themselves part of a vulnerable minority. Occasionally, however, something occurs that draws together all the diverse effort for change and gives it formal approval.

The GCSE had just that effect. Determination to revise the examination process at 16+ brought about a nationwide re-appraisal not only of how to assess what is learned but also (and perhaps more importantly) of what school is for and why certain fields of knowledge and experience should find a place in the curriculum at all. Discussions that led to the formulation of subject criteria were especially significant. Here we had, for the first time, a national agency charged with, among other things, sorting out strengths and weaknesses in current practice within the various disciplines and bringing them into focus – a process now carried forward into the formulation of the National Curriculum.

When the GCSE was introduced it was the subject criteria that promoted new educational ideals and helped to give credibility to ideas which were still to some extent regarded as experimental. Thus, in addition to criterion reference and assessment functions, both the National Curriculum and the GCSE have become important influences for change in the design of the secondary curriculum. And because crucial public examinations occur during secondary schooling, developments there tend to affect the whole range from the primary school to higher education.

Interestingly, in music the changes have been more radical than elsewhere; but, compared with the pros and cons of other curriculum matters, news of a revolution in music education is unlikely to cause much of a stir. It is not difficult to see why this is so: in spite of the fact that music is so much in evidence around us (few people get through a day without hearing some music somewhere), its contribution to general education has, broadly speaking, been undervalued.

At one time the content of an average school music lesson was, at best, little more than a cultural additive, injecting a few facts of musical theory and history. In an educational system predom- inantly geared to teachers passing on information, music tended to conform. In any case, it was difficult to see how music-making (other than massed singing) could be accommodated in the classroom. Therefore direct involvement with the real artistic excitement of music found no place in the general curriculum, and was relegated to out-of-timetable sessions, mainly for talen- ted instrumentalists.

Gradually views on music in schools changed. Eventually, the criteria for music in the GCSE capitalised upon two long-term though not deliberately connected developments. First, the Local Education Authorities' investment in widening access to instrumental lessons which, as well as expanding and enhancing out-of-timetable ensembles and youth orchestras, made class- room performance a realistic option. And secondly the work of those teachers who for many years had advocated composition as a prime element of class music teaching. The new examination's requirements for composition and performance were clearly a formal acknowledgement that music demands imagination, active involvement, and creative commitment; and it is to be hoped that this view will remain prominent in the National Curriculum key stages for music.

However, the value – or even the possibility – of encouraging creativity in music education is still for some a contentious issue; no doubt in part because the word 'creativity' itself has been overworked and to some extent discredited by misuse and misunderstanding. This is unfortunate because creativity should be at the heart of all the affective areas of the curriculum.[1] Its context is imagination, origination and invention; but it goes beyond that to include interpretation and personalised imitation. Characteristically it calls upon preference and decision to a greater extent than other modes of thought. It is especially important as 'a way of coming to know' through independent, innovative responses to ideas and to the means of expression. Thus it differs substantially from received knowledge and from skills acquired through rule-directed learning.

No doubt a strong case could be made for a school curriculum limited to literacy, numeracy and communication – the tools that enable us to move into and around other areas of interest and expertise. Wider understanding in every sphere is in some degree dependent upon those core skills; so that everything else might reasonably be regarded as additional, to be fostered through specialist opportunities outside the school timetable for those who want to be involved. Yet it is also arguable that formal education should stimulate students' interest in things they may not be motivated to discover for themselves, and which they might otherwise miss altogether; and that includes the ability to recognise and deal with their own feelings.

[1] E. P. Torrance (*Guiding creative talent*, Prentice Hall, 1962, p. 139) defines creativity as 'The emergence of a novel relational product, growing out of the uniqueness of the individual on the one hand and materials, events, people and the circumstances of his life on the other'. These are elements which would seem to be of paramount concern in every area of affective education.

On the one hand we need to affirm and confirm our cultural heritage. At the same time, we should be aware of the subtle changes in the world around us, be able to understand the responsibilities that life presents, and be equipped to react sensitively and with imagination. Susanne Langer has pointed out that our existence is fundamentally sensory, and Robert Witkin warns that schooling which neglects 'the intelligence of feeling' is in danger of educating only half the child.[2]

Considerations of this kind are among the reasons why artistic creativity has an important part to play in education, strengthening awareness of the totality of our global community and of the range of relationships we have with it. The arts do not have a monopoly of creativity, but palpably they stand for an innovative view of the world. Their processes of thinking and making highlight elements of risk and challenge which are likely to be of importance to future generations. Attempting to make concrete in poetry, dance or music some of the volatile and intangible relationships our senses identify can be a powerful means of developing fresh perceptions of self and environment, people, places, ideas and the scope for action.

Yet there are other and, perhaps, even more compelling reasons why artistic creativity should have a place in the curriculum; reasons which become clear when we look closely at the characteristics and qualities of music itself.

[2] Susanne K. Langer, *Philosophy in a new key: a study of the symbolism of reason, rite and art* (Cambridge, Mass., Harvard University Press, 1942, 3rd edn 1969), p. 260.
Robert W. Witkin, *The intelligence of feeling* (London, Heinemann Educational Books, 1974).

Composing, performing and listening

Music is both a creative and a re-creative art, and a lot could be made of these distinctions. Music is widely regarded first and foremost as entertainment, contrasting on the one hand the inventiveness of composers and improvisers with – at the other end of the spectrum – the passivity of the receiving listeners. In the middle are the re-creators – the performers – clearly contributing something of themselves but by and large serving the interests of composers in order to give pleasure to the listeners.

This conventional picture may be a reasonably accurate description of the day-to-day operation of the music business, but that doesn't mean that it is necessarily the way to get the most out of music; nor does it suggest that the situation must remain unchanged. Indeed, given the initiatives now gaining ground in musical education we may realistically expect to see a growth in active, creative involvement with music.

A composer's work is very obviously creative. But – more than may generally be acknowledged – the interpretative role of the performer also calls for inventiveness. Research in music psychology has shown how expression is derived from structure; how expressive changes in particular parameters (e.g. tempo) during performance are based upon structural properties of the music, and therefore depend upon the performer's imaginative understanding of the whole constructive scheme. Admittedly the structural information has to be integrated (e.g. from notation or from some other source) before the performer can work out a strategy of interpretation; but the strategy, when it is devised, will have come only from the performer's imagination and, as with all other artistic activity, represents 'a radical form of ambiguity and creativity', the 'boundless possibilities' of which intrigue us and play a large part in convincing us that it is worth continuing to listen to music.[3]

We assume that those who compose and perform have substantial intellectual grasp of the potential of musical ideas and their scope for development. The intellectual overview sorts out the options, but it must be allied to a sensitive ear in order to make the artistic decisions that put the structural elements in place with the most effective emphases. However, do we recognise that both processes depend even more upon acute and attentive listening? This is the mainspring of musical understanding.[4]

Naturally, many people feel they need music in their lives without having to make the conscious effort of listening to it: they ask no more than that it shall be there. Moreover, some music is composed specifically to serve that purpose; to provide a comfortable and undemanding background for, say, shopping or travelling. Whether we like it or not, this is now one of music's functions, possibly the one which comes closest to so-called passive listening. Yet it need not stop at that. The overriding importance to musical creativity of having a 'good ear' suggests that we shall derive deeper significance from the experience of music if we cultivate the skill of attentive listening. Since this skill is a *sine qua non* for musical understanding in those who make music, surely it must be also for those who receive it? Passive listening may be an observable social phenomenon, but artistically it makes little sense. As music has now developed, it is the artistry of music that offers us so much.

Among the special features of musical experience, creative listening emerges as a key factor, not only in the invention and presentation of music, but also in the concert-goer's or record-listener's appreciation. That too demands a commitment of imagination through which, as it were, the composer's sound-world is re-made within the individual. It may be a different kind of creativity from that of the composer but it is, nevertheless, a creative act. The listener participates ('If I could have made this music, this is exactly how it would be') and the experience becomes an adventure which provides both a sense of self-sufficiency and the recognition of a driving force beyond us. It is as though we had projected into the music something of

[3] Edward Clarke, in John A. Sloboda (ed.), *Generative processes in music: the psychology of performance, improvisation and composition* (Oxford, Clarendon Press, 1988), p. 24.

[4] Compare Debussy's vehement attack on the music conservatoires for failing to recognise this: 'Foule ahurie! N'êtes-vous pas capable d'écouter des accords sans demander à voir leurs cartes d'identité et leurs caractéristiques? D'où viennent-ils? Où vont-ils? Faut-il absolument le savoir? Ecoutez. Cela suffit.' ('Insensitive rabble! Can't you listen to chords without demanding to see their identity cards and characteristics? Where have they come from? Where are they going to? Is it absolutely necessary to know this? Just listen. That's enough.') (André Boucourechliev, 1972, *Debussy*, p. 84)

ourselves which now has a life of its own. We can aspire to the artifice of art; to its completeness and to its inner logic.[5]

Responsibility for leading anyone to make such a commitment must lie partly with the composers whose organisation of the materials should, presumably, commend their music wholly to our attention. But this presupposes that we are disposed to get to know certain pieces of music in the first place; at the very least, to be happy to be where we cannot avoid listening to them. The position is somewhat different for music as part of the school curriculum. That implies a responsibility to help young people benefit from more than a casual acquaintance with the art of music. The question then is how can creative listening be taught?

Is it a matter of introducing students to suitable music? If so, what is 'suitable'? There are so many different kinds of music, serving such a multiplicity of purposes, some more lastingly significant than others. Music inspires us, entertains us, provides a blissful relief from the pressures of existence, calms us at moments of anxiety and comforts us in times of distress. Music can appear to change a person's mood or state of mind; to carry an emotional charge which prompts every shade of feeling from deep sadness to overwhelming elation. All conscious musical experience is concerned with adventures of feeling, imagination and invention. These features link composing, performing and listening, and should presumably be given some prominence in music education. Unavoidably, the central fact about music is that access to it is sensory and subjective. Related information can provide support but, on its own and divorced from 'the intelligence of feeling', has little to do with art and the reality of musical experience.

There is an old axiom which says, 'Never teach anything you may subsequently have to un-teach'. In other words, be wary of explanations which circumvent what seem to be deep or difficult aspects of a subject. Those explanations may get you off the hook for the time being, but before long students catch up, and you find yourself having to explain away the original explanations. Quite apart from anything else, that damages credibility. In the arts particularly, it is worth taking a little time to come to terms with the deeper implications of appreciation and understanding – in this case to investigate, as far as possible, the nature of music and musical experience and why it appears to be universally important. The outcome could well affect the content of your teaching and your expectations of pupils.

[5] This is consistent with our contemporary view of how the human mind acquires knowledge. Two hundred years ago educators thought of the mind essentially as absorbing or reflecting the external world. Today we see it as active; contributing creatively to the process of understanding (cf. John Dewey: 'Education is active; it involves a reaching out of the mind').

Why does music matter?

Several years ago the Performing Right Society, which collects and distributes income due to composers and authors for public performances of their works, made a film drawing attention to the widespread tendency to take music for granted. The opening sequence showed people enjoying music: a boy on roller skates swinging along to the accompaniment of music from his Sony Walkman; a motorist in a traffic jam soothing his frustration by switching on the car radio; and the happy atmosphere of a party with people dancing. Suddenly and dramatically in each situation the music was removed. As might be expected, the resulting surprise and anger was very evident!

The object was, of course, to remind us that the pleasure we receive from music is the result of someone's inventiveness, skill and effort which, like any other labour, should be properly rewarded. Unintentionally, perhaps, the film also highlighted the way in which the very quantity of music now available may dull our appreciation of it.

Music is so much part of everyday living that it is hardly surprising that many people accept it without question; and certainly without ever wondering what kind of commodity it is. It is clear that music is experienced through listening, and that there is a distinction between listening to it and merely hearing it. But what more can be said? Surely music is . . . just music?

To be given some information about those who perform the music may help us to feel closer to it. It can also be stimulating to explore the historical or sociological background and to discover something of the life and times of the composers. That kind of knowledge may enhance appreciation, but still it does not reach the heart of the musical experience. What deep-rooted need in our lives does music satisfy – and satisfy as nothing else can?

What does music communicate?

Some pieces we like, some we dislike. Are we merely responding to the sensuous attraction (or otherwise) of particular musical sounds or styles? Or does it go deeper; and if so, is it conceivable that there could be an explanation that applies to all music, irrespective of style and provenance?

It is obvious that the interpretation of musical meaning differs widely from one person to another and from one place to another, and that throughout history there have been conflicting views about the significance and function of music. In certain circumstances music appears to conjure up visual and dramatic images, or to be capable of carrying or reinforcing specific social, cultural and political messages. Moreover, in addition to allowing such referential possibilities, we frequently speak of the *language* of music. Does all this confirm that music is indeed a medium for conveying the kind of ideas we also communicate in words? Or are we deluding ourselves if we think that music has anything to say to us? At least one great composer, Stravinsky, appears to have thought so:

> I consider that music is, by its very nature, powerless to express anything at all, whether a feeling, an attitude of mind, a psychological mood, a phenomenon of nature, etc . . . if, as is nearly always the case, music appears to express something, this is only an illusion, and not a reality.[6]

[6] Stravinsky (1936), *Chronicle of my life*, pp. 91–2.

Strong words which no doubt still challenge many people's conceptions of how music works. But Stravinsky's forthright statement is also a useful reminder that the appreciation of music is fundamentally subjective and intuitive. Whatever he meant by those words he must surely have expected his music to produce some sort of reaction in those who heard it? There can be little doubt that music appears to create sensations in the mind; and that something is expressed – in the sense of being projected – by the music in performance; and something is received. What, then, is it that we experience? Pleasure? Delight? Satisfaction? How, and in what way, is music satisfying?

Curt Sachs points out that it has all been going on for a very long time, and that the origins of music are obscured by an extensive overlay of techniques:

> However far back we trace mankind, we fail to see the springing up of music. Even the most primitive tribes are musically beyond the first attempts.[7]

[7] Curt Sachs, *The rise of music in the ancient world, East and West* (London, J.M. Dent & Sons, 1944), p. 20.

In the quest for the real import of music, the surface appearances – the multiplicity of styles and referential meanings – can help us only so far. We must look beyond them for the quintessential feature that is common to all music. For it is difficult to believe that anything of such complexity and variety could have been developed and sustained throughout thousands of years without having a significance that embraces all its functions and interpretations. Music does matter, world-wide, and clearly has done so for as far back as we can see across the centuries. Could its hidden significance be that it acts to mitigate a deep-rooted concern, even though that relationship may not be immediately apparent?

Structure and sound

Because the mind finds it difficult to tolerate uncertainty, the inconsistency of existence is a perennial problem for humanity. In our attempt to overcome the effects, we swing first one way and then the other. Periods of liberalism and non-conformity gradually come to be regarded as permissive, weak and unstable, ultimately to be countered by some form of authoritarianism – which in turn disappoints, because that too fails to resolve the ambiguities once and for all. Reforming conviction which pointed the way to a new decisiveness becomes yet another barrier to fresh thinking; the uncertainties remain, and so the pendulum swings again.

Uncertainty is our problem: making models of perfection is our answer. Pyramids and paradigms; utopian orderings for the living and the dead: tracing our ancestry, we see bewildered humanity trying to give meaning to existence by forcing intractable diversity into forms that can be retained or that might in some way give the illusion of resisting the uncontrollable extent of space and the unstoppable flow of time. On the walls of caves, hunters painted pictures of the creatures they pursued; the quarry trapped for ever in idealised two-dimensional images. Later generations sought a kind of permanence for humanity itself by mummifying the body and presenting it, transmuted, in 'eternal' outer coverings, or by sculpting the perfected human form in seemingly indestructible marbles.

At another level it is a problem of scale. We feel lost in the very vastness of existence, and so we look for evidence of pattern and order in the cosmos. The movements of stars and their measurable relationships take on more than practical importance; and we clutch at the apparently scientific certitude of numerical patterns. Even when their interpretations are overtly superstitious or magical, numbers seem to make highly significant structures. These entirely abstract, symbolic forms suggest a hidden world of pure – and therefore possibly eternal – order, beyond the earthbound representation which commonly characterises most of our other models and images. Of all that we can organise and make manageable by our own efforts what, apart from numbers, could more surely bring within our grasp that which is beyond the reach of time and decay? So, our lives are structured in calendars and anniversaries; and, notwithstanding the advanced technology that cocoons us, the shifting number patterns of days, months and years have a strange fascination. Do we hope that, one day, time will 'stick'?[8]

Science or non-science, sense or nonsense, the wide-ranging importance that patterns and structures have for us can hardly be overestimated. Hence the particular significance of works of art. For although on the one hand the arts may seem to celebrate *im*permanence – in that it is not the business of artists to establish a status quo but rather to take risks and to devise new means of expression to match new modes of perception[9] – at the same time it is through artistic structures that we glimpse a different kind of existence, outside the continual flux of time and space. These works appear to control the space/time dimensions. Painting and sculpture fix visible and tangible form within defined and measurable limits. Architecture supremely demonstrates how space can be captured and managed. Similarly, a poem or a narrative encompasses and holds our experience of

[8] St John's vision of ultimate perfection is represented by 'Alpha and Omega . . . who is and who was and is to come'. α plus (i.e. imposed upon) ω makes – should we be surprised? – ∞, a figure 8 on its side; a symbol of eternity (comparable, perhaps, with the Chinese circular yin-yang figure symbolising the source of order and harmony).

[9] Cf. Hans Keller: 'Anything predictable is not art.'
Also, Sigfried Giedion: 'The opening up of new realms of feeling has always been the artist's chief mission' (*Space, time and architecture: the growth of a new tradition*, 5th revised edn, Cambridge, Mass., 1967, p. 431).

time; and film directors and dramatists juggle with the unities of time and place in order that we shall believe what is presented to us. But in every instance, whatever the extrinsic reasons for the work displayed in the artist's response to feelings and ideas, the central intrinsic reason, to which all technique is directed, is the creation of a singular coherence; a model that reveals something new about time/space existence, or at least helps us to make more sense of it. What the artist finally presents, in order to achieve this, is a heightened, unattainable 'reality' that can never become what it reaches for. But then, that is part of its fascination. As someone once remarked of poetry, it should awaken 'a sense of possibility beyond the words'.[10]

Obviously, this is not the way most of us habitually think about works of art and the pleasure we receive from them. It is likely that we respond principally to the overall stimulation and/or to the sensuous qualities of details: mellifluous texture or melody, or stirring rhythms. Features which immediately catch the eye or ear are frequently delightful in themselves, although this may also be because their characteristics are associated with other things we find pleasurable. For instance, warm colours, smooth sculptural forms, gently flowing melodic lines and rich instrumental timbres – such as the lower registers of the clarinet – may all evoke sensations of peacefulness, comfort, affection, belonging, freedom from disturbing or intruding harshness, and so on. Similarly, the clean lines of classical architecture, the balanced phrases of classical music, the clear timbre of flutes and oboes and the coolness of blues and greens can be satisfying because of the association with uncluttered orderliness, disciplined thinking and well-regulated organisation.

Yet, however much the individual elements give pleasure through association, it is unlikely that we should ever find deeper satisfaction in them were it not for their structural consequence within a work of art as a whole. It is unfortunate that we categorise some art and music as abstract, and seem thereby to imply that it is likely to be less appealing – perhaps because its associative or evocative possibilities are suppressed. Strictly speaking, all art is abstract; indeed, that is its prime justification. Painting, sculpture, dance, a poem or a piece of music: every art object in fact, even when its content relates directly to what we can observe and recognise, is an abstraction from the 'real' world, a formalised construction of its creator's imagination. It is not nature itself but what nature might be; and the deepest satisfaction we can receive from art comes from the total acceptance of these abstracted forms. The details draw us in, intrigue us, beguile us and charm us, but their main function is to 'describe' the structure. That is to say, all the nuances of colour, shape, word patterns, story-lines, movements, gestures, and sounds are there in order that we shall receive satisfaction and insight from

[10] Similarly, Messiaen, writing of the process of musical composition, observes that 'One point will attract our attention from the outset: the charm of impossibilities.' (*Technique de mon langage musical*, Paris, Leduc, 1944). In this context it is, perhaps, useful to expand the points already made about architecture; not only does it show how space can be managed but it also enables us to grasp (i.e. metaphorically to take hold of) the space it defines, and thereby to understand the concept of space itself. In this way the great medieval cathedrals were able to make the infinity of space intelligible. As Professor Patrick Nuttgens has pointed out, these buildings were intended to be 'like nothing on earth'.

the way in which they interact. It is (as John Cage informs us) rather like the objects in a Japanese stone garden: they are there so that we shall notice the spaces in between and, when we have seen them all, understand the wholeness of what is there. Each event has its own importance, of course; but where it happens, when and in relation to what is even more important.

Structures in dance, drama, visual art, poetry and literature are made with the same materials that are commonly employed for normal, everyday description, but set apart from the ordinary by the artist's skill and imagination. Yet, even in avowedly non-representational works, a degree of realism may frequently be used to capture attention and to make us take notice of the work's viewpoint (i.e. relating to what is familiar and easily understood). There is, then, an understandable expectation that the visual arts will show us things 'as they are' and in 'lifelike images'; that the action of a play shall be naturalistic; that poetry and literature will have strong narrative elements; and that dance, through movement and gesture, will tell stories that make realistic sense. Certainly, works of art can be enjoyed in those terms, and there is no reason why that should not be so; most of us like a good story well told. Nevertheless, the extent to which an art form can or cannot represent ideas, locations and events is probably the least important of its qualities.

We should be wary of taking realism as the only touchstone of success for any work of art, but with music such judgements are out of the question; music is different. By itself (i.e. without the addition of words, titles or whatever) music cannot relate to tangible or visible reality. Although, like other arts, its materials may have more commonplace uses (e.g. police sirens, standard telephone tones, alarm signals), they should not be confused with the musical use of sound. There are, of course, examples of composers imitating bird calls and other familiar sounds, but these are usually idealised and occur at exceptional points in a work for reasons other than the purely musical.

Literal imitation is not one of music's essential attributes. Even those works which refer to a story or a 'programme' rarely use direct imitation. The story is no more than a starting-point for the musical structure – which is where the true aesthetic adventure is to be found. For instance, although Dukas's famous symphonic scherzo *L'apprenti sorcier* is based on a poem by Goethe, it would be impossible for a listener who did not know the title to follow the narrative from the music alone; and it is unlikely that the composer thought of this work merely as telling a story. What he wanted was that we should immerse ourselves in the music he had so painstakingly constructed.

Regrettably, in schools and concert halls we still find a misleading emphasis upon the literal interpretation of music. Stories, pictorial ideas, notions of mood and 'atmospheric' meaning, programme notes and peripheral information have been pressed upon us in the name of musical understanding for so long that we have reached a stage where it is difficult even to question this practice. The assumption is that these aids make it easier for people to listen to music; and although, up to a point, we may be persuaded that they do, in fact they take us more or less in the opposite direction.

Nowhere is this more blatant than in the way music is likely to be treated on television. It will be argued that television is a visual medium and that the first concern of those who work with it must be to present interesting visual images. But in that case why emphasise tenuous pictorial or literary associations in dealing with an art which is essentially aural? Diverting attention away from the rhythmic vitality and the sumptuous, shimmering textures of Messiaen's *Turangalîla* with pictures of Indian carpet patterns, or – while a performance of the work is actually in progress – attempting to explain the words of Walton's *Façade* with film biography of Edith Sitwell, can only destroy the wholeness of the music and deprive us of the pleasure and insight which that wholeness alone can give. It also displays a serious misunderstanding of the status of experiences and events which, in one way or another, function as starting-points for a composer's musical thinking.

Rather than assisting musical understanding, the television treatment all too often places barriers between the listener and the music; barriers which, unfortunately, quite a few listeners (viewers!) are unaware of. Based, as it seems to be, upon the misguided assumption that a composer's hard-won musical organisation is not sufficient in itself but needs the support of pictures or other information, this is hardly the path to creative listening. Indeed, it completely overlooks the challenge music offers us – to develop an attentive ear.[11]

It cannot be said too strongly that the process and purpose of musical composition is not to translate into sound-pictures experiences, historical events, literary or visual ideas, or anything else that may happen to stimulate a composer's imagination. Once the imagination has been stirred the musical considerations take over; and although a composer may want to recall the starting-point and to hint at it in, say, a title or some other literary reference, there can be little doubt that it is the musical continuity we are intended to follow for its own sake, not as an analogue of ideas that can be better expressed in another medium.

Music's lack of descriptive power of the kind associated with words and visual images is not a weakness; it is its strength.[12]

Unhampered by problems of representation, composers, performers and listeners engage directly with the sound relationships and their onward movement in the musical timescape. It is

[11] Of course, it doesn't have to be like that. Occasionally we are privileged to see sensitive and effective television presentation of music, and there is clearly scope for a great deal more research into the potential of this relationship. It is not simply a matter of better film music or better films about music. Rather it suggests a fundamental review of the immensely exciting possibilities for linking visual creativity and ambisonic sound diffusion. The technology is advancing by leaps and bounds, but little is being done to exploit it artistically.

[12] Again Debussy: 'Je ne suis pas tenté d'imiter ce que j'admire dans Wagner. Je conçois une forme dramatique autre: la musique y commence là où la parole est impuissante à exprimer; la musique est faite pour l'inexprimable.' (I'm not tempted to imitate what I admire in Wagner. I conceive dramatic form quite differently: beginning where verbal expression is powerless; music is made for what is inexpressible). (Quoted in Boucourechliev, 1972, p. 48).

these varied and subtle relationships which give us delight; and it is the sense of completeness in a successful piece of music which gives us satisfaction (and, conversely, the lack of coherence – incompleteness – which disappoints us in an unsuccessful work). This applies as much to rock music, Gilbert and Sullivan operas or the Indonesian gamelan as it does to Bach or Monteverdi. Little wonder it has been suggested that 'all art constantly aspires to the condition of music'.

Thinking and making

In following this line of argument we may seem to have strayed a long way from the practicalities of the school classroom. But, like music itself, a curriculum must have an essential unity to which all its elements relate convincingly. A careful examination of the roots of our musical experience is the first step towards deciding the content of the programme. Too often we have ignored the deep structure and in consequence have ended up trivialising music, reducing it to superficial theory and fact that has little to do with artistic reality. Hans Keller believed that an essential part of his work with students was 'to cure them of their A levels and return them to music!'

Music and musical understanding are the priorities. Before all else we have to find suitable ways of helping students to engage with the hierarchy of elements and with questions of continuity that work together to make each piece of music a whole.[13] Words alone can do very little to explain what it means to inhabit a musical timescape. This is where we need the skill of creative listening; and one of the best ways of acquiring it is through first-hand experience of asking the questions and taking the decisions which produce music – both in performance and in composition. As Herbert Read suggests, 'Appreciation . . . is not acquired by passive contemplation: we only appreciate beauty on the basis of our own creative aspirations, abortive though these be.'[14] The education of an artistic eye or a musical ear begins when we start to explore the means of expression, simultaneously encountering and learning to enjoy the creations and presentations of others, which then further inspire our own attempts.

There are not two kinds of musical education, the one participatory (for the talented) and the other a passive appreciation (for the 'non-musical'!). Participation and appreciation are complementary aspects of the same thing, and they must work together, at suitable levels of technique, whatever the previous musical experience of the students.

Because its forms have no responsibility to tangible reality, music lends itself to wide-ranging inventiveness more readily than most other means of expression – which may explain its

[13] Cf. Hans Keller: 'Great music diversifies a unity, mere good music unites diverse elements' ('Chamber music' in *The Mozart companion*, p. 90).

[14] Sir Herbert Read, *Education through art*, 3rd edn (London, Faber & Faber, 1956).

universal appeal and variety. Experience of improvising and composing is helpful in the development of all creative and interpretative techniques. Whether the music is notated in minute detail or created by means of improvisatory empirical composition, the structural problems are solved primarily by aural sensitivity to the quality of musical ideas and to the nuances of sound through which structures can be controlled.

Whether this is the outcome of individual exploration or of group activity – in which composing can be rather like a brain-storming discussion – the principle is the same. To begin with it is useful to have at least some idea of the overall direction and duration of the music. From there on, musical starting-points have to be thought about and agreed; possibilities examined; ideas generated; structural procedures tried out; and preferred routes confirmed by frequent repetition, judging carefully, as the work proceeds, how specific features – such as melodies, rhythmic patterns, combinations of instrumental or vocal colour, and dynamic changes – might be extended, developed, transformed, or made to give way to fresh thoughts.

No externally imposed rules can answer these questions. Every piece of music is a new adventure of thinking and making in which – almost without realising it – we become intensely aware of things that matter to us; of our commitment to ideas and our determination to see the task through to the end and to stand by the decisions we take. Each piece must work by commending itself to us when we listen to it in its completed form. That is to say, the first people who must be satisfied with finished pieces of music are those who compose them.

Challenge and achievement: the case for creativity

All over the world people invent music and preserve their musical traditions. While the circumstances of making and presenting music, the cultural conventions and the learning processes, vary immensely from one place to another, the essential reality of music remains the satisfying wholeness of its sound-structures.

Uncertainty about the role of music in the school curriculum has been part of a larger problem of the place of arts generally, exacerbated by a tendency to accept without question a curriculum style in which factual information and objective description take precedence over other forms of knowledge and expression – such as those typified by art and music. Yet we know that, for the most part, individuals relate to their world both objectively, in clinical and absolute terms, and subjectively, through the indefinable but no less important mental processes of emotions. And just as topics which require a linear approach to learning make an essential contribution in their own way to the totality of general education, so the arts, representing a very different and essentially holistic mode of perception, offer students something which would not otherwise be available.

The misunderstandings that have arisen around the promotion of creativity in education are unfortunate. Although we now see a greater willingness to draw upon students' originality, imagination and inventiveness, and widespread agreement that the development of lateral, creative thinking is important for society's future, there are still many who find this a disquieting notion. They see creativity either as an impossible and pretentious goal (because they regard it as the province of a few very special minds) or as an open invitation to lawlessness, unproductive freedom and lowering of standards.

Surely it is by now difficult to ignore the plentiful evidence we have of school students' creativity in music, quite apart from the other arts? All of which seems to bear out Wilfrid Mellers' belief that:

> in a healthy society all men should be artists to some extent and in some way, in proportion to their capacity to live creatively.[15]

[15] Wilfrid Mellers, *Music and society* (London, Dennis Dobson, 1946), p. 10.

As to the other point, it is quite true that, without the support of a well-organised course, what passes for creative activity can leave students wandering in circles, never producing anything of the slightest merit. Standards have to be established in education and we should expect to see worthwhile productivity in every part of the curriculum. Again, we must look to the National Curriculum to define appropriate stages of attainment, but at the same time not to sacrifice the very essence and integrity of the work by forcing it into unsuitable moulds.

One of the clearest signals of danger appears when a quite proper desire to maintain standards begins to elevate teaching and examining above the processes of learning. In spite of any beneficial effects the goals and examinations may have (e.g. as formative influences upon the programmes of individual teachers), when expectations lean towards more and more certification, education loses its sense of challenge and takes on a placatory role, satisfying ambition with nothing more than a proliferation of degrees and diplomas: laurels upon which we can all rest.

However, life doesn't rest; and there is more to it than educational qualifications. We continually aspire to achievement, especially the kind that truly represents us as individuals. The challenge of creativity provides that very special sense of overcoming, and does so more lastingly than anything else. To have made something which is yours, and yours alone, is real achievement.

Using this book

Sound and structure is a practical guide; but it is not a course nor is it a 'method'. The intention generally is to re-present the case for creativity as a basis for the music curriculum, and specifically to argue for greater emphasis upon structure in the kind of composition teaching now expected in schools.

Everything we do in education aspires to an expansion of the intellectual life. Music is not inferior in this respect; thinking and making with musical sounds gives rise to 'ways of coming to know' and 'ways of telling' different from those in other disciplines but no less important to intellectual development. Thought meets thought in the sharing of our own creativity and in performing, listening to and understanding the output of other people's inventiveness.

A flow chart of this activity would reveal a network of interaction within which one might take any direction so long as it passed through the central point:

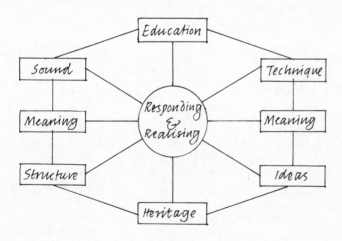

Every point in this vibrant world resonates with others. At the centre is the aural response which links creating, performing and listening, and which exists only through the seemingly unlimited relationships ('Infinite & Eternal', as William Blake thought them to be) that can be set up between sound, time, ideas, and artistry to produce stimulating and satisfying musical structures. This book explores those relationships.

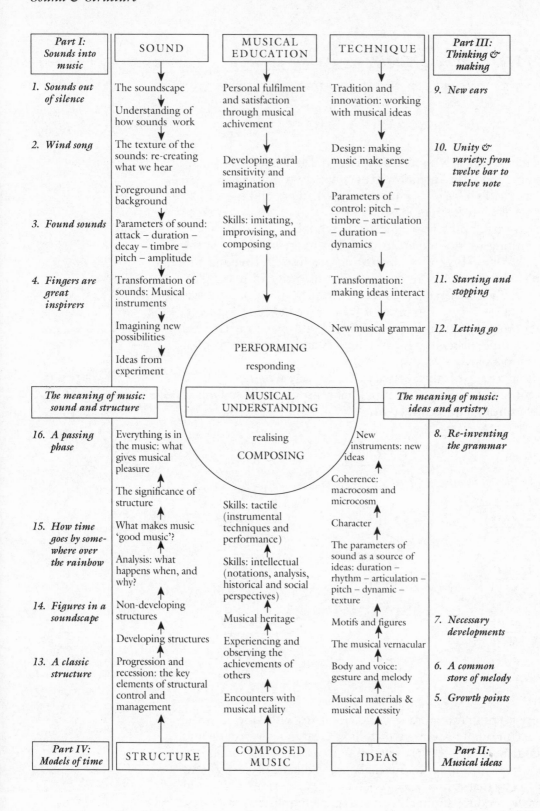

Part I:
Sounds into music

SOUND

MUSICAL EDUCATION

TECHNIQUE

Part III:
Thinking & making

1. *Sounds out of silence*

The soundscape

Understanding of how sounds work

Personal fulfilment and satisfaction through musical achivement

Tradition and innovation: working with musical ideas

9. *New ears*

2. *Wind song*

The texture of the sounds: re-creating what we hear

Foreground and background

Developing aural sensitivity and imagination

Design: making music make sense

10. *Unity & variety: from twelve bar to twelve note*

3. *Found sounds*

Parameters of sound: attack – duration – decay – timbre – pitch – amplitude

Skills: imitating, improvising, and composing

Parameters of control: pitch – timbre – articulation – duration – dynamics

4. *Fingers are great inspirers*

Transformation of sounds: Musical instruments

Imagining new possibilities

Ideas from experiment

Transformation: making ideas interact

New musical grammar

11. *Starting and stopping*

12. *Letting go*

PERFORMING
responding

MUSICAL UNDERSTANDING

The meaning of music: sound and structure

The meaning of music: ideas and artistry

realising
COMPOSING

16. *A passing phase*

Everything is in the music: what gives musical pleasure

The significance of structure

New instruments: new ideas

8. *Re-inventing the grammar*

Coherence: macrocosm and microcosm

15. *How time goes by some-where over the rainbow*

What makes music 'good music'?

Analysis: what happens when, and why?

Skills: tactile (instrumental techniques and performance)

Character

The parameters of sound as a source of ideas: duration – rhythm – articulation – pitch – dynamic – texture

14. *Figures in a soundscape*

Non-developing structures

Developing structures

Skills: intellectual (notations, analysis, historical and social perspectives)

Musical heritage

Motifs and figures

The musical vernacular

7. *Necessary developments*

13. *A classic structure*

Progression and recession: the key elements of structural control and management

Experiencing and observing the achievements of others

Encounters with musical reality

Body and voice: gesture and melody

Musical materials & musical necessity

6. *A common store of melody*

5. *Growth points*

Part IV:
Models of time

STRUCTURE

COMPOSED MUSIC

IDEAS

Part II:
Musical ideas

Each project identifies with a certain part of the pattern, which can be entered at any point. The most obvious route would be to start with the raw materials (sounds), and from there to look at ways in which sounds become musical ideas and lead us to develop the means of artistic control which in turn make possible the production of whole pieces of music.

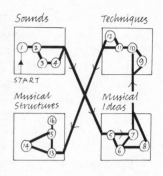

Other routes are equally valid. For example, you could start with fully realised forms (existing pieces of music) and, having examined the way certain pieces work as a whole, move on to projects which explore control mechanisms in greater detail. It would then be useful to see how musical thinking has reached that point by way of the potential of natural sounds and musical ideas.

Or yet again, by beginning with simple tunes generated, as it were, off the top of the head from that common store of melody we all inherit, work through other ways of producing musical ideas to the moment when it is reasonable to ask 'what next; where can music go now?' From there, return to the point at which the meaning of sounds links intuitive reactions with imaginative experiment, and – leaving aside, for the moment, the overlay of techniques and composed music – work backwards to the natural soundscape. From there it would be feasible to jump to those projects which focus on the means of control, completing the scheme with examples of fully realised pieces.

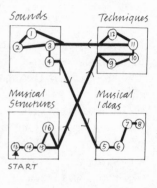

Because the aim is mainly to explore processes by which a great variety of forms can come into being, there is no suggestion of coverage in the range of topics. Each offers a particular view of the musical world and, in various ways, can be made to relate to others. Overall the projects represent ways of thinking about those relationships, and it is hoped that this will stimulate teachers to research other examples of musical structure and devise their own projects.

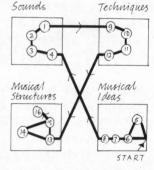

The student assignments in each section are included principally as a way of explaining a style of teaching appropriate to the aims of the book. They can, of course, be taken as lesson topics but, perhaps, not as lesson notes. Almost certainly they will need adapting to meet differing age-ranges, circumstances and the special interests of students.

It is no more possible to provide recipes for successful music education than it is for composing pieces of music. There are far too many variables – different pupil and teacher interests; environmental influences; differences in timetable, organisation and ethos from school to school; varying resources; varying degrees of support from parents, head-teachers, local education authorities and inspectors; opportunities to hear live music;

differing critical opinions and the continuous change of musical fashion. No book could cover every eventuality or propose schemes that would work in any and every classroom come what may. None the less, it is possible to make some general observations about management of the 'workshop' style of teaching envisaged in this book.

Organisation and resources

In school music education there is now a substantial background to creative work stretching over more than a quarter of a century. The literature on this subject is extensive, and throughout the last twenty years the classroom techniques for developing improvisation and composition with related performance and listening have undergone considerable refinement. Yet the key to the whole thing remains simple aural awareness and a sense of adventure in making and presenting pieces of music.

Older class-teaching patterns have gradually given way to different arrangements, more appropriate to the new activities. In the small-group workshop, for example, it is usual for the teacher to start with a proposal for the groups to explore. What the teacher offers at this point may be little more than a brief statement, although it can include some demonstration of possibilities. Either way, it is advisable to make it no longer than three minutes, and to ensure that it presents a challenge to the students' imagination, something they can all act upon. Immediately after this the class quickly divides into small groups to begin making music.

Ideally each group should have a separate work-space close to the main music room, so that from time to time they can all be brought together quickly and without fuss. Instruments and other equipment must be on hand as the groups begin to work; and there ought to be a reasonable choice to allow each group the opportunity to experiment until they have matched ideas and instruments satisfactorily.

The quality of instruments is very important. Classroom percussion has served us well for many years but much more sophisticated equipment is now available and should be used. Synthesizer keyboards are especially useful because they offer scope for both melodic and harmonic exploration. With the addition of varied timbres, MIDI and other electronic devices this has become a powerful tool for creative experiment. Used with headsets, these keyboards also encourage an easy transition between group compositions and individual work.

The workshop in action

To begin with, group activities are a helpful way of generating ideas (i.e. by brainstorming). They also make it possible to create, quickly and easily, complex and interesting textures of instruments and voices which the group can experiment with and change. The disadvantage is that inevitably there are subtle bids for leadership, and the ideas of certain members are likely to prevail over others. You can get round that problem to some extent by judiciously reorganising groups from time to time for particular musical reasons (e.g. selecting players of a certain kind of instrument to make a group piece). But the better way is to move towards individual composing when everyone can have time to work out their own ideas.

No one should be expected to work with inadequate resources. On the other hand, a great deal can be done with voices and with quite simple equipment (e.g. 'found' sounds). If you wait for perfect conditions you may never start anything. Therefore it is probably better to begin with what is available, even though ideals may have to be modified and limited. Having said that, none of us wants to be taken for granted, or to get a reputation for being able to work wonders under difficult conditions and never ask for anything better! It is essential to build quickly upon even modest successes.

The teacher's role is vital to the success of a composition workshop. Nothing can be left to chance, and there is no substitute for good planning. It is crucial to anticipate the kind of guidance most likely to be needed (on the reasonable expectation of what will be produced in response to given starting-points). At the same time, we must allow for the unexpected and be ready to encourage it when it appears. It is important to know – from personal experience – what *may* happen. That means being active ourselves in creating and performing, and being inventive and innovative in our teaching.

Anticipating the response also means being ready with appropriate recorded examples to demonstrate other uses of techniques or developments discovered by the students. Music listening is most valuable when it can be associated with pieces performed or composed in the classroom.

Above all, students must be able to feel that they are working purposefully within a framework they can grasp. Without such a focus interest is quickly lost and the whole exercise becomes aimless. Suitable frames for developing inventiveness might be:

- composing within a limited range of pitches or for a particular sound-source

- composing with specified techniques (e.g. certain harmonic limitations, canon or free imitation, a distinctive procedure in orchestration – for example masking, see page 73)

- using techniques derived from Afro/Caribbean/Asian musics – for example, resultant melodies (melodies formed by combining the fragmentary contributions of two or more parts)

- making instrumental arrangements and song accompaniments for specified players

- inventing and constructing completely new musical instruments, and composing music for them

- composing for a particular mode of instrumental articulation (e.g. harmonics on the piano, 'Bartók' snap pizzicato on stringed instruments, flutter-tonguing on the flute, etc.)

Even when an activity is brief, or mainly experimental, the aim should be to make pieces of music, not merely to explore possibilities. At the heart of all this is the creation of musical structures, and as often as possible students should be able to feel that they have made something which is complete in itself.

When a piece is finished it's a good idea to suggest that it is given a title (if a title has not already been used as a starting-point). That will add to the sense of achievement – much in the same way as it would to display a completed painting, for example. Even so, music exists only at the moment when it sounds; it cannot be preserved in a once-and-for-all finished form like a painting. Music can be recorded, of course, but that's not the same thing; it depends upon live presentation for its most telling effect. That is why there is a special satisfaction in having completed a composition which can then be brought to life whenever you choose to perform it.

Do not, however, overlook the value of improvisation – both as an art-form worth cultivating for its own sake and also as a training ground for composition (e.g. listening and imitating; listening and responding; channelling ideas and shaping their development musically). All composition begins with some form of improvisation, even if it is a silent process in the head. Thereafter ideas have to be worked out systematically, with care and patience, until the composer is completely confident of the overall direction of the music. Students should learn by experience that first thoughts are not necessarily the ones that will ultimately be used. It is often necessary to make several fresh starts before discovering ideas that can usefully be developed.

The teacher must help those beginning to compose to find the courage:

- to pursue an idea until it yields the best opportunities for taking the music forward, or

- to abandon it, even after extensive exploration, if it looks like being a dead-end.

This is not wasted effort. The mind needs to work on possibilities, sifting and sorting. Preliminary trial-and-error is an essential part of the process. Some particular points that arise from experience of working in this way are worth noting. For example, on the handling of the workshop:

i. Get the groups working as quickly as possible. Too much talk from the teacher at the beginning can kill enthusiasm.

ii. With the groups in their various working places and started, visit each in turn very briefly, making sure they know what they are supposed to do and have the resources they need.

iii. After a few minutes, stop the activity and call the groups together. Ask for some (not all at this stage) to report on their progress, not by talking about it but by performing what they have produced so far. This is not the moment to invite comments from the other groups; it is, though, the point where the teacher must teach. As a group presents whatever has been achieved, however rudimentary it may be, notice particular ideas that may usefully be developed. Draw attention to these points: 'Did you all notice how they started with . . .?'; 'That's a strong idea because . . .'; 'They've got a lot of interesting possibilities here; perhaps too many ideas; they'll have to decide which are the best or even which *one* is the best to go on with . . .'

In making such comments we are not composing the pieces for the groups but pin-pointing the kind of questions they must learn to ask for themselves. We are also drawing the attention of the other groups to the wealth of possibilities that exist in the chosen starting-point.

iv. Send the groups back to continue their compositions, and during the next part of the workshop spend more time with certain groups – having made a mental note of any that especially need help or encouragement. Try to avoid explaining too much. The key is to ask the right kind of questions – as often as possible about structure: 'How is the piece starting? How might it finish? Can you think of ways of making that idea (or technique or development) a very special feature of this piece? How can you make the music push ahead here? How can you avoid it sounding as though it is going to stop altogether when you really only want it to relax a little at that point? Are there too many/too few instruments for the effect you are wanting to create?' And so on.

Much will depend upon the deployment of the groups and the ease with which they can be brought together; but within those limitations there should be a reasonable number of opportunities throughout the workshop for them to share further progress reports and for the teacher to comment.

It is not necessary to hear every group on each of these occasions, but they should all be heard at least once before finally presenting their completed compositions. For the students, an important part of the process is learning to stand by decisions taken; and that needs working at. The report and discussion points can help with this. Comments should of course be supportive, but should not exclude criticism: it is vital to maintain an atmosphere of purposeful creative endeavour.

In the initial stages it is generally necessary to bring everything to a neat conclusion at the end of each workshop, giving everyone a sense of having achieved something during that time. But once the workshop format has become established (perhaps after a few weeks), it should be possible to set up projects of longer duration, carrying work over for three or four weeks and having groups and individuals engaged on compositions for as long as is needed, presenting the completed pieces whenever they are ready for performance.

Teaching points

In each of the projects in this book the Student Assignments are followed by Teaching Points. Once again, there is no suggestion of covering every eventuality; these notes indicate just some of the ways in which you might follow up aspects of the students' work. More importantly, perhaps, they range widely around the project topics; just as you might do in the classroom whenever the opportunity arose, encouraging students to see composition as an adventure that leads in many unexpected directions. Some points are expanded with additional references, printed in the margin – rather like asides, not crucial to the argument at that juncture but possibly providing useful background to it; or taking off at a tangent; or simply offering more food for thought.

You can, of course, ignore the teaching points entirely! But if they serve any wider purpose it is perhaps to say that there is really no end to what might be done with musical composition and it is essential that we all keep open minds. Tovey pointed out that fugue is a procedure not a form, and by the same token it has to be emphasised that what is set out here is a view of music education and not a method of teaching music. Indeed, this is one area where methods are to be avoided, because they are the very antithesis of the creative mind. When you find you've developed a system for teaching composition, that is the moment to give up!

Part I

Sounds into music

Project 1

Sounds out of silence

Sound, time, ideas and technique are the four corners of musical experience. Music results from dynamic relationships between them.

To understand music we need to understand these relationships: to know how sounds work; how they can become musical ideas; and how those ideas, transformed by artistic techniques, can structure time.

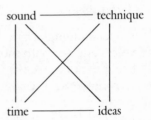

Student assignments

Assignment 1

a. Sit very still: what can you hear? Identify all the sounds that can be heard where you are.

b. Identify only the natural sounds (e.g. breathing, wind rustling leaves). Is this possible from where you are, or do you have to go somewhere else to hear any kind of natural sound?

c. Identify sounds that result from human activity, invention and construction (e.g. work sounds, mechanical and electrical sounds, recorded or electronically transmitted sounds).

d. Identify sounds produced by natural forces reacting with human constructions (e.g. wind whistling in overhead telephone or power lines).

e. Identify patterns of sound.

f. Identify highest and lowest pitched sounds.

Assignment 2

Understanding a sound from the 'outside': find out how it is produced (i.e. what force reacts with what substance and under what circumstances to produce the sound?).

Assignment 3

Understanding a sound from the 'inside' by imitating it as closely as possible. Record a sound. Listen to it many times to find out how it works. Notice particularly the start of the sound (attack), how it goes on (envelope) and how it finishes (decay). Then try to imitate it exactly with one or more voices. Record the imitation and compare it with the recording of the original sound.

Assignment 4

Understanding sound textures by re-creating a sample (a) with voices and (b) with musical instruments. Either individually or in groups (not more than five to a group), sample (by *listening*, not recording) 30 seconds of what can be heard where you are. Note carefully *when* in the 30 seconds particular sounds start and finish; which are high and which are low; which are in the foreground and which are in the background. Remember any special features. By imitating the sounds and the way in which they combine, try to give as accurate a representation as you can of the 30-second 'timescape'. Rehearse it and record it.

Assignment 5

Create in sound an idealised representation of a particular location (e.g. a room in which certain kinds of sounds can be heard, a large hall, a swimming pool, field, wood, seashore, street, alley-way, public square, workshop). The location must be accessible; i.e. it is not sufficient merely to imagine it: its soundscape must be experienced, if possible over a period of some hours either by remaining there or by visiting it from time to time. At the location listen attentively for, say, three minutes. Make careful observation of the qualities and characteristics of every sound heard. Keep an accurate record. Allow a little time to pass, then take another three-minute sample.

Continue in this way for as long as possible, gradually building up a detailed sound-file of that location (like a photograph resulting from many exposures of the same piece of film). Notice in particular the sounds that occur most frequently in all the samples: did those sounds give a special character to the place?

From all this evidence, devise a plan for making a texture of sounds that will suggest to a listener the essence of the place visited.

- How long should the pattern of sounds last? (Bear in mind the things that must be included.)

- Which sounds will start?

- What will be the steady state of the texture? Will some sounds come and go, or reappear?

- How will you end it?

Lay out this organisation of the sounds on a piece of paper (you could invent symbols to represent the different sounds and arrange them along a time-line; the higher-pitched sounds above the line, the lower-pitched below). When all the detail of what happens (and when it happens) has been decided and carefully placed, experiment to find the best ways of imitating the sounds. Work at individual sounds and at combinations of sounds until the whole structure can be performed satisfactorily using voices alone or voices and musical instruments. When you can produce a distinctive and definitive sound evocation of the place visited, record it and present it to an audience.

Assignment 6

Create in sound a new and unusual imaginary landscape. Imitate (or use recordings) of easily identifiable sounds but organise them together in a short textural piece that evokes a strange and unreal place.

Teaching points

These assignments are not in themselves musical but, from simple exercises in attentive listening to exploration of how sounds are made and how they evoke atmosphere, the project can develop into a wide-ranging investigation with imaginative use of sound textures that parallel important features of music. It would be useful to draw out these parallels, either in preparation for subsequent projects or (if you have started with other projects) to present previous work in a new light.

An understanding of the inner structure of sounds links easily with the 'opposite corner' of musical experience (see figs 1 and 2 above) because the substance of every musical idea rests in the special characteristics of the sounds chosen. Every tiny nuance of pitch, duration, amplitude and articulation can have a momentous effect. Coming to understand the morphology of everyday sounds around us, by imitating them carefully and building up textures of the imitated sounds, is an important step towards evolving and developing musical ideas.

Assignment 5 could be an introduction to the concept of style. First the soundscape is observed as it is in reality, then it is stylised – rather like finding a statistical norm. As with statistics, musical style embodies a generalised truth which does not represent any particular reality. That is why, when we have heard a lot of music from a certain historical period or place (e.g. Vienna in the last quarter of the eighteenth century), we can, without too much difficulty, identify the period (and perhaps the place) by recognising the general style qualities of composers at that time. Individual works will vary greatly in detail but particular features will stand out – probably because, in one guise or another, they appear most frequently. Those features take root in the mind as the most representative because they have the characteristics most quickly recognised, and so present the generalised view – the statistical norm. It would be possible to take a selection of those features and string them together to make a piece of music sounding passably like a work from the period in question – even of a particular composer. Pastiche composition of this kind is a good way of getting to know how musical styles work.

In Assignment 5 students are asked to focus upon the sound style of the chosen location.[1] An alternative way of tackling this would be to sample the actual soundscape in a series of short tape-recordings. Then, having noted the most significant and frequently occurring sounds, to edit those elements into an idealised version of all that was recorded. In other words, by using the most strongly characteristic sounds – those that immediately evoke the atmosphere of the place – to create on tape the soundscape *as it might be*. This is not nature, in which textures are formed by the accidental coming together of sounds, including industrial sounds; this is art, the tape montage presenting a singular, idealised soundscape.

Now we are in the world of imagination; and Assignment 6, although it uses found sounds, requires them to be structured into what is essentially a musical frame. The sounds must be plotted carefully in time to create the desired effect. If the structure is too short the ideas will be gone before their meaning can be absorbed; if it is too long the mystery and unreality of the imaginary landscape may be dissipated and destroyed.

As a follow-up to this assignment the group could listen to *Visage* by Luciano Berio. Composed in 1961 for the soprano Cathy Berberian, this work combines vocal and electronic music to create what the composer described as 'a sound track for a "drama" that was never written'. It is based on the shadowy meanings of vocal gestures and inflexions (only one complete word is ever used, 'parole' – Italian for 'words'), and it conjures up strange sequences of almost-ideas and almost-events which could have many different interpretations. Berio has said of his use of these ideas in musical composition: 'I am not interested in sound by itself, even less in sound effects . . . sighing and breathing are vocal gestures and not sound effects, and thus they carry meaning.'[2]

Cathy Berberian was herself a composer, and her work *Stripsody* – a rhapsody on comic strips, cartoon figures and their conventional onomatopoeic words (Pow! Ugh! Zoom! Splat! Zowie!) – for solo voice, could also link usefully with Assignment 6: 'The score should

[1] See also R. Murray Schafer, *The new soundscape: a handbook for the modern music teacher* (1969, BMI Canada/ Universal Edition London; incorporated with *The thinking ear*, 1986, Arcana Editions, Toronto, Canada). Schafer, one of Canada's most distinguished composers, has written extensively about the soundscape (a term he coined) and its potential in music education.

[2] *Visage* was recorded in 1967 on TV 34046S (Decca).

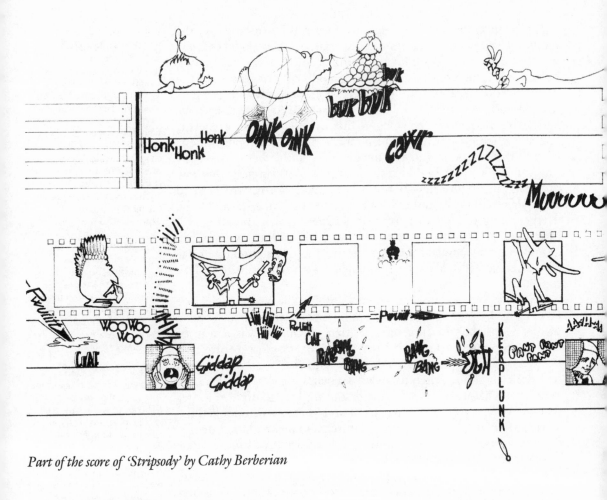

Part of the score of 'Stripsody' by Cathy Berberian

be performed as if by a radio sound man, without any props, who must provide all the sound effects with his voice.'[3] An extract from *Stripsody* is included on the accompanying tape (track 1).

Trevor Wishart's *Journey into Space* is a tape composition which uses – and dramatically transforms – an enormous variety of everyday sounds, creating a strangely dreamlike 'imaginary landscape'.[4] Two extracts from *Journey into Space* are included on the tape (track 2).

[3] Cathy Berberian, *Stripsody* for solo voice (Edition Peters, No. 66164, 1966).

[4] Trevor Wishart, *Journey into Space*, Parts One and Two. (1972: Realspace Musics, 83 Heslington Road, York). '. . . the allegorical journey of a man towards self-realisation. It begins in a strange landscape of Birth from which emerges the cry of a baby. The man, as if waking from a dream, sets off in his car with the sounds of a space-rocket launch on his car radio. The two journeys coalesce in his mind as he continues through many strange musical landscapes . . . *Journey into Space* was made using the most diverse methods of sound-production and tape-composition. Real-world events were collected via portable tape recorders. Miscellaneous sound-sources were collected from metal workshops, toy shops, builders' yards, etc. Some of the material for the original source-tapes was group improvisation on these collected objects, and/or instruments and voices . . . some very free, others less so, and yet other sections strictly notated. Other sound-sources were recorded individually and mixed later in the studio.'

The relationship between art and nature is intriguing. At the simplest level, nature supplies the raw materials – sounds, colours, stone, wood, the possibility of controlled physical movement. Nature also suggests shapes, forms, growth of structures and the behaviour of special features (e.g. recession, observable in perspective and audible in the natural decay of sounds). At another level we find artists frequently returning to nature as a source of energy. Some may think of this as inspiration, the natural phenomena stirring the emotions and the imagination. Others emphasise the ways in which art builds upon nature, transforming the raw materials to produce new symbolic structures; forms which stand for a perceived inner reality.[5] Rather than being struck dumb by the overpowering majesty of nature, it is expected that the artist will intervene; and in this sense the musician can enter into the morphology of sounds, transforming them into temporal organisations that 'go on' – and, thereby, engage with the ultimate reality, time.[6]

Certainly the fundamentalism of nature – the way in which it takes us back to first principles – can be a powerful source. For the painter Constable the directness of that encounter was a way of clearing his mind, ensuring that he applied his imagination afresh to his ideas and did not merely rely upon knowledge of what others had done in similar circumstances. 'When I sit down to make a sketch from nature', he wrote, 'the first thing I try to do is to forget that I have ever seen a picture.' He admired artists who looked for 'perfection at its primitive source, nature', and he had little time for those who were 'intent only on the study of departed excellence or what others have accomplished'.

Exactly the same thing applies in music. We can, of course, benefit from examining closely other composers' ways of dealing with certain kinds of problem, or other performers' interpretations of particular works, but we must also learn to use and to trust our own aural imagination, and to approach every composing and performing opportunity afresh.[7]

[5] The German Romantic writer and music critic E. T. A. Hoffmann believed that a mere copy of nature would be 'as miserable, awkward and forced as an inscription in a foreign language copied by a scribe who does not understand it and who laboriously imitates characters which are unintelligible to him'. By contrast, it was the mission of all the arts 'to seize nature in the most profound expression, in the most intimate sense, in that thought which raises all beings towards a more sublime life', because artists, writers and musicians had received 'the gift to transpose emotions into works of art'. (E. T. A. Hoffmann in the story 'Die Jesuitenkirche in G': *Nachtstücke I*, 1816)

[6] 'That which is within us entering as far as possible into the external reality of things.' (Theodore Rousseau, *c.* 1837).

'The purpose of all musical labour, in thought or in physical activity, is to create and develop the illusion of flowing time in its passage . . .' (Susanne Langer, *Feeling and form*, p. 120).

[7] Music-making is an *intelligent* response to feeling; and the hallmark of intelligence is, as Piaget has shown, 'an assimilation of datum into structures of transformations, from the structures of elementary actions to higher operational structures . . . These structurations consist in an organisation of reality, whether in act or thought, and not in simply making a copy of it.'

Project 2

Wind song

Poets may use phrases like 'the music of the sea' or 'wind's song', but natural sounds do not really have much in common with musical sounds.

Music is closest to nature in its textures: some sounds in the foreground, some in the background, some growing louder while others fade. In the varying textures of orchestral music we can find some affinity with the way we hear sounds all around us. With timbre too: just as we can recognise and identify the instruments of the orchestra, so natural sounds have their distinctive and memorable colours. Nature also has its regular rhythms: the walking patterns of people and animals; the regular thud of a horse galloping; pulse and heartbeat; waves on the shore; water bubbling over stones in a brook. But none of these sounds and sound patterns is exactly like music; and when we come to consider pitched sounds the link is even more tenuous.

Melody is the most contrived, and therefore the most un-natural feature of music. Pitched sounds in nature are nowhere near as precise as they are in music; the distinctive calls of birds are a long way from the structural completeness of a tune.[1] Notwithstanding this, musicians throughout history have been fascinated by birdsong and other melodic ideas in nature, and have not hesitated to make reference to them in music. To do this they have had to stylise the natural sounds. In other words, they have had to make them more clearly musical.

[1] Nevertheless, there is evidence that some birds do extend and develop their songs. The American composer and flautist Robert Dick recalls an occasion when he sustained a lengthy improvisation with two birds, both of which appeared to respond to ideas which he introduced.

Student assignments

Assignment 1

On a windy day (or, better still, a number of windy days) record several different examples of wind making pitched sounds (cf. tape track 3). Investigate the various pitches and the ways in which they rise and fall. Make careful notes of all that can be discovered about the character of the sounds. Then, *either* by imitating the sounds with a group of voices *or* by mixing down suitable parts of the recording, invent a way of using the most distinctive features of the pitched sounds to create a short piece called *Windsong*.

Assignment 2

Working as in Assignment 1, collect water sounds that have distinctive pitch. Analyse the sound characteristics and identify the pitches as closely as possible (they are unlikely to match exactly any notes on the keyboard, so take the notes nearest in pitch to the water sounds). Then use these notes and the other sound characteristics to make a piece called *Water song*. Once again, this may be done either by tape editing and mixing or by using suitable musical instruments.

Assignment 3

Record the singing of one bird whose song is particularly prominent. If possible, transfer the recording to an open reel tape and – if you can find a tape recorder that will do this – change the speed to lower the pitch. If the original recording is transferred at 19 c.p.s. it can be played back at 9.5 c.p.s. This will lower the pitch one octave and make it easier to hear the individual notes clearly.

(Alternatively, use the birdsong recordings provided on the accompanying tape, track 4.)

Find these notes (or notes as close as possible to them) on a musical instrument. If the birdsong included sliding between notes, think of a way of simulating that on the instrument. Listen carefully to the rhythm patterns in the slowed-down version. Practise playing your version of the bird's song in that rhythmic pattern. Play it at different speeds – some faster, some much slower. Try to play exactly the same shape of tune starting on a different note (i.e. transpose the tune, making sure that the intervals between notes remain exactly the same). Play it at many different points on the instrument.

Then have three or four players (perhaps on one or more keyboards) play this melody together each using a different transposed version. This will create harmony: three- or four-part chords, the parts moving in parallel. Experiment with a number of versions to find the most interesting chords.

Add other instruments (again, all playing the same line of notes in the same rhythmic pattern but each using a different transposed version, high or low). Experiment too with the combinations of the instruments to vary the colour of the chords.

Now make up a piece of music based upon these experiments. Perhaps the same idea is repeated several times with different groupings of instruments. There could be interludes in which the rhythm pattern only is played by a group of non-pitched percussion; but the emphasis should be on deriving as much as possible from the birdsong notes and rhythms.

Assignment 4

Either by collecting natural sounds on tape, *or* by using those on the accompanying tape (track 5: various animal calls), transcribe and imitate the pitches and rhythm patterns of these short motifs. Few of them will exactly match the notes on standard musical instruments, but in your imitation try to get as close as possible to the main features of the original sounds.

Now, using all or some of these motifs, make an interesting piece of music. Which is the best motif to start with? What will make a good ending? What ways are there of using the different rhythm patterns or (as in Assignment 3) of combining several transposed versions of the same motif to make chords that move in parallel? How can your finished pattern of sounds be made to sound like a whole and complete piece?

Teaching points

These are all relatively long-term assignments. Ideally students should spend some days collecting the natural sounds on tape because this will stimulate greater interest in those sounds and increase the students' powers of discrimination. However, if that is not possible, the material on the accompanying tape can be used. The tape also includes (track 6) examples which might usefully be matched with the new pieces produced by the students.

The suggested title, *Windsong*, is borrowed from a film score by the American composer Harry Partch (1901–76). Partch was an 'original' in every sense of the word. Self-taught, he turned away from conventional musical ideas to explore monophony (as opposed to the harmonic traditions of European music), natural sounds – including so-called natural tuning systems such as 'just intonation' – and antique and oriental scales. Much of his music was composed in a microtone scale of 43 notes to the octave.[2] Using sometimes the richness of rare and exotic woods and at other times everyday objects such as light bulbs, liquor bottles and vehicle hub caps, he re-created ancient musical instruments and invented new and totally unorthodox ones.

Windsong (later recorded as *Daphne of the dunes*) was composed in 1958 as the sound-track for a film directed by Madeline Tourtelot. Its melodic material is largely in the form of short, recurring ideas in

[2] See Harry Partch, *Genesis of a music*, 2nd edn (New York, Da Capo Press, 1974).

ever-changing rhythmic patterns; very close in spirit to the natural world depicted in the film.

> The music, in effect, is a collage of sounds. The film technique of fairly fast cuts is here translated into musical terms. The sudden shifts represent nature symbols of the film . . . dead tree, driftwood, falling sand, blowing tumbleweed, flying gulls, wriggling snakes, waving grasses.[3]

The banshee, by Henry Cowell, is not directly connected with the whining of the wind, although that sound may not have been far from the composer's mind.[4] The weird sounds are made by running the fingers swiftly along the length of the piano strings while the sustaining pedal is held down. The piece depends on careful control of contrasts in tone quality and of dynamics. It was composed in 1923, in some ways anticipating the sound world of electro-acoustic music that was to appear much later in this century.

Since the pitched sounds of nature rarely match those of our conventional musical instruments, and natural rhythm patterns (e.g. in birdsong and the calls of wild creatures) are often very irregular, if we want to make use of these ideas in music we must compromise by stylising the rhythm patterns and matching the pitches to the closest notes. This can often be surprisingly effective, creating exciting short motifs which can be used in many different ways to make musical structures.

It is possible that the motifs of natural 'song' were the starting-point for human music-making.[5] The melody-shapes and rhythms of birdsong in particular could well have suggested simple repetitive musical forms; and the later history of music includes many examples of composers imitating or simulating birdsong. For example, the cuckoo in 'Sumer is icumen in' (thirteenth century), in Daquin's harpsichord piece 'Le coucou' (1735), and in Delius's *On hearing the first cuckoo in spring* (1912). In the harpsichord music of François Couperin ('le Grand') there are several pieces which, in stylised forms, imitate natural sounds ('les sons non-passionnés', i.e. sounds devoid of human feeling). These include the lovesick nightingale ('Le rossignol-en-amour') and the gnat ('Le moucheron'). The nightingale and the cuckoo, along with the quail, also appear in the slow movement of Beethoven's Sixth Symphony. Among other composers who have created birdsong-inspired music are Janequin, Handel, Vivaldi, Liszt, Vaughan Williams and Respighi – whose orchestral work *The pines of Rome* (1924) incorporates a recording of the nightingale.

By far the most extensive and consistent reference to birdsong is to be found in the music of Olivier Messiaen.[6] Rather than merely imitating the songs for atmospheric effect, Messiaen derives fundamental melodic and rhythmic material from a vast range of often very complicated birdsong motifs. The opening section of *Couleurs de la cité céleste* (1963) demonstrates well this use of such motivic material. The form of this work is dependent upon the 'colours' that arise from various combinations of instruments. Here the intervals

---

[3] Partch, quoted in Danlee Mitchell's sleeve notes to the recording *The world of Harry Partch* (Columbia Records MS 7207) which includes *Daphne of the dunes*.

[4] Henry Cowell (1897–1965) was of Irish descent but was born and brought up in California. Many of his early compositions were based on Irish traditions and mythology. A banshee is 'a fairy woman, a woman of the Inner World, who comes at the time of a death . . . She is uncomfortable on the mortal plane, and wails her distress until she is safely out of it again.' (from the album notes for *The piano music of Henry Cowell* (1963), Folkways Records FM 3349).

[5] 'Nature's capacity to create, nourish and stimulate is the starting-point for all music; rhythm informs the beat of the heart, the thrumming downpour of rain and the thud of horses' hooves; melody is evoked in the mind by a bird-call or the howl of a jackal; form can be produced quite casually through repetition or memory. The first music was born independently of man, yet it was man who created genuine music from natural sounds . . . the two elements of music, pitch and rhythm, were both carried in the human body as natural, cosmic phenomena.' (Bence Szabolsci, *A history of melody*, Barrie & Rockliff, 1965, p 1.)

[6] 'In my hours of gloom, when I am suddenly aware of my own futility, when every musical idea – classical, oriental, ancient, modern, ultra-modern – appears to me as no more than admirable, painstaking experimentation, without justification, what is left for me but to seek out the

and rhythms of the New Zealand Tui-Bird and the Bell-Bird are used to make parallel chords, vividly contrasting the colours of woodwind and brass, solo piano, and ensembles of xylophone, marimba and tuned cow-bells. This and other works of Messiaen could be used as follow-up to Assignments 3 and 4.

If, for Assignment 3, it proves too difficult to record suitably distinctive birdsong, that on the tape (track 4) could be used. The first example is from the original recording. This is then reduced to half speed (and, consequently, lowered an octave). On the recording a number of birds can be heard but one is particularly distinctive. This song features four motifs separated by short periods of rest. The first and third motifs have the strongest characteristics for musical purposes, but the whole sequence is interesting, not least because the silences between the four phrases appear to be more or less of equal duration. Notated in a slightly stylised form so that it can be played on a normal musical instrument, it might look like this:

true, lost face of music somewhere off in the forest, in the fields, in the mountains or on the seashore, among the birds.' (Olivier Messiaen, *Le Guide du concert*, 3 April 1959).

As suggested in the assignments, by adopting a technique similar to that used by Messiaen, parallel chords can be made using transposed versions of these motifs. For example:

Project 3

Found sounds

We are surrounded by all kinds of sounds that are just waiting to be made into music. In this project we explore the different characteristics of sounds produced by everyday objects.

Student assignments

Assignment 1

a. How many different sounds can you produce from all the things made of wood in one room (excluding conventional musical instruments)? If several objects make more or less the same sound, choose the best and reject the others. (How will you decide what 'best' means in this case?) When the investigation is complete you should have a range of contrasting sounds. Make a list of the different ways in which these sounds can be played, e.g. all together; individually; two together having a musical conversation; three together having a musical argument; in extended patterns on one, two or three of these 'instruments'; loud; soft; and so on.

b. A group of five players improvises with the most interesting of the found sounds. Don't let this be too short; keep the improvisation going long enough to get the most out of the individual sounds and various combinations of them.

c. Compose pieces of different style and character using these found wood-sounds. In what ways do the sounds themselves suggest musical things that can be done with them?

d. Invent a notation for this music. The symbols should be able to indicate the different ways in which each sound is to be played. (Remember to include a sign for silence.) Each group should now notate the pieces already made up in such a way that the intentions will be absolutely clear to another group performing those pieces.

Assignment 2

a. Taking cassette tape recorders, collect the sounds of modern commerce. For example, the electronic sounds of a supermarket check-out; cash registers; telephone ringing tones; the differently pitched sounds of some push-button telephone dialling systems; car phones – and any other pitched or rhythmic mechanical or electronic sounds connected with buying and selling.

b. Make a second collection consisting of sound signals – police; ambulance; pedestrian road-crossing; the call-signs that precede train announcements on some railway stations; locomotive horn/whistle; bells of any kind that signal something; radio signals; ice-cream van identity tunes; and so on.

Analyse both recorded collections. Notice the rhythmic patterns, and also the precise pitches in any melodic fragments (e.g. the exact notes of the ambulance siren). Memorise these signals, or write them down; then practise imitating them with musical instruments or with your voices.

Now, using these imitations of the rhythms and melodic fragments you have collected, make two sound collage pieces. Construct these by choosing the best of the fragments you have collected and by devising ways of linking them; repeating some, perhaps using one as a surprise, and so on. Think carefully about how the sounds can be used to make something that, as it goes on, will be continuously interesting. It is not necessary to make either piece into a story; let the sound ideas (motifs) speak for themselves. The main interest should be in how they are used, individually and in combination. It is particularly important to think about (and try out) ways of starting and ending each piece. Give the finished pieces appropriate titles.

Assignment 3

Each member of the group finds one object that makes a single *beautiful* sound. (Before setting out to look for these objects it would be best to decide what 'beautiful' means in this connection. How much does it have to do with familiarity, on the one hand, and surprise, on the other?) Listen to all the sounds and talk about how they can be grouped. Which go best together – and why? Experiment with different combinations of the sounds, and then use each grouping to make a piece of music that exploits the special (i.e. 'beautiful') qualities you have identified. Then devise a plan for making a large-scale piece that uses all these found-object sounds together.

Assignment 4

A project called 'Materials and instruments', in which you gather materials – wood, glass, metal; whatever can be made to produce sounds – in order to invent and build new and unusual musical instruments. Be as imaginative as you can. Forget that you've ever seen a musical instrument of any kind! But do try to ensure that every instrument you build has a range of different pitches, and that it can be played in a variety of ways (loud, soft, short sounds, sustained sounds). When several instruments are completed, explore each one thoroughly and develop its playing techniques. That will probably suggest musical ideas. Make up pieces of music for the instruments individually and in groups.

Assignment 5

a. Make a piece for 20 metronomes.

b. Make a piece for 10 alarm clocks.

c. Make a piece for 8 radios.

d. Make a piece for 100 tea-spoons. (How can you get a really good sound out of them?)

e. Everyone in the group brings one device that works by electricity and makes a distinctive sound when it is switched on. Choose one of these to be a solo 'instrument'. The rest form an 'orchestra'. As a group composition, make a concerto for the solo instrument accompanied, as appropriate, by the orchestra.

Assignment 6

The traditional music of Java and Bali is for the gamelan, an orchestra of mostly metal percussion instruments – gongs and metallophones of various sizes. Generally, the low-pitched instruments play slowly; and the higher the pitch of an instrument the faster the music given to it (tape track 7).

Use this principle to make a 'found-objects gamelan'. Collect things made of metal that sound well when they are struck. Arrange them in groups: the largest and lowest-sounding in one group, the smallest and highest in another, and the middle-pitched sounds together in a third group. Make sure there is sufficient contrast in the kind of sounds that can be made with what you have collected.

Listen again to the tape of the Javanese gamelan (track 7). Without knowing anything more about how that music works than what you can hear in the recording, and using your three groups of found objects played together, make up a piece of music that has some of the characteristics of the gamelan sound.

A Javenese gamelan

Assignment 7

Design and build a sound-sculpture. It must be as fascinating to look at as it is to listen to. In what ways can the sounds be made to match the theme of the sculpture? Can you, perhaps, make use of electronic sounds?

Teaching points

Composing is first a process of selection and rejection; of reviewing the strongest features in the materials at our disposal and then choosing what is best. That could, of course, mean a number of different things: best for a specific purpose, such as making music for a particular event or occasion, or to accompany some other art-form, such as a film; best because the sounds selected are those that you specially like; best because all concerned agree that the sounds chosen have an inherent beauty – as opposed to the inherent ugliness of those not chosen (but again, terms like 'beauty' and 'ugliness', and the extent to which familiarity affects our judgement, will need to be discussed).

Assignment 1 focuses attention on selecting and grading sounds found in a limited field. Having agreed on a way of taking the decisions, it is essential to go on to make music. The first stage is likely to be a group improvisation; for its own sake – i.e. because it is a musically valuable thing to do – and also because it reveals further possibilities. Improvising helps to draw out the musical potential of the sounds and to relate them to one another; and it encourages the players to think imaginatively and quickly with those resources. Composing then concentrates upon the refinement of forms, and the relationships between specific features which can be elaborated through creative experiment. Attempting to find a suitable form of notation – and thereby experiencing the conse-quences when others try to perform the music from that notation – will provide further opportunities for detailed analysis of the sounds and their musical potential.

Assignment 2 is in some respects an extension of work suggested for Project 1. Once again, the intention is that students should become involved with the sounds by analysing the recordings so that they can appreciate the detailed characteristics and be able to imitate them. This time, however, the aim is not to make an environmental sound picture – i.e. not to represent the sounds in a real, if idealised, setting – but to use the musical qualities of the collected rhythm patterns and melodic motifs (even brief two-note sirens) to create an abstract collage which is interesting for its own sake rather than for its association with the original sources of the sounds.

In this assignment, thinking of a suitable title for each finished piece is very much part of the composition. But in no sense are these pieces meant to be programme music. The point is that, because a title may refer back – however tenuously – to whatever it was that started the train of thought towards musical forms, it can provide an important confirmation of wholeness in the completed music. It unifies all the sensations and 'vibrations' received from the original stimulus. For example, a suitable title for the first piece might come from some aspect of commerce – trade, money-making, market forces – or from a pun, e.g. 'Twenty-pence Piece'. And for the second piece, perhaps an idea that suggests warning, signalling, or controlling.

For a composer, a title is more likely to symbolise the process by which stimulus (inspiration?) has been transmuted into musical ideas and subsequently worked out as a piece of music, than to signify any translation into a sound-story.

Similarly, for listeners a title should not normally be anything more than a link with the composer's starting-points or with some kind of overview of the musical structure. To know that a piece resulting from this project has some general connection with commerce may help a listener to place the sounds used; but it should not raise expectations of a 'programme' or a story; nor should it seem to invite the listener into a guessing game where every musical event must be related to something in the real world. Music doesn't work like that.

Music cannot describe as words or visual images describe; and we must be careful never to give students the impression that it can. We do them a disservice if we lead them to think that music may be no more than a sound-effects translation of experiences that can just as well be described in words. This is not to say that we should avoid literary or pictorial starting-points as a way into composing. It is simply that we should be aware of the dangers and of the possibility of misunderstanding.

The necessary 'literary-ness' of so many aspects of music (and particularly of learning about music) can, if we are not careful, become a barrier to understanding the musical function of music. Therefore it is worth clearing the ground at the first opportunity by talking about the relationship between titles, and other visual/verbal expressions, and completed pieces of music. As well as confirming the unification of musical ideas, a title may itself be a starting-point, prodding the imagination to generate everything from tiny motifs to whole structures. But titles must not be allowed to obscure the significance of the sound-forms themselves.

The writings of R. Murray Schafer and Trevor Wishart offer further ideas for using found and environmental sounds as a basis for music.[1] It could also be useful to refer to the work of John Cage[2] – perhaps the best known figure in a musical movement of the 1950s which often eschewed conventional musical instruments, drawing instead upon the haphazard ambient soundscape. Cage's *Williams Mix* brings together recordings of many different sounds from city and countryside in a strange collage controlled by games of chance.

As an extension of Assignment 3 students could be encouraged to perform one or more of the pieces in *Prose Collection* by Christian Wolff. For example:

STONES

Make sounds with stones, draw sounds out of stones, using a number of sizes and kinds (and colours); for the most part discretely; sometimes in rapid sequences. For the most part striking stones with stones, but also stones on other surfaces (inside the open head of a drum, for instance) or other than struck (bowed, for instance, or amplified). Do not break anything.[3]

This could lead to further discussion of notation. In this case we have a verbal score; what are the advantages and disadvantages of preserving musical ideas in such a form?

Assignment 4 develops another line of imagination. This time the found objects are materials which must first be made into musical instruments. Avoid too many non-pitched percussion sounds; they will be the most obvious, but they will also be the most limited.

[1] R. Murray Schafer, *The new soundscape* (1969) and *The composer in the classroom* (1965) (BMI Canada – available from Universal Edition, London) – both incorporated with additional material into *The thinking ear* (1986) (Arcana Editions, PO Box 425, Station K, Toronto, Canada M4P 2G9).

Trevor Wishart, *Sun: creativity and environment* (1974) and *Sun: a creative philosophy* (1977) (Universal Edition).

[2] John Cage, *Silence* (Cambridge, Mass., MIT Press, 1966).

[3] Christian Wolff, *Prose Collection* (London 1968, Vermont 1969).

Encourage students to explore pitched sounds that can be precisely controlled. To be musically useful an instrument should have a distinctive sound quality and be capable of producing, within that same quality, a range of sounds. These do not have to be identifiable pitches – they could be various timbres – but pitched sounds that also have interesting timbres will normally offer greater musical scope. Some craft skills will be helpful for this part of the project, perhaps through links with craft and design departments.[4]

For the 'found-objects gamelan' (Assignment 6) the formal organisation is dependent upon what can be discovered about the Indonesian gamelan conventions merely by listening to the tape. The aim is to capture the character of gamelan sound rather than to learn the precise techniques:

> In the glittering peal of this strange orchestra one can distinguish the plain and solemn melody of the basses, its paraphrase and loquacious figuration in the smaller chimes, and the punctuation of the gongs, of which the smaller ones mark the end of shorter sections while the powerful basses of the large gongs conclude the main parts. The two drums guide the changing tempo.[5]

The sound-sculptures made by the brothers François and Bernard Baschet are beautiful objects in their own right, but they are also instruments on which children and adults are encouraged to make musical improvisations.

[4] See also: David Sawyer, *Vibrations: making unorthodox musical instruments* (Cambridge University Press, 1977); John Paynter, *Music in the secondary school curriculum* (Cambridge University Press, 1982), pp. 114–16; David Toop, *New and re-discovered musical instruments* (London, Quartz/Mirlton, 1974); Andy Jackson, *Instruments around the world* (London, Longman, 1988); *The glass world of Anna Lockwood* (recording).

[5] Curt Sachs, *The rise of music in the ancient world, East and West* (London, Dent, 1944), p. 152. See also, by the same author, *The history of musical instruments* (London, Dent, 1942), pp. 237 ff. Further information on the gamelan can be found in William P. Malm, *Music cultures of the Pacific, the Near East and Asia* (New Jersey, Prentice-Hall, 1967), pp. 15–35.

Sound-sculptures by the Baschet brothers

'Ode til lyset': sound-sculpture at Storedal, Norway

At the Storedal Cultural Centre, set in the countryside of eastern Norway, there is a huge sound-sculpture, 'Ode to light', created by Arnold Haukeland and the composer Arne Nordheim. The Centre is dedicated to working with blind people, and the sound-sculpture symbolises two arms outstretched towards the light. Photo-electric cells placed at various points on the sculpture react to the slightest changes of light in the sky, and this controls the sound. When the light changes – with the sunrise, with the coming of dusk, or with the movement of clouds – the impulses from the photo-electric cells activate a computer controlling two pre-recorded tapes which in turn send music appropriate to the quality of the light to twenty-six loudspeakers housed in the sculpture.

Musical instruments extend the sounds we can make by clapping hands, stamping feet and singing; but what made people devise musical instruments? It is unlikely that there was a conscious moment of invention. What we should now regard as simple percussion instruments were probably in use for many thousands of years, emphasising the hand-clapping, feet-stamping and singing of ritual dance and chant long before anyone had the idea of manufacturing instruments as such for musical purposes.

Doubtless we shall never know how music and musical instruments began, but we can see that, all over the world, people continue to make instrumental music just by adding rhythmic accompaniments to their own singing and dancing; and presumably that – or something like it – has been happening for as long as the human race has existed.

We are not, then, talking about a process of evolution from the primitive to the sophisticated, but observing that, fundamentally, music is music-making. However much it becomes complicated by elaborate notations and painstakingly thought out structures, music is basically what it always has been: people being moved (quite literally) to make patterns of sound that convey emotion. And because the emotions are strongly felt, so the patterns of sound are in various ways made larger than life; exaggerated particularly in the rhythmic features which mark the passing of time.

Today we are more than ever made conscious of music as music; music as entertainment, existing independently of other aspects of living. Yet people still respond with movement, even to the disembodied sound-patterns created by computer synthesizers and transmitted via tape, radio and television. And, notwithstanding all the technological wizardry, a vast amount of the world's music goes on being made, as it always has been made, by people who have no conventional musical education (in the current high culture sense) simply singing, playing, repeating and remembering what comes into their heads and what bodily movements suggest.

Some anthropologists believe that rattles, as they are used in many musical cultures, attached to the ankles, knees or waist of a dancer to emphasise rhythms that would not normally be audible, are among the world's oldest musical instruments. We should not think of that as primitive music-making; it is an elegant solution to the problem of how to stress complex rhythmic articulations. But in a wider view of musical instruments, the design and sound of the rattle has probably not changed much since people first thought of using gourds for that purpose. Other instruments, though, have been refined and developed over many thousands of years, partly to produce greater variety and range of sounds (particularly pitched sounds) and more precise ways of obtaining exactly the sound wanted at any particular moment, and also to provide greater subtlety of tone quality.

The latter is a very important ingredient in music's appeal. The suggested discussion of what constitutes 'beauty' in sound (Assignment 3) could, perhaps, come some way towards identifying the sensuous qualities that delight us as we listen to music. Inventing and building new instruments is, in a way, an extension of that discussion.

From the initial instinctive rhythmic response and sensuous delight in timbre and melodic shape musicians develop their fascination with pattern – with structure. That is the real beginning of composing.

Composing consists in dealing with the flow of music rather than with particular instants of sound . . . The musician is working with a constantly flowing stream of sound – so that how you make the stream flow and what obstacles you put in to stop it from flowing or to modify the flow, and so on, become fundamental.[6]

[6] Elliot Carter, quoted in Allen Edwards, *Flawed words and stubborn sounds: a conversation with Elliot Carter* (New York, W.W. Norton, 1971), p. 37.

Even when composing with the random sounds of found objects, that is a most important consideration.

Project 4

Fingers are great inspirers

Musical instruments themselves inspire musical ideas, not only by the quality of the sounds they produce but also by the way they are constructed and played. The outward appearance of an instrument often seems to invite you to place your fingers on it in a way that will produce interesting arrangements of sounds.

For example, the harp's strings suggest long sweeping movements across them – and that is perhaps one of the commonest and most characteristic uses of the harp in orchestral music. A whole piece of music for solo harp could be made from a series of those glissandi.

Student assignments

Assignment 1

For guitarists. The guitar seems to invite broken chords: one hand holding down three or four strings against the frets while the other plucks them separately, one after another. Choose a fingering pattern for any chord (or make up a new one) and then, keeping that hand shape, move it, fret by fret, up and down the finger-board, plucking the strings individually or strumming gently across them. Include one or more open strings to produce a series of different chords, some of which will probably sound unusual. Develop this into a short piece of music that contrasts the different kinds of chord obtained.

Assignment 2

For keyboard players. The arrangement of the keys suggests certain hand shapes. The hand sits quite naturally over the white keys, so that musical figures such as

are almost created by the instrument itself. Make up a piece of music simply by repeating such figures and moving them up and down the keyboard.

Quite an extensive piece can be made out of a relatively simple sequence of chords:

J S Bach, Prelude 1, *Das Wohltemperierte Klavier*

Assignment 3

For players of the violin, viola, cello or double bass. Because – unlike the guitar – these instruments do not have frets on the finger-board, the movement of the hand up and down the finger-board is very easy; and that suggests *sliding* along the strings:

Bartók, String Quartet No. 3

Make up a piece – preferably for a large group of players – using sounds produced (arco or pizzicato) by sliding along the strings.

Assignment 4

More for keyboards:

a Make more hand-shape pieces, perhaps beginning on the black notes which, because they stand up clearly in twos and threes (or fives?), seem to invite us to use them in those patterns.

b Go on from there to find other arrangements of keys which lie easily under the hand. Take care to remember precisely what you discover and the musical ideas that come to you: repeat them (exactly or slightly changed – i.e. developed), and keep going. Music will begin to take shape.

It is surprising how often an idea can be repeated without becoming boring. For example, begin as before with fingers of the right hand on the notes C, E and G. Play them as a downward broken chord, one after the other from highest to lowest. Then move up one note and play the same shape on the notes A, F and D. Move up one note again, and so on, repeating the simple three-note figure higher and higher. Add something new: for example, playing a black note each time simultaneously with the first (highest) note of the right-hand pattern:

Experiment with this idea, repeating it at various points on the keyboard, high and low. Play it softly. Play it loudly. Play it as fast as possible. Start at different points and leap over gaps:

Devise other ways of using this combined left-hand/right-hand idea: for instance, making the left-hand note more forceful and letting it come before the descending right-hand notes:

c There are many examples of specific techniques being used as starting-points for Studies. The way an instrument is played can stimulate ideas just as much as its physical appearance and mechanical arrangements. Any technical point could become the basis of a composition, e.g. chord playing, arpeggios, staccato/legato, pianissimo/fortissimo, pedalling.

One of the first things we learn on the keyboard is how to play scales smoothly by tucking the thumb under:

Make a piece using that simple movement of the thumb as the principal idea. Use the entire range of the keyboard.

Invent other musical ideas based on points of keyboard technique.

d On the piano, choose any three low notes. Depress the keys very gently so that the notes do not sound. This will lift the dampers from the strings. Holding down those keys, strike sharply another note or group of notes higher up the keyboard. The notes of the held-down keys will sound like an echo, in sympathy with the harmonics of the notes struck sharply.

Use this effect to make a piece of music in which the sympathetic vibrations accompany a melody. With the left hand, hold down silently a triad or any group of notes. Make up a melody with the right hand. Playing the melody will vibrate the open strings of the notes that are held down with the left hand. Make pauses in the melody so that the mysterious effect of the harmonics can be heard.

A musician sits in the pavilion door

John Paynter

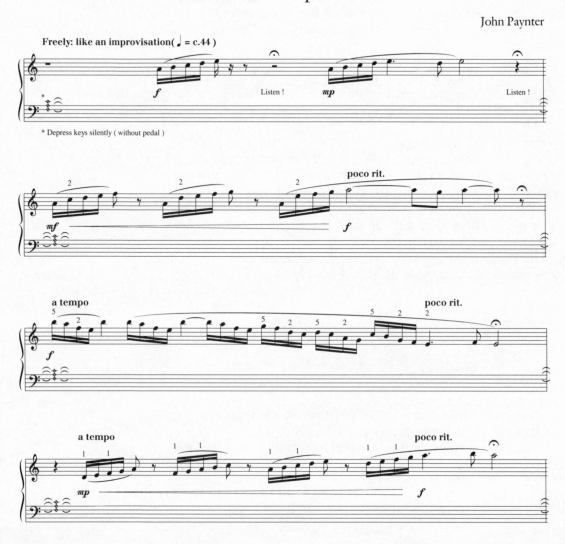

e 'Prepare' the harmonics of a series of notes and then compose solo and duet pieces for 'prepared' piano. (See below under 'Teaching points'.)

Assignment 5

More for strings:

a Experiment to discover as many different ways as possible of producing sounds, bowed and plucked. Include the standard techniques. Make a list and demonstrate all the techniques listed. Compose a piece that uses every one of these techniques.

b Using only four unusual techniques, compose pieces for solo instruments and for groups. In each of the group pieces, have a recurring section which is played by everyone together, alternating this with solo and duet sections. Remember the value of silence in music: silences are essential parts of the composition but they must not hold up the flow of the music. You must manage the silences so that they do not give the impression of the music stopping. Discuss ways in which that can be done.

c Make a group piece which uses only the lowest string of each instrument but includes a variety of bowed and plucked techniques.

d For advanced players. Make up pieces of music that exploit various bowing techniques, individually and in combination (e.g. *sul ponticello, sul tasto, tremolando, martellato, saltando, portato, col legno*).

e Compose a suite of 'Four characteristic pieces' for strings (i.e. each short piece exploiting a particular technique). For example:

i fast and entirely pizzicato;

ii slow, quiet and mysterious, playing tremolando, *sul ponticello*, at the point of the bow throughout;

iii moderate speed, all four players glissando throughout;

iv fast and disjointed, playing always on the far side of the bridge.

Assignment 6

For percussion. Arrange a large number of percussion instruments *either* close to one another to form a 'sculptural' group *or* spaced out like a theatre set. Think carefully about where each instrument should be placed and how each relates to those nearest to it and to the group as a whole. Make a series of improvisations using different numbers of players (from one upwards) and discuss the results. In what ways did the arrangement of the instruments affect the nature of the music produced? Next, make individual and/or group compositions for the same layout of instruments. Try to introduce an element of theatre into the way the players perform on the instruments.

Assignment 7

Experiment with many different musical instruments to discover the ugliest sounds they can make. Compose a piece with these sounds (*molto brutto!*). Give it a suitable title.

Teaching points

This motif for two clarinets, from the third tableau of Stravinsky's ballet *Petrushka*, was originally intended to be part of a piano concerto. The piano would be like 'a puppet, suddenly endowed with life, exasperating the patience of the orchestra with diabolical cascades of arpeggios'. The motif is made of two arpeggio chords – C major and F♯ major – played simultaneously. The physical relationship of the idea to the composer's hands on the keyboard is very evident: one hand on the white keys the other on the black. In spite of all that has been written about the polytonality of this famous musical idea, it was probably just discovered by Stravinsky doodling at the piano. In his *Chronicle of my life* he refers to many other instances in which his creative imagination was stimulated by the mechanics of the keyboard itself. Writing about *Piano-Rag Music* (1919) he says:

> What fascinated me most . . . was that the different rhythmic episodes were dictated by the fingers themselves . . . Fingers are not to be despised: they are great inspirers, and, in contact with a musical instrument, often give birth to subconscious ideas which might otherwise never come to life.[1]

[1] Quoted in Eric Walter White, *Stravinsky: the composer and his works* (London, Faber & Faber, 1966), p. 242.

The first assignments in this project are intended to produce ideas in that way. Even complete beginners can appreciate the pattern arrangements of the keyboard; indeed, making up a short piece on the lines suggested could be someone's introduction to the piano. Most children are fascinated by pattern pieces on the piano and even those who have never had lessons will struggle to play 'Chopsticks', or this:

However, the more technique anyone has the better will be the control of the patterns. A player with a reasonably secure technique at about Grade V might produce something like this for Assignment 4(b):

The following pattern piece, based on triads and octaves, was made by an 18-year-old doodling at the keyboard. He had never taken piano lessons and in no sense could he be called a pianist. Nevertheless, he became fascinated by the possibilities of this pattern and continued working at it until he had made a piece he could remember. He notated it very simply using the letter names of the notes. The following is a staff notation transcription.

Andrew Wood

This is uncomplicated music. Even so, it reveals an intuitive feeling for design, in that the whole structure derives from the minim bass notes of the first four bars. The triads and the octave leaps form the principal musical idea; and the recurring sequential figure (bars 9–14, 19–24, 29–end) is also initiated by the octave (sometimes two-octave) leap. It is clear from the way the cycle of upward-moving triads and descending sequences ultimately arrives back on the low C – the note with which the piece began – that the composer appreciates the wholeness of this piece. Notice too his obvious delight in the rich, low sonority of the bass; in the potential for changes of rhythmic emphasis; and in harmonic subtleties such as the augmented 4th in bar 21 – which occurs because of the self-imposed limitation of making the pattern on the white keys only. Although such details are probably intuitive rather than pre-conceived and thought out, a teacher, offered a piece like this, should not hesitate to discuss them with the composer.

The next example is of a piece produced in response to Assignment 2. The composer has developed the technical point (the triadic form that seems most natural to the hand shape) into music of striking individuality. The style is aggressive – violent, even – characterised by those moments when the notes of the triad are sounded together as staccato chords contrasting with the forceful but legato broken chord pattern. Having made such a piece, the composer might well appreciate some of the piano music of Béla Bartók – in particular, the *Allegro barbaro*, the Piano Sonata (1926), and 'Chase' from the suite *Out of doors*.

Valerie Mills

The piano music of Debussy will also provide useful examples to match with students' compositions. Where suitable, it would be helpful to study the printed music first and to discuss the forms of the hand-shape ideas before hearing music such as 'Doctor Gradus ad Parnassum' (from the suite *Children's corner*), 'Jardins sous la pluie' (from *Estampes*), and 'Feux d'artifice' (second book of *Préludes*). Even if it is not practicable to discuss detailed points from the printed music, it would still be profitable for students who have made pattern pieces to listen to performances of this music – preferably live performances so that they could observe how the hand shapes relate to the musical ideas.

For anyone learning to play a musical instrument, composing for that instrument should be part of the process. As new technical points are encountered (e.g. for woodwind, particular methods of articulation such as flutter-tonguing) they can become the basis of creative experiment and composition. Creativity and skill-acquisition should go hand in hand. If possible, arrange for instrumental teachers to become involved with the class music teaching – working on some of the more unusual techniques with student players and advising groups or individuals exploring technical points as a basis for composition.

The 'prepared piano'

In the twentieth century, composers have extended the range of techniques to take in many sounds that previously would have been regarded as unusable. These include – on stringed instruments – playing beyond the bridge, and – on wind instruments – using special fingerings to produce chords, a technique known as multiphonics.

One of the most notable (some would say notorious!) twentieth-century extensions of this kind is the 'prepared piano'. The normal piano sound is changed by inserting small pieces of metal and wood carefully between the strings. Although this may seem a barbaric thing to do to a fine instrument, it is in fact only a device to make it possible for a pianist to play harmonics, something we take for granted on every other instrument that has strings (and, indeed, now accept in the multiphonics of, for example, the clarinet). Used sensitively, the harmonics of the piano strings are amazingly effective; they have a clear, pure quality which is unlike any other musical sound.[2]

The guitarist produces beautiful bell-like harmonics by touching the string very lightly at the twelfth fret (i.e. not pressing it right down) and then plucking the string sharply to let it ring. Harpists can similarly produce harmonics by plucking the string while at the same time touching it lightly either with the right hand (the side of the palm) or with the left hand (first joint of the index finger, plucking the string above it with the thumb). In each case the hand forms a kind of artificial bridge which damps out the fundamental tone that would be produced by the full length of the string. Violinists, viola players, cellists and double bass players all make frequent and easy use of the unusual and often mysterious effects of harmonics. So, why not pianists as well?

Quite simply because it would be very difficult to touch the piano strings at the correct points and at the same time to play on the keys. It is possible to make use of piano harmonics to a limited extent by holding down keys with the left hand (i.e. putting them down silently to raise the dampers of those notes without letting the hammers strike the strings) and then striking other keys normally. The struck notes activate the harmonics in the strings of the held-down keys, producing an echo-like aeolian harp effect (see Assignment 4(d) above). Beyond that, the only possibility for extensive use of piano harmonics in a way comparable with what can be achieved on other stringed instruments is to dedicate specific strings to that use by preparing the harmonics beforehand.

[2] For example, John Cage, *Sonatas and interludes* for prepared piano, recorded (1974) by John Tilbury on *Mr John Cage's prepared piano* (Decca HEAD 9).

The point at which the string is touched is crucial. Every vibrating string has a number of nodes (points at which the string is, or could be, stationary – i.e. not vibrating), and it is at these points that the 'preparation' is made. Precisely which node to use and the nature of the preparation (e.g. metal, wood, rubber) is a matter for experiment; it will depend upon the musical effect you want. Great care must be taken not to damage the strings when you insert a screw or whatever between two strings. (Well-sharpened pencils can be just as effective as screws and, twisted down gently between two strings, are less likely to cause damage.)

If you want to use only the harmonics, then it will probably be necessary to prepare a good number of notes. In that case, the prepared sounds would become virtually an instrument in their own right. Dispensing with the rest of the piano, the very special qualities of the prepared notes could be allowed to suggest the style and form of the music in its entirety. Alternatively, it could be equally interesting to use just a few prepared notes for special effect in a piece conceived mainly for the normal piano sound.

Part II

Musical ideas

Project 5

Growth points

A musical idea may be nothing more elaborate than a very short motif or figure. It could even be a single note; but then it would need special attributes to make it a memorable idea. An idea of that kind is rather like a seed; it contains features that will become the distinctive characteristics of whatever grows from it. It is a starting-point from which you can draw out and develop those special qualities one by one, or by taking the motif as a whole and extending it in various ways.

Student assignments

Assignment 1

Choose any one note and give it some easily recognisable characteristics – duration (e.g. long or very short); articulation (a special way of starting and finishing the note); dynamic change (e.g. starting it very quietly and getting dramatically louder); some kind of decoration (e.g. a trill or a mordent). Whatever you decide to do, it will need to be exaggerated to make the single note idea really memorable. Go to extremes!

Assignment 2

Choose any two notes. Experiment with distinctive ways of playing them. From this experiment derive a two-note musical motif and explore ways of keeping it going, using changes of dynamics and articulation to vary it and to make it grow and develop. Try a number of possibilities; some fast, some slow.

Assignment 3

Invent a strongly characteristic motif as in Assignment 1 but using groups of 3 or 4 notes. Transpose this motif to different parts of the instrument, sometimes by leaping to a very high or very low point, at other times simply by moving the whole motif up or down a single step. Explore ways in which this idea could be made into a whole piece of music.

Assignment 4

Invent a musical motif using only drums, wood blocks, claves, maracas and non-pitched 'found' sounds. Try to discover ways of exaggerating the contrasts of dynamics and articulation so that you can keep up the interest as the idea is extended and developed.

Assignment 5

For a group of 5–10 players with instruments of contrasting timbres. Each player makes up a short (2–3 seconds) figure which includes strong and unusual features. Eventually all the figures are to be played simultaneously to make a single dramatic gesture; that is to say, a distinctive and memorable group of sound-ideas, complex (because of the many different things happening at the same time) but self-contained (because the motifs and figures are not, at this point, developed or extended in any way, but simply stated once; like a single, highly expressive gesture of the hands, emphasising some particular point).

The musical gesture will be all the more powerful if its individual parts have unexpected features. At the same time, since it will probably last for only two or three seconds at the most, no one part should stand out too obviously; and they must all fit together as naturally as possible. You will have to experiment to see how that can be done without destroying the most interesting features of individual motifs. It is important, therefore, that players work not only on the individual motifs but also on how those motifs can go together.

A quality which may be useful here is the rate at which different sounds fade away. For example, the short, dry wooden sounds of xylophones die away quickly, whereas other instruments (such as bells, cymbals, the piano with the sustaining pedal held down) continue vibrating so that the sounds take much longer to disappear. Then there are instruments on which the sounds can be sustained just as long as is necessary (e.g. any stringed instrument played with a bow) but which can also produce very short, spiky sounds (e.g. strings played pizzicato). And again, wind instruments which can go on sounding as long as the breath lasts. Try to make use of these different rates of decay to allow certain features to be more prominent than others in your group motif.

When everyone in the group is agreed on how the combined gesture should sound, explore ways of making it go on – but without changing its special features too much – to make a whole piece of music. For instance, you could repeat the motif several times with certain features only very slightly changed. Or you might extend individual players' ideas, bringing in the complete motif (i.e. all the instruments together) every now and again as a kind of punctuation mark.

Teaching points

An interesting idea can be made from a single note, but only if the note is given some distinctive characteristics of attack and dynamic control. For example:

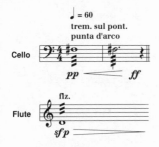

Ideas like that can be developed by repeating on different pitches, and with varied durations and dynamics:

While it is possible to make something interesting from only one note, adding a second note opens up a much bigger range of possibilities.[1] A bright and forward-driving motif could be created simply by quickly alternating any two notes, for instance:

[1] Cf. Delacroix: 'One line alone has no meaning; a second one is needed to give it expression.'

– perhaps getting louder all the time:

or moving from soft to loud in waves:

That is not particularly elaborate; in fact, it's very simple! But it *is* an idea, and it does have a certain character. (And will, incidentally, make a different impression depending upon the instrument used. Improvise with it on several different instruments to see which produces the most interesting possibilities.)

Other ways of using the same two notes might be:

1. to create a different character by lengthening one of them ▷

2. to make contrasts of articulation (e.g. staccato, legato, trilled, etc.):

3. to play the notes with a variety of articulation on several different instruments in turn or overlapping with one another to produce interesting contrasts of timbre and dynamics:

Even with the limitation of just two notes it is possible to create some very distinctive ideas because the other features (loudness, duration, attack, timbre) can be combined in so many ways. In addition, either or both of the notes can be decorated with trills, repetitions and rhythmic figurations, for example:

An idea is not merely a starting-point for elaboration; it can also be the germ of an entire organic structure. In classical Greek ἰδέα (idéā) was associated with a similar word meaning 'to see' – from which, presumably, we have come to think of an idea as 'the look' of something: 'I *see*; that's how it will be!' or 'So *that's* what it's going to be like!' In this way, a musical idea can reveal, from the start, the essential nature of a piece.

It need not be elaborate. If it has strong characteristics it can be quite short. This is what is looked for particularly in Assignment 5, where the group must work together to invent an idea which lasts for no more than one or two beats, but which combines different instrumental timbres, articulations and decorations in such a way that, short as it is, it makes a very big impression.

The term usually applied to such a short but distinctive musical utterance is 'gesture'. Just as we can convey our intentions with expressive bodily movements (an urgent or intense physical gesture may be a complicated combination of hand and arm movements, fingers, raised eyebrows and grimacing – all happening more or less simultaneously!), so we can make involved and exciting musical gestures by combining complementary ideas on several musical instruments. The musical gesture *in toto* is heard as a single idea. It may subsequently be developed in various ways, or merely repeated (with only minor changes) and contrasted with similar ideas – in which case, we might refer to the musical style overall as 'gestural'.

As is suggested in the assignment, when several instruments are involved the differences in rate of decay can be particularly useful in allowing certain features to come through the texture – and so make the overall composite idea more interesting.[2] For example, in a musical motif such as the following there are significant points of interest in what each instrument plays, but the musical effect is created by the complexity of the combined ideas.

[2] Pierre Boulez, in a programme note for one of his works (*Eclat/Multiples*), asks the audience to take special note of this feature: 'Analyse, I hope with pleasure, the contrast in decay between sustaining instruments and percussive ones.'

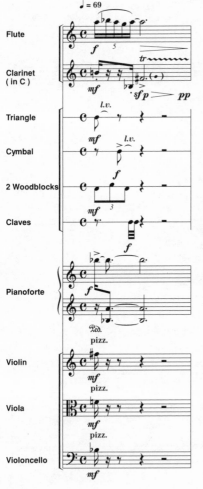

This combination of sounds creates a complete musical idea. The instruments play together in a single gesture which has a number of distinctive features, all of which could be exploited in an extended piece of music based on this idea. The loud, incisively dissonant chord of 2nds and 7ths masks the percussion, which is sustained – and therefore emerges only gradually from 'behind' the first chord. The clarinet sustains the G and F♯ trill but, after its *sfp* start, quickly reduces the breath to dissolve to *pp*.

Timbre is an important quality, but one that is frequently overlooked by students when they are concentrating on melodic and rhythmic ideas. Doubtless many good tunes sound perfectly well no matter what instruments they are played on. Handel and his contemporaries, for example, were for the most part content for their instrumental sonatas to be played by flute, oboe, or violin, according to what was available. For Stravinsky, on the other hand, melody and timbre were inseparable. Although, throughout his life, he generated ideas at the piano, he maintained that he never invented a melody without immediately hearing in his imagination the instrument that would play it.[3] The rightness of certain timbres for particular kinds of musical idea is worth exploring; although with a severely limited choice of instruments the problem has to be approached the other way round: what can we do with what we've got; what are the characteristics of the timbres available to us? What kind of melodic ideas do they suggest?

Discuss the details of all the ideas made up during the project as they are presented. Emphasise the special musical qualities and draw attention to features that are really distinctive and capable of being developed. Experimenting with the first two-note idea should indicate possibilities for extension and development such as

[3] For example, the bassoon solo at the opening of Stravinsky's *The rite of spring*. This folk melody was originally from Lithuania. As Stravinsky sets it, in an unusually high register of the bassoon, its oddly penetrating quality evokes the remoteness of a primitive world. It is within the range of the cor anglais, and might be played more easily on that instrument, but the timbre of the high bassoon is a unique and unforgettable sound which is now forever associated with this tune.

- repeating the figure in different octaves:

- keeping the fast rocking shape but changing to two other notes a 3rd apart (perhaps with some recognition of the different impression given by major or minor 3rds):

- varying the dynamics and the instrumentation:

Simple as this first idea is, it can be developed without losing its essence. It gives us a strong starting-point for an extended piece in which the character of the original idea can always be identified. A starting idea needs some distinction if anything extensive is to grow from it; but that doesn't mean it has to be complicated. Some of the most striking ideas are the most straightforward.

What must surely be one of the world's most memorable tunes springs from a four-note idea: two notes making a downward inflexion, then a short leap up to two other notes which again make a downward inflexion. (Or is it really just a two-note idea? ▷)

This is expanded into four phrases:

I.

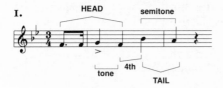

The dotted anacrusis figure prepares us for the strong beat a whole tone higher, adding strength to the downward inflexion. This 'head' is then echoed in the 'tail' a 4th higher. From the point of view of development, the most useful features are the dotted rhythm, the upward leap and the downward movements.

2.

The same 'head' with a different 'tail' (the leap of a 4th now extended to a 5th).

3.

Again the dotted rhythm to 'kick off' the phrase, but now the upward leap is dramatically extended to an octave, and the downward inflexion developed into a line of notes combining the downward inflexions of both head and tail (i.e. semitone and tone).

The dotted-rhythm head, now lifted, gives unexpected variation and reinforces the descending phrase which signals the approaching final cadence.

The forward impetus of the first phrase, which derives from the dotted rhythm, the whole-tone lift (F G F) and the leap (F Bb), carries through the whole tune. In one sense phrases 2, 3 and 4 are variants of the first phrase. But there is more to this melody than a mere string of semi-independent phrases. The principal idea is stated in phrase 1, established by a modest development in phrase 2, driven suddenly to a dramatic climax in phrase 3, and brought gently home in phrase 4. There is a clear satisfaction in the *wholeness* of this pattern. Quite apart from the structural strength of the overall design, the tune's basic idea has an internal strength of its own (the head motif generating the tail motif); and a major feature of the development – the descending line of notes in the third phrase – is made by overlapping two three-note phrases, both of which relate to the two-note downward inflexion. The first three-note phrase opens up that feature by expanding the interval to a 3rd, and the second pulls it together again into semitone followed by whole-tone (the same intervals as are found in the original idea):

Different sorts of musical idea lend themselves to different forms and directions of development – but potential for development also relates to the *quality* of a musical idea. It's worth spending time working over an idea, shaping and reshaping even short phrases and motifs to produce a final version that has character and distinction. Encourage students not to settle too easily for first thoughts. Instead, they should look for rhythmic features that can be improved (i.e. made more strikingly characteristic) and melodic points that could become the basis for extension and variation. Really good ideas can be made to unfold with continuing interest and yet never lose their identity. Weak ideas, on the other hand, can generally only be repeated, and so become boring because they yield very little for development.

Project 6

A common store of melody

Although we may not be aware of it, each of us carries around in the memory a store of melody ideas from which we can make tunes in much the same way that we are able to draw upon a common stock of phrases and sentences for our everyday conversations. This musical vernacular has, like the language we speak, grown up over hundreds of years and is being changed and added to all the time. Because it is very largely associated with songs, it can be triggered quite easily by presenting someone – anyone – with a verse or two of poetry and asking them to sing the words instead of saying them.

Student assignments

Assignment 1

Here is a selection of short and simple rhyming verses. If you can't find anything you like among these, choose others; but try to keep to verses of about four to six lines.

The camel has a single hump;
The dromedary, two;
Or else the other way around.
I'm never sure. Are you?
Ogden Nash

I'll race you down the mountain,
I'll race you down the mountain,
I'll race you down the mountain,
We'll see who gets there first.
 Woody Guthrie & Marjorie Mazia

A tail behind, a trunk in front,
Complete the usual elephant.
The tail in front, the trunk behind
Is what you very seldom find.
A.E. Housman

Three wise men of Botham
Went to sea in a bowl:
And if the bowl had been stronger,
My song would have been longer.
anon., 18th century

I never saw a Purple Cow,
I never hope to see one;
But I can tell you, anyhow,
I'd rather see than be one.
Gelett Burgess

The country is a funny place,
I like to look it in the face.
And everywhere I look I see
Some kind of animal or tree.
Ogden Nash

If you should meet a crocodile,
Don't take a stick and poke him;
Ignore the welcome in his smile,
Be careful not to stroke him.

For as he sleeps upon the Nile,
He thinner gets and thinner;
And when you meet a crocodile
He's ready for his dinner.

anon.

I caught me a wild aminul,
Jing jing jing-a-ling;
Caught me a wild aminul,
Yow, yow, yow, yow!
I caught me a wild aminul,
Bear and a monkey,
A woof and a camel:
I caught me a wild aminul,
Jing jing jing-a-ling.

Woody Guthrie

The man in the wilderness asked of me,
How many strawberries grow in the sea?
I answered him as I thought good,
As many red herrings as grow in the wood.

anon., 17th century

There was a witch
The witch had an itch
The itch was so itchy it
Gave her a twitch.

Another witch
Admired the twitch
So she started twitching
Though she had no itch.

Now both of them twitch
So it's hard to tell which
Witch has the itch and
Which witch has the twitch.

Alexander Resnikoff

The sun was shining on the sea,
Shining with all his might:
He did his very best to make
The billows smooth and bright–
And this was odd, because it was
The middle of the night.

Lewis Carroll

The whole group sits in a circle. Everyone chooses a verse (or a group of verses if they make a sequence). Then, going round the circle, one by one *sing* the verses to whatever tunes come to mind. Just make them up on the spur of the moment. Don't stop to think: this is exactly like reciting the verses except that instead of speaking the words you sing them. You'll find it's quite easy to do.

When everyone has sung a song, divide into small groups (four or five in a group) to make accompaniments for the songs. There may not be time to work on every song, but each group should see how many of the tunes made up at the start they can remember, and then decide which are the most suitable for adding accompaniments (e.g. those with the most memorable characteristics).

The accompaniments can be quite simple: hand-clapping rhythm patterns, or some more colourful rhythm backing using percussion instruments. Alternatively, experiment with chords on keyboards, finding out by trial and error the chords that fit best with the tune. In each group some can sing the tune while others play the accompaniment. Leave enough time at the end to perform as many as possible of the songs with their accompaniments.

Assignment 2

If you play a musical instrument, it's just as easy to make up tunes on your instrument as it is to sing them. Fingers 'remember' the most commonly used groups of notes and the ways in which they go together. Set yourself a tempo – not too fast – in 2, 3 or 4 time. (Count carefully, keeping the pulse absolutely steady in your mind all the time; or ask someone else to keep the rhythm going on a drum; or accompany yourself with a synthesizer drum machine.) When you have the beat firmly in mind, just play; and keep going! After a while you'll find that some of the phrases that come out are really quite memorable. Try to play them again. See if you can work one of them up into a complete tune that you can remember and repeat. If you've been working on a keyboard, try now to discover harmonies that will fit your tune.

Teaching points

As an elementary form of composing, working from this common store of melody has distinct advantages. It provides a basis for discussing, at various levels, the nature of musical ideas and musical style. It is also a good confidence-builder, because the activity is immediate, it requires hardly any prior explanation, and there's something everyone can do. Some may hesitate to sing but generally they'll be drawn in by the success of the less reticent members of the group.

Having been round the circle and had everyone make a song, very little need be said before moving to the next stage – remembering the most distinctive tunes and adding simple accompaniments. Simple rhyming verses spontaneously bring the familiar melody shapes instantly to mind, often to the surprise of those singing them; and that generates confidence. Using keyboards or tuned percussion (the latter, perhaps, with bars arranged to form primary triads), the same technique can fairly easily be applied to creating suitable accompaniments. The common language of tonal harmony is as familiar and as much in everyone's memory as the melody forms.

Even at the very simplest level, spontaneous melody-making is an important creative step, because the music will flow naturally from those making it. Although the common language provides a secure framework, nobody is exactly working to a formula; the achievement is real and it is relevant.[1]

How was it done?

When it is appropriate to do so, discuss the process. Everyone should try to be objective about what happened; how was it possible to make up these songs so easily? The words were read and immediately the tunes came to mind. Maybe some melodies were unusual, but most will have had things about them that sounded familiar. This is because we have all heard an enormous amount of music that goes with simple poetry of this kind; and, almost without knowing it, we have in our heads a large number of phrases – like a musical pattern book of ideas that can be put together in many different ways.[2]

The similarity between this and the way we use language is striking. To communicate with other people we don't have to invent a grammar for making words go together: we simply draw upon a common stock of ready-made phrases and, without having to think about it, we know they can be joined in various arrangements to make sense.

[1] A lot has been written about the relevance of subjects and topics in the school curriculum. In music this is often associated with style features (e.g. Top Twenty pop is 'relevant' because it represents music styles that most teenagers listen to). We need a broader view than this. In the first place, something is not necessarily relevant to our education simply because we are already familiar with it. All kinds of unfamiliar things can become relevant (in the sense that they then matter to us) when we develop intellectual and emotional involvement with them. It is part of a teacher's professionalism to help bring about that involvement. More to the point, however, it is the activity and the achievement that is relevant. It is there that we see students claiming as their own the emotional and intellectual growth that is the real hallmark of education. Independently of anything we can teach, we should recognise the educational value of the sociability, esteem, and relationships inherent in corporate musical activity, as well as the enjoyment, delight, and insight deriving from personal achievement. The humble level of artistry evident in spontaneously generated vernacular melodies is relevant to education because it is at least a step towards that state where 'Whoever is creative in a truly original sense . . . aims at being self-sufficient.' (Max J. Friedlander, *On art and connoisseurship*, Boston, 1960, pp. 242–3).

A. H. Maslow (in *Motivation and personality*, New York, Harper & Row, 1970) describes a 'hierarchy of basic needs' in which 'self-actualisation' – the need for self-fulfilment – is identified as the ultimate 'growth need'. We cannot function normally as human beings if we lack physiological and psychological security, affiliation, affection and a reasonable measure of self-esteem born out of some competence and its recognition. But such things only ensure that we get by in the business of living; beyond that we need to grow through self-actualisation (Jung called it 'self-individuation'). Music is one very important way of achieving this. The music is within us. All we need are the opportunities for it to flow out, to form itself – in the first instance, as naturally as possible.

[2] For detailed information on these and other topics covered in this project, see the account by Mária Sági and Iván Vitány of recent research in Hungary (in J. Sloboda (ed.), *Generative processes in music: the psychology of performance, improvisation, and composition*, Oxford, The Clarendon Press, 1988, pp. 179–94). This research builds upon theories propounded in the early years of this century by Béla Bartók and subsequently developed in his book *The Hungarian folksong* (first published 1924; recent English edition, Albany, State University of New York Press, 1981; see in particular pp. 2, 3 and 99).

Developing language

Occasionally it is necessary to say something in a special or unusual way, and that calls for more careful thought, not only about our choice of words but also about the way the phrases are constructed and how they should be joined together. This is more like the inventive and painstakingly-composed writing of novelists and poets. Over the years some of the special words and phrases from literature filter through into the established patterns of everyday conversational language, expanding and changing the common store. At the same time, other words drop out; phrases that were commonplace a few years ago now sound dated, so we consciously avoid using them. And if we want to be accepted by certain groups of people we may find ourselves quite deliberately using the expressions currently fashionable with those groups. The 'vernacular language' of music also develops in this way; but such changes as there are do not make too much difference, so it remains a way of making music that everyone understands and feels comfortable with.

It should be easy enough to identify 'common language' phrases in the songs made up during this project. Possible 'solutions' to the song-making activity might be:

The sun was shining on the sea, shining with all his might:— He did his very best to make the

bil - lows smooth and bright— And this was odd, be - cause it was the mid - dle of the night.

We could think of these songs as variations on well-known patterns, or on musical ideas we have heard and liked and feel we can re-use or re-shape in our own ways.

Going further

Other assignments in this project could include more music-making by the same process in various styles that draw upon common-store musical ideas. For example:

- the rhythmic vernacular of Afro-Caribbean and Asian music
- blues-jazz-rock melody (and, of course, the standard scheme of blues harmony which permeates all this music)
- R & B, country and western, show music, etc.
- the vernacular of European folk music, and the ways in which it has provided creative starting-points for composers such as Bartók, Kodály, Vaughan Williams, Janáček and Berio
- the words of folk-songs as evidence (perhaps the only evidence we have) of what ordinary people thought about events and conditions in previous centuries (use some of these words to invent new tunes)

A worldwide vernacular

Almost anyone can make up songs by singing words, and people have done this for many hundreds of years. Perhaps there is less incentive today for us to make our own music when television, radio, discs and cassettes seem to provide all we need. Nevertheless, the powerful influence of common-store musical ideas is evident. Afro-American and Afro-Caribbean music has become the twentieth century's most widespread and significant musical voice, simply because the melodic and harmonic idioms are, in the main, rooted in the musical vernacular. Listening to this music, it is not necessary to go outside the limits of what any of us might think we could do for ourselves musically. The familiar elements are quickly recognised, so that, notwithstanding any original and adventurous features, it is still easy to identify with this music. Its styles change frequently, but normally within well defined limits because if the music ventured too far from the familiar vocabulary it would no longer seem to be the kind of thing people could make for themselves; and that would immediately create a barrier, hindering the understanding and acceptance of the music.

This is true also of popular classics. Complicated development sections of symphonies, for example, leave some listeners feeling bewildered. Yet even without formal musical education, they can still enjoy the music because some parts of it (e.g. the principal themes) are clearly in a language everybody recognises. Once again, these melodies are of a kind that sound as though we might be able to make them ourselves.

New musical language: meeting our expectations

When we come to the more advanced music of the twentieth century there is little that can be identified as belonging to the vernacular. The problem is not merely that the music of Schoenberg, Webern, Bartók, Boulez or Stockhausen may appear to be discordant, harsh and 'difficult': the real problem is that the music does not connect in any way with what is known or expected; its sound world is not the common language of music, and most people could never imagine themselves making music that sounded like that.

Even so, such music does meet some expectations: the expectations of its own grammar; or, to be more precise, its own grammars, because a striking characteristic of music throughout the twentieth century has been the variety of styles and techniques of composition. Novelty now has a high priority, and we might even say that one of the expectations of today's music is that there shall be no expectations!

How can we get inside this music?

If, then, there are new musical languages to be learned – languages substantially different from those of popular music past and present – how can we learn them? More participation in music-making would certainly help; but again, there are problems.

Sitting silently and listening carefully to music is a relatively modern idea. Two hundred years ago or more, much of the most frequently heard music was actually serving other interests: the theatre, the church, public celebrations and grand occasions. Even at designedly musical events such as the opera, members of the audience were inclined to walk about and talk to one another. On the other hand, if they wanted music in their homes, they had to make it themselves; and in that way they did get to know a lot about musical ideas and styles.

Composers were well aware of this, and on the whole, as they explored new forms of expression, were careful not to abandon completely the musical language that most people understood. Amateur musicians kept in touch with the latest developments by playing chamber music, and that helped new forms to filter through into popular music-making. In this way there was continuous interchange between the various kinds of music; symphonies incorporated the forms of popular dances while, simultaneously, folk ballads and dances aspired to the forms of composed concert music. This two-way traffic in ideas and techniques meant that virtually the whole range of musical language was within anyone's grasp.

Unfettered exploration

Gradually – but most noticeably from the late nineteenth century into the first decade of the twentieth century – the balance shifted. Composers, freed from the obligation to serve other interests, followed their inclinations to explore entirely new musical possibilities. Eventually sound recording provided a means of disseminating definitive performances, but it also created an ever-increasing demand for technically superior singers and instrumentalists able to give as nearly as possible perfect presentations of difficult new music.

One way or another, through its most radical developments, twentieth-century music has distanced itself from the common language. Relatively few amateurs can play even the classics of twentieth-century chamber music (e.g. the string quartets of Bartók, or Schoenberg's *Pierrot lunaire*), let alone the most adventurous music of today's avant-garde. This is music for highly skilled professional performers. So we have, for the first time, a repertoire made largely to be listened to.[3]

Experience and understanding

If indeed it is listened to, that cannot be bad. We must believe that composers have always wanted people to listen to their music, even though, in earlier times, they knew that it would often have to be a background to something else. The dramatic increase in complex

[3] This needs some qualification. In past centuries chamber music was more often than not commissioned by aristocratic amateurs. Even if not commissioned, such works would probably be dedicated to those influential patrons who were also potential performers of the music. It was exceptional for a composer to produce music speculatively, without some immediate prospect of performance, and this meant that to a large extent the musical language needed to be capable of easy assimilation.

Nevertheless, some notable exceptions do come to mind. In 1788 Mozart announced the publication of three string quintets, for sale by subscription. His action is surprising when we recall that not only was the popularity of his music waning at that time, but also these works contain some of his most difficult musical language. They would certainly have been out of tune with the current Viennese taste. The subscription failed and the publication had to be postponed.

There is no doubt that audiences in the late 1780s did find Mozart's changing style hard to accept. Yet in spite of his growing personal difficulties and debts (or, perhaps, because of them), he seems to have eschewed what was fashionable, retreating into himself and producing music of great power and depth that was beyond the technique of the average amateur player. (See H. C. Robbins Landon, *Mozart: the golden years 1781–1791*, Thames and Hudson, 1989, pp. 192–5.)

However, the difference between such an extreme and exceptional example from the eighteenth century and the output of chamber music in the twentieth century is that Mozart really did expect to sell his quintets to amateur musicians, whereas so much of our contemporary chamber music is aimed solely at the highly skilled professional.

and unfamiliar information which characterises so much twentieth-century music obliges us – if we are to make anything of it at all – to listen in new ways, and above all to listen attentively. Unfortunately, it doesn't always work out like that. Deprived of learning about the music through the experience of performing it, listeners become totally dependent upon programme notes and record sleeve notes – the writers of which seem sometimes quite determined to widen rather than close the gap between the music and the public![4]

Broadly speaking the two main branches of contemporary music have gone their separate ways, although the links are fascinating and worth exploring. The world force in music today is Afro-American rock, harmonically and melodically rooted in the 'common tongue',[5] but its most recent developments owe a lot to advances in music technology, spearheaded by composers from the other branch (as it were) working in electronic music studios. Similarly, some modern orchestral works have been influenced by the energy of rock music, as well as by the sonorities of other world musics (African, Indian, Indonesian); but those features are never strong enough to surmount the basic inclination of most composers of concert music to move away from the vernacular.

[4] Cf. Bernard Levin's dictum: 'Those who can understand it do not need it, and those who need it cannot understand it.'

[5] '. . . rock has not only gone out through the whole world but has also been in a constant state of development, change, and, in particular, synthesis.' (Christopher Small, *Music of the Common Tongue: survival and celebration in Afro-American music*, London, John Calder, 1987, p. 377).

Tasting the mustard seed

Discussion of these topics is unlikely to be conclusive, but simply raising questions about musical language, style, expression and communication may help to show why there can never be a single 'right' way in music. Anything is possible for those who are prepared to open their ears to it. Moreover, it's a challenge we can meet with our own inventiveness by creating more of our own music. What we produce may not match the originality, enterprise and expertise of the professionals, but it may draw us closer to the ways in which they invent and use musical ideas.

There is an Indian proverb that says, 'The man who has bitten upon the mustard seed knows more about its taste than he who has seen a whole elephant-load.' So, whether it is extending the familiar vocabulary or more adventurously inventing new ways of making music, the important thing is the doing of it. Either way, it will not be long before precise decisions have to be taken about what should happen and when; in other words, how to make musical ideas grow into musical structures.

Further reading

Graham Vulliamy and Ed Lee (eds), *Pop music in school*, 2nd edn (Cambridge University Press, 1981). In particular, the activities described by Piers Spencer in 'The blues: a practical project for the classroom' and 'The creative possibilities of pop'.

Graham Vulliamy and Ed Lee (eds), *Pop, rock and ethnic music in school* (Cambridge University Press, 1982).

Graham Collier, *Jazz workshop* (London, Universal Edition, 1988).

Lionel Grigson, *Practical jazz* (London, Stainer & Bell, 1988).

Roy Palmer, *The Oxford book of sea songs* (Oxford University Press, 1988).

John Shepherd, Phil Virden and Trevor Wishart, *Whose music? A sociology of musical languages* (London, Latimer, 1977).

John Blacking, *How musical is man?* (Seattle, University of Washington Press, 1973).

Project 7

Necessary developments

Music is made by extending and expanding sound-ideas. To a large extent an idea itself will show what needs to be done to develop it into a complete piece of music; and the more characteristic (i.e. distinctive) the idea, the more clearly it will suggest the overall musical form it needs to become.

As with all artistic ideas – in painting, sculpture, poetry, dance, drama, film – it is important to establish the scale (i.e. size, duration and manner) in which the idea is most likely to work out satisfactorily. The process can also be reversed: if you know the scale of the music you want to make (perhaps even precisely how long it ought to last – if it's for a particular occasion), you can try to invent ideas that have the characteristics needed for that kind of development. Either way, you will have to work on those features that make the ideas really distinctive.

Student assignments

Assignment 1

How would you describe the character of this idea? What are its main features? What instrument seems to suit it best? What could we do with it to develop it into a complete piece of music? What sort of music would that be (big and broad and lasting a long time; or something of a different nature on a smaller scale)?

Assignment 2

With instruments, and working in pairs or in groups of three, invent a musical idea with the characteristic of continuous rising and falling movement. This must be something much more distinctive than merely running up and down scales. You have at least two instruments, so make them work together in an interesting and, perhaps, unusual way. Don't be content with the first thing you think of; try as many possibilities as you can. Listen carefully to what you do in your experimenting, and be as precise as possible. When you discover something that sounds right, go back over it and work at it to make it as distinctive as possible. Remember exactly how the idea is made, so that you can repeat it.

When you are satisfied with the shape and style of the idea, use it to make an improvisation – continuously renewing it, changing it very slightly, driving it onwards, weaving the sounds around one another. Keep going for as long as seems right – and in any case, don't let it stop too soon. Go on improvising to see how much you can make out of this single idea. Try to let the idea itself suggest the directions it needs to take.

Remember, you must maintain the character of the musical idea you started with. There is no story attached to this music; it is quite simply an improvisation that uses and extends the musical idea you have invented. If the main characteristic of that idea is really strong, it should be possible to hear it coming back in various ways throughout the improvisation.

Assignment 3

Here are two short poems by Edwin Morgan. The first thing to notice about them is that they must be performed; i.e. they must be read aloud because the sounds are a vital element. What do those sounds tell you about the way each poem should be performed? (How quickly or slowly should it be read? Do any of the letters require a special kind of pronunciation, and why? Are some features to be sounded louder than others?)

Siesta of a Hungarian Snake

s sz sz SZ sz SZ sz ZS zs ZS zs zs z

Chinese Cat

p m r k g n i a o u
p m r k g n i a o
p m r k n i a o
p m r n i a o
p m r i a o
p m i a o
m i a o
m a o

Although the first poem consists of only one line, a lot happens. There is a sense of completeness: starting, going on and finishing; developing a single idea but staying firmly in character throughout. How many things can you identify that contribute to the character of the principal idea? What is snake-like about it? How do we know that the snake is Hungarian and that it's having a siesta? (In other words, how does the main idea work?) Do you need any special information or technique before you can perform the poem?

'Chinese Cat' is also based on one highly characteristic idea. What is that idea, and how does it work out to form the complete poem?

Assignment 4

Use all or some of the suggestions given below as starting-points for inventing musical ideas. When you've tried out the possibilities and decided on what you feel is a good idea, make an extended improvisation with it on a solo instrument or with a group of instruments.

Don't try to make up stories about the topics you choose. They are intended only as starting-points; each one can be a way into inventing a characteristic musical idea that could become the basis of an improvisation.

    i. a pebble dropped on the calm surface of a pond
    ii. bubble
    iii. mirror
    iv. surprise
    v. interruption
    vi. cycle
    vii. dead-end
    viii. blunt
    ix. sharp
    x. stranger
    xi. 'The King is coming'
    xii. hesitate
    xiii. wasteland
    xiv. busy
    xv. signals

Assignment 5

Using a musical instrument you play well, experiment with the characteristics that make it different from any other instrument. Invent a short but distinctive musical idea that exploits those characteristics. It must be complete in itself, and memorable. It might be a tiny melodic shape, curling back on itself or leaping strongly up or down; or an unusual rhythmic figure; or a group of very high or very low sounds. But above all it must feature the instrument.

When you are satisfied with what you have invented, improvise on it, extending it and developing it in any way you think appropriate; but make the main features prominent, so that the music is always recognisably linked to the starting idea. Keep the improvisation going for as long as possible, bringing it to a satisfactory end.

As you improvise, try to exaggerate the most striking and unusual parts of your idea. That will maintain the interest. If an idea doesn't seem to have enough in it to make a really substantial improvisation, abandon it and think again. You can only find out by trial and error which are the strongest ideas and those most likely to be fruitful for music.

Assignment 6

Invent (a) a very grand or very serious idea, and (b) a small-scale, amusing or light-hearted idea. Improvise first with one and then with the other, taking care in each case to maintain the characteristics you gave them to start with. Then give them different treatments: e.g. use the 'wrong' instruments or try fitting the large-scale idea into a very short space of time, with just one or two instruments; try to make the light-hearted idea sound bigger and more serious than it was intended to be.

Assignment 7

Invent musical ideas for others to improvise upon.

Teaching points

Beginning with improvisation

In this project the emphasis is on inventing musical ideas of strong and recognisable character as a basis for individual or small-group improvisations.

This may suggest a type of free music-making not exactly compatible with the school classroom – almost by definition a place for analysis and discussion, imposing a degree of limitation which improvising musicians are likely to find unacceptable. Derek Bailey, in his excellent book on improvisation, is critical of the idea of improvisation classes. Understandably, he feels this is not something you can teach: it is quite simply something you do. Trying to teach improvisation, he says, usually leads us into the trap of talking about it and analysing the process; and 'if there is anything which is singularly inappropriate for treatment in this way it must be free improvisation'.[1] Surely no one would disagree. What he identifies as the 'purely practical character of the activity, avoiding the establishment of a set of generalised rules, always allowing an individual approach to develop', would certainly be difficult to achieve under the normal conditions and expectations of class teaching. (Although, it must be said, a different attitude towards classroom activities could easily create an appropriate atmosphere for music improvisation; nothing is impossible.)

However, we are not talking here about improvisation for its own sake. That really is another matter altogether; a very worthwhile creative musical experience, but outside the scope of this book.[2] Our immediate concern is with the first stages of composition teaching: finding out what can be achieved with musical materials, and why and how some musical structures appear to be more successful than others.

This is not the same thing as trying to teach improvisation. Composition has to be simultaneously a process of analysis and synthesis which cannot avoid 'the establishment of generalised rules' for each new work. Only when we are able to make such generalisations do we begin to learn how to handle structures compositionally. As far as possible, students should discover structural processes for themselves and make their own generalisations by working with sounds. Discussion as a follow-up to those discoveries can help to focus technique; but the first step is for the students to make music.[3]

Improvisation, of a kind, is probably the only way of learning to evaluate ideas. Many have recognised it as a first stage in composition; for example, Stravinsky: 'Improvisation sows the seeds of musical ideas.' Composition is rarely an entirely silent process;

[1] Derek Bailey, *Improvisation: its nature and practice in music* (Ashbourne, Moorland Publishing Company, 1980), p. 137.

[2] See Richard Addison, 'A new look at musical improvisation in education' in the *British Journal of Music Education*, vol. 5, no. 3, November 1988 (Cambridge University Press), pp. 255–67.

[3] As a commentary on the underlying educational principle the following quotations are, perhaps, instructive:

'To cultivate technique and increase knowledge without a comprehensive perception of the importance of developing the individual in self-confidence and awareness is a negative process.' (The industrialist and composer Ernest Hall, 1984)

'The least piece of writing, if the teacher has established the context for proper "giving", will be a "meant" gift. Of course, it depends on what the teacher's attitude is to human beings. If he cannot believe that every human being has an inward need to find himself, in a struggle . . . between the subjective and objective worlds, then he probably won't get given poetry.' (David Holbrook, *Children's writing*, Cambridge University Press, 1967, pp. 8–9)

'One learns practically nothing about the actual functioning of music by sitting in mute surrender before it. As a practising musician I have come to realise that one learns about sound only by making sound, about music only by making music . . . The sounds produced may be crude; they may lack form and grace, but they are ours.' (R. Murray Schafer, *Ear cleaning*, BMI Canada, 1967, p. 1)

'. . . students who are talented performers but who are unable to compose even a simple piece of music, thus demonstrating a total lack of practical knowledge of the very basis on which their art is founded.' (Peter Tahourdin, 'Electronic music in the classroom' in *Australian Journal of Music Education*, April 1968) nobody can imagine something 'out of the air', because anything heard in the head must have some basis in sounds already experienced. Indeed, for all musicians there is a continuing cycle of improvisation, composition/interpretation, rehearsal and performance with each element of the cycle in some way feeding back into the others. The ability to 'hear music in your head' comes only from involvement with all points of that cycle.

Through improvisation students can learn to appreciate the scale and quality of their musical ideas. Although there can be no rules about such things – and, in any case, composers of unusual talent or insight may easily confound us with extensive but manifestly appropriate treatments of seemingly slight ideas – we can and we should draw attention to the importance of testing the potential of ideas through improvisation before embarking on a composition as a whole. Eventually students will develop the confidence to test ideas in the much more extensive field of the imagination; but, as a beginning at least, working directly with sounds and sound-ideas is always instructive and never wasted effort.

Musical ideas and ideas of music

Where do sound-ideas come from? Absolutely anything can stimulate the musical imagination – things seen, heard or read about; events current or historical, natural or supernatural; a glimpse of something beyond what is immediately or clearly perceptible; other examples of artistic expression; other music and techniques and concepts of form; or combinations of all these things. But no matter what it is that in the first instance stimulates invention, it is the resulting musical idea alone that must then be worked upon to produce music. Any suggestion that the purpose of music is in some way to describe, portray or make an image of the original stimulus, or that it can narrate details about whatever first stirred the composer's imagination, must be erroneous. Such things are outside the scope of music: music's power lies in quite different directions.

This applies as much to programme music as it does to other genres. It is inconceivable that anyone would go through the immense labour of creating a large-scale orchestral work merely in order to find an alternative way of telling a story! The story (the 'programme') provides the composer with a stimulus (call it inspiration if you like) for musical thinking, but in the finished work it is surely the music we are intended to experience. To be able to identify the composer's starting-point may be interesting or in some other way helpful to listeners, but ultimately it can have very little genuinely musical significance.[+]

Sooner or later students must come to understand the relationship between, on the one hand, the invention and development of musical ideas and, on the other, experiences and thoughts, verbally or visually expressed, which, while they may have great importance

[+] Why is it that 'Music Appreciation' teaching so often features programme music, apparently in the belief that it will quickly capture the imagination and draw the

in themselves, are for musicians not ideas as such but merely starting-points for the generation of musical ideas.

Titles

Some composers like to start from a title; it can help to focus thoughts and give rise to musical ideas or even to complete musical forms. But that is not to say that the music itself becomes a description of whatever the title refers to. Nor can it tell a story based on the title. Used in this way, a title merely provokes musical thinking.

From another point of view, choosing a suitable title when a composition has been completed can give the music a context. It seems to encompass not only the starting-point but also the entire process of working upon the musical ideas, expanding and trans-forming them and bringing the whole structure to a satisfying conclusion. For school students this is a particularly important use of titles because it brings a feeling of substance to intangible musical forms: it represents achievement.

Quality and scale

The realisation of musical ideas is the beginning of every musical process. For the performer and the listener it means being able to accept what the composer has set down as the principal materials of a work. There is no argument about that; if we cannot find, for ourselves, artistic potential in the ideas, we shall never enjoy the music.

Composition must, of course, begin with the inventing of ideas; and that too involves an appreciation of artistic potential and quality in the possibilities being explored.[5] Perhaps such things can't be taught; but, as we've already suggested, they can be learned. Finding out how to assess the quality of ideas is largely a matter of experience, a great deal of trial and error, and taking risks by pursuing trains of thought which may turn out to be fruitless.[6]

No one can give us rules for inventing good ideas. A musical idea is only 'good' to the extent in which the individual or group using it can think of ways of making interesting music with it. In a sense this reverses the old saying 'necessity is the mother of invention'; for here we must first make a stab at putting sounds together and then examine what we have produced to discover what is necessary for its development. If we give it a chance, an idea will reveal its potential to grow into music. Once we recognise what needs to be done, we are free to take whatever action we choose to achieve it. That action will itself involve some kind of self-imposed limitation. It may be broad, it may be narrow; but it must be able to channel our thinking

uninitiated closer to understanding music? Unfortunately, by focusing upon extra-musical ideas, it tends to steer the uninitiated right away from genuinely musical considerations. The practice is much more evident than it should be on record sleeves, in school-books and in concert programme notes. Worse still, the writers frequently choose avowedly non-programmatic works to label as 'programme music'; for example Debussy's 'Clair de lune' and Honegger's *Mouvement symphonique no. 1* 'Pacific 231'. Cf. *The New Grove Dictionary of Music* (London, Macmillan, 1980), vol. 8, p. 679: 'When the subject of *Pacific 231* (a steam engine) brought the piece an easy popularity, Honegger was not impressed; he desired rather that the work, like the sequel *Rugby*, should be heard as absolute music, and he left the last member of the triptych without a descriptive title as *Mouvement symphonique no. 3*.'

[5] Cf. the painter John Constable: 'No one can see anything he does not already understand.' Understanding comes largely from trying things out; for example, in the way children learn language by playing with words and getting things wrong. It is the balance between that kind of 'failure' and the essential reinforcement of success that leads to understanding – at which point things fall into place and are seen (or, in the case of music, heard) in context.

[6] Richard Hoffman: 'The composer is not an "apostle" who clings to formulae, but an artist who "shapes his own ideas" independently and takes risks by entering unknown territory' (quoted in Rufer, *Composition with twelve notes*, 1969, p. 186).

and experimenting towards an overall coherent musical structure; in other words, to make what happens in the music make sense.[7]

It is now, before the extended process of composition begins, that questions of scale have to be faced. Very simply put, there is a danger that broad, dignified or very serious ideas will sound unfulfilled, pompous or even slightly comic if they are dismissed in too short a time or played on inappropriate instruments (e.g. a combination of swannee whistles and kazoos!). Similarly, light and unpretentious ideas will lose their appeal if they are kept going too long or are unsuitably padded out with a lot of instruments.

This is, of course, a generalisation, and should not be taken as anything other than a rule of thumb. A Beethoven or a Bach would almost certainly find unsuspected depths in an idea the rest of us regarded as simplistic. But that is not to say that Beethoven or Bach habitually disregarded implications of scale. On the contrary, the skill of Bach's formal judgement is frequently evident in just such matters. Compare, for example, his treatment of the subjects of fugues 1 and 4 in the first book of the '48'. The subject of the first fugue is relatively slight; light-hearted and 'un-serious' (in character, that is – this is not meant to be a value judgement):

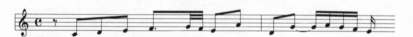

By contrast, the subject of the fourth fugue is weighty and solemn in character; a large-scale idea in spite of its mere five notes:

Again, this is not to suggest that the first fugue lacks substance or musical importance, but merely to notice that Bach has assessed the scale and style of the subject he has invented, and has decided that it would be inappropriate to overdo its significance. He limits the scope of the fugue to two pages of lively, imaginative but nevertheless straightforward classic fugal techniques, avoiding elaborate episodes, never venturing beyond the closely related keys, and keeping the entire texture more or less in the middle of the keyboard. In fugue no. 4, however, Bach assesses the potential of the subject on a very different scale. This short but noble theme is full of possibilities, and is accordingly given the space it needs. It is combined with subsidiary themes and elaborated in five parts, with four substantial episodes and some dramatic use of texture-space (e.g. unexpectedly extending the upward-downward range of the texture, as at the bass entry at bar 73).[8]

Stimulus and action

The most obvious characteristic of the idea given in Assignment 1 is the choppy, brittle effect produced by the staccato quavers. This

---

[7] Cf. Hegel: 'Freedom is the awareness of necessity.' And Solzhenitsyn: 'Freedom is defined by its limitations: otherwise it becomes licence.' In passing, it is perhaps worth noting that, irrespective of what has been said above, necessity quite frequently *is* the mother of invention in musical composition; as, for example, when a composer is commissioned to write for particular instruments, or even particular players, to compose music for a film or play, or to a specified duration. In school, too, this kind of necessity may help to generate musical ideas, e.g. when only certain instruments are available. Then it is no bad thing for students to have to accept that they must do what they can with what they've got.

[8] Cf. the first subject of the double fugue in the second movement of Stravinsky's *Symphony of Psalms*:

(transposed into C minor for comparison)

The opening four notes clearly have a relationship with the subject of Bach's 4th fugue in the '48'. There is a similarly 'antiquated' solemnity which seems to require extended treatment, achieved in the Stravinsky by continuing to work out (from figure 5) the instrumental fugue simultaneously with a choral fugue on a different subject.

characteristic is enhanced by the *p* dynamic, the fast tempo, the rests which interrupt the forward drive, and the dissonance – not only of the D/C♯ but also of the D♯–G♯ leap which seems not to belong with the opening figure. The essence of the whole idea is fragmentation: things are out of joint and unrelated; but, perhaps, never very serious.

An idea that goes by fits and starts can hardly produce sonorous, flowing music. You could, of course, imagine a contrasting idea, smoothly melodic, for which this disjointed, chirpy motif could act as a foil. But the assignment is to concentrate on what the given idea suggests about its own development. The following is just one possibility. It doesn't attempt any great depth of feeling but maintains its carefree, 'fragmented' character just long enough for the idea to establish itself without becoming frustrating (if it went on too long in this vein the effect would wear very thin).

The Edwin Morgan poems (Assignment 3) neatly demonstrate the relationship between characteristic ideas and 'necessary' development. In the first, the printed letters themselves form a snake-like line (made fatter in the middle, by the use of capitals, than at the head or tail) which gives the structure a visible coherence. In fact, the principal idea is a sound-idea (is this a poem or a piece of music?): the snake's normally powerful hiss softened to a gentle 's' as the creature dozes in the afternoon heat, then gradually and sleepily transformed into the abrupt final 'z'. Can we assume that the capital letters suggest a slightly louder sound, perhaps also drawn out a little? And that the whole effect, the real exploitation of this simple but vivid idea, requires us to pronounce the letters as they would sound in Hungarian?

> **s** like *sh* in shame
> **sz** like *s* in son
> **zs** like *s* in pleasure (like *j* in French *jour*)
> **z** as in zip

In a similar way, 'Chinese Cat' transforms, little by little, the sounds of the seemingly unconnected string of letters that form the first line. Read aloud and pronounced individually, these letters at first suggest a gentle but, perhaps, distant purr (the 'r' must surely be rolled) ending in something like a conventional cat cry, the two things held apart, as it were, by the 'k', 'g' and 'n' sounds. As the pattern systematically reduces itself, those intervening letters are lost and the others begin to merge, as though struggling to become real words. We have the impression of the cat's image slowly coming into focus, until at last the letters can be joined to make two unmistakable words: one clearly indicating 'cat', the other – a simple variation of the first – an equally powerful evocation of 'Chinese'. But it is the sound-idea and its transformation that tells us everything.

Assignments 4 and 5 are, again, principally concerned with devising short and strongly characteristic musical ideas. If, as suggested, the ideas are then developed through improvisation, it is important for students to concentrate on the musical elements and to avoid what they may see as the dramatic implications of a literary stimulus.[9] In this connection, it may be helpful to observe how classical composers of the late eighteenth and early nineteenth centuries were able to make so much of tiny but powerful motifs. Working with melody fragments to build up whole movements is characteristic of virtually every great work of that period, but two outstanding examples that will always repay careful study are the finale of Haydn's 'Drum Roll' Symphony (no. 103 in E♭, 1795) and, of course, the opening of Beethoven's Fifth Symphony (1808). As an approach to the detailed study of what Haydn and Beethoven make of their ideas, students could use those same motifs as a basis for their own improvisation (by way of addition to Assignment 7).

[9] The composer Morton Feldman argued against what he saw as a damaging 'literary' perception of music. Forms, structures and procedures were too strongly biased towards verbal description, and this had come about because increasingly composers found it easier to think about music in words than to work directly with sounds or to allow the sounds themselves to dictate musical direction. Feldman acknowledged the problem-solving aspect of composing but deplored the use of elaborate pre-compositional analyses to explain the 'solutions', often before a single note of music had been composed!

Whether or not one agrees completely with Feldman's view, there clearly is a tendency for many of us to take refuge in words about music or words associated with music, if only because the sound-patterns themselves are elusive and intangible. In general we have come to accept that the only way to examine musical phenomena is by using words; but then even the technicalities and the notation take on a kind of literary importance and prevent us from getting close to the music. Sometimes it appears almost more important to be able to recognise and label a sonata or a fugue than to delight in the music. It's hardly surprising that many people have the impression that music is merely a translation into sounds of other experience – a kind of sound-story or sound-picture of things heard of, read about or seen – and that, to be properly understood, music needs verbal description. No doubt something of this lies behind Derek Bailey's emphasis upon 'the purely practical character of improvisation' (and cf. the method of functional analysis pioneered by Hans Keller in the 1950s).

Project 8

Re-inventing the grammar

It is one thing to invent a musical idea, but quite another to make it go on in time to become a substantial and coherent piece of music. As an alternative to starting from a musical idea which is a tiny cell – or perhaps just the first phrase of a melody – and developing that by extending it, expanding it and decorating it in various ways, you can begin with an overall view of the way the music will work. This is rather like inventing the grammar for a language; deciding how the various parts will function together, and then inventing the words to fulfil those functions.

Student assignments

Assignment 1

Devise a way of making a piece of music that will 'work' like a pyramid, i.e. not a piece of music about pyramids, but a method of putting musical sounds together that resembles as closely as possible the way in which stones were put together to make the ancient Egyptian pyramids.

Think about the structure. It is built of individual blocks; its base has four corners and is the most extensive area. As it grows higher, the area of each successive layer diminishes until there is only one stone at the top. At the same time all the lower layers remain in place.

When you have thought of a way of making this idea work with sounds, experiment to find the most suitable musical sounds to use as building blocks for your musical pyramid. Using the sounds you have chosen, invent a short musical motif to build with. You then have a number of possibilities for working with this figure, for instance:

i. building up a complex texture gradually (figure by figure; instrument by instrument; layer by layer; corner stones first, then fill in the rest of the layer)

ii. using all the instruments, with the same figure or different versions of it, all together so that the structure is created in one go and simply 'stands' there.

The first option could make it easier to maintain the musical interest because it is a process that goes on. But is there some way in which the second possibility could also be made to go on in time and be interesting to listen to even though the pyramid is (in a sense) 'complete' right from the start? (N.B. it does have four sides.)

Assignment 2

Devise a way of making 'strata' of musical sounds behave together like this geological formation. As with the pyramid idea, there are a number of possibilities. The formation could simply exist (in which case, how could the sounds be made to go on in time; how would the music start and finish?). Alternatively, we could hear the strata 'flat' at the beginning (see opposite, above) and then 'folded'. Or again, having folded, the top might be gradually eroded – as happens with the tops of hills and mountains – revealing features of the layering that were orig-

inally hidden. What feature(s) of the sound layering, formerly masked or in some way underneath, could then be revealed? Remember that, unlike the pyramid, although the various layers keep their positions relative to each other, they all move up (are they also stretched?) as they fold. What does that suggest for the layers of musical sound?

Assignment 3

Not a piece about a volcano (i.e. it doesn't have to be violent, nor should you try to imitate the sound of a volcano), but a way of making musical sounds work so that, like the strata in Assignment 2, a feature that is at first overlaid by other sounds, suddenly (unexpectedly?) works up through the texture and dominates the whole.

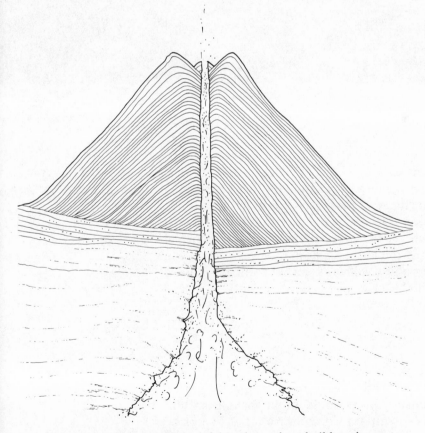

Over the years, with each explosion of the volcano, lava builds up layer upon layer, and the shape of the land is changed.

Assignment 4

Use the form of a delta as a way of controlling a musical idea.
What would you expect the idea to be doing just before the delta
begins? The delta splits the river into several separate strands, yet
it remains the same river. How would your musical idea branch
out into several strands yet remain recognisable as the principal
idea? What would cause the idea to split in this way? When you
have decided how your music will work, invent a suitable musical
idea to be treated in this 'delta' form.

Assignment 5

Inside a car you seem to be sealed off from the rest of the world.
All kinds of extraordinary things could be happening around
you, but you can go on with a quiet conversation – or just be
alone with your thoughts! Does this suggest a way in which a
piece of music could be made to work?

Assignment 6

A piece of music to be called *100 mph*. What does the title suggest for the overall progress of this music? Invent musical material that can be treated throughout in the same way but will go on being interesting.

Assignment 7

A piece of music for a solo instrument that uses only the following notes:

accompanied by a small group of contrasting instruments whose music is restricted to these notes:

Make another piece with similar restrictions but choosing your own sets of notes. Decide first on a theory for selecting the notes. That will determine the overall sound-world of your music. Will the choice of notes also affect the choice of instruments/voices?

Assignment 8

A haiku is a very short poem of a type invented by the Japanese in the mid sixteenth century. Normally there are 17 syllables (although there may be fewer). The aim is to focus in a concentrated and witty way upon a particular feature of the poem's subject. A haiku can be a useful starting-point for a musical idea; for example:

> Right at my feet –
> and when did you get here,
>   Snail?
> *Issa, translated by H. G. Hendersen*

This haiku gives us a single, concentrated image of someone looking down suddenly and seeing a snail; where did it come from and how long did it take over the journey? It could suggest an unexpected meeting of two individuals who set out together along the same path, one moving much slower than the other but in some mysterious way catching up so that they both arrive at the same time.

In musical terms this could mean two instruments (or voices) that play or sing either the same line of melody or one which has more or less the same shape in both parts, one moving in fast notes the other in slow notes. They both set out along the same melodic path, and although the slow-note part would not complete the phrase, it would arrive ('Right at my feet . . .') at a point where it was very close to the fast-note part; and this same point should feel like a conclusion. This is the 'grammar' of how the piece would work. All you have to do now is to find the notes and create the structure. Perhaps it would be something like this:

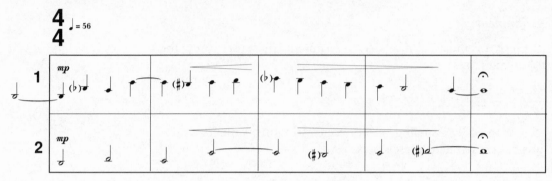

> Two small groups of singers:
>
> **Group 1:** One singer from group 1 decides the pitch of the first tone; the other singers join in with that tone and sing the melody line gently and steadily, trying as far as possible to sing the same pitches as each other, following the shape of the melody as shown by the signs. All singers must listen very carefully to each other as they sing and try to get as close as possible to a unison melody (But it will not matter if some of the tones are pitched slightly higher or lower so that the voices create 'accidental' chords). Sing all on a single vowel sound.
>
> **Group 2:** All singers listen carefully to the solo voice which pitches the first tone for group 1. Then group 2 singers join in, trying to relate their melody line as closely as possible to what group 1 singers are singing. As with group 1, singers must also listen very carefully to the others in their group, and try to pitch their tones as closely as possible to a unison, following the shape of the melody as shown and the duration of the tones. Sing all on a single vowel sound (but different from the vowel chosen by group 1).

or, in more specified notation:

or:

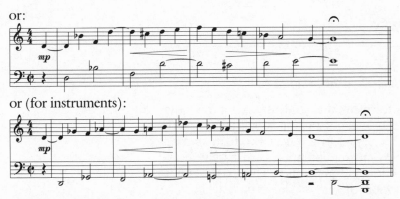

or (for instruments):

Below are some more haiku. What kind of musical organisation does each suggest? First you must decide what is the main feature of the haiku. Then think how that idea might characterise the way you organise the musical sounds. Finally, think of the detailed musical ideas for the piece. Try several possibilities and then work carefully at each haiku until you have a series of short pieces of music (i.e. like these short, witty poems themselves) which can be performed as a sequence, one after another.

Sneezing,
   I lost sight
      of the skylark.
Yaya, translated by R. H. Blyth

            Rain drums on the pane
               and runs down, wavering the world
                  into a dream.
            James W. Hackett

Snow melts,
   and the village is overflowing –
      with children.
Issa, translated by H. G. Hendersen

            In my new clothing
              I feel so different
                I must look like someone else.
            Basho, translated by H. G. Hendersen

A whale!
   Down it goes, and more and more
      Up goes its tail.
Busou, translated by H. G. Hendersen

            A flitting firefly!
              'Look! Look there!' I start to call –
              but there is not one by.
            Taigi, translated by H. G. Hendersen

Teaching points

Another way of deciding how the music should go

Once again it is important to ensure that students do not think they are being asked to make music about pyramids, volcanoes, or the 'story' of a haiku. These literary ideas are no more than starting-points for musical thinking, and the intention is that they should stimulate ideas about structure and procedure. This needs emphasising. The widespread notion that music in some way portrays visual and verbal ideas hampers musical education by focusing on non-musical matters. At the same time we have to recognise the value, to composers, of literary and visual stimulus.

First, a theory

In the earlier projects of this section we saw how a certain kind of stimulus could help to produce a musical idea – a brief gesture, a few notes, a short rhythm pattern or a phrase of melody suggested by the rhythm of words – and how that might be developed in a variety of ways, first through improvisation and then by working on points of melodic or rhythmic detail, keeping the idea going and extending it to make a complete piece of music. That way of working starts at the beginning, with an idea already formed in musical sounds, and allows it to shape its own progress.

In this project we look at a different kind of musical idea; a theory for each piece of music which will determine the behaviour of all the sounds and motifs that eventually go into the piece. We tend to talk about *the* theory of music as though there were one theoretical basis for all music. It would be more accurate to say the theory of *a* music because, in world terms, there are many different musics, each with its own theory.[1]

---

[1] This could be the point at which to introduce a wider discussion of the cultural influences that produce the different theories of music. African music, for example, is essentially a 'people' experience, not a 'person' experience; audience participation is expected and is therefore part of the theory of that music:

'Westerners trying to appreciate African music must always keep in mind the fact that the music is organised to be open to the rhythmic interpretation a drummer, a listener, or a dancer wishes to contribute. The music is perhaps best considered as an arrangement of gaps where one may add a rhythm, rather than as a dense pattern of sound.' (J. Chernoff, *African rhythm and African sensibility*, University of Chicago Press, 1979, p. 113)

'African music is not just different music but something that is different from "music". For a westerner to understand the artistry and purpose of an African musical event, it is necessary for him to sidestep his normal listening tendencies . . . It is a mistake to "listen" to African music because African music is not set apart from its social and cultural context.' (Chernoff, p. 33)

This is not simply a matter of how music is used, or the purposes to which it is put. Nor is it a question of structure. The decisions we are considering here are still very much within the realm of musical ideas, and must be taken prior to any thoughts about structure. There is a sense in which every piece of music has its own theory. That is to say, the composer's first task is to decide how the music will work in the light of the ideas from which it starts. If the first thing to be considered is mechanism – an understanding that the sounds will relate to one another in a particular way and exclude all other possibilities – that is rather like agreeing upon grammatical functions (e.g. the way verbs must function in relation to nouns) before inventing the words that will express the details.

Musical grammar, old and new

With normal spoken and written language the functions are universally agreed. A writer can go straight to the point of using words, confident that everyone who reads the book, the poem or whatever will know what the grammatical conditions are, and won't confuse verbs with nouns! In much the same way this is true of well established musical procedures. For example, we have certain expectations of the 'grammar' of classical harmony: the sense of key and key relationships, the effect of different types of cadence, textural homogeneity, and so on. We quickly notice if chords are misplaced, if a modulation or a cadence is clumsy or the texture of harmony unbalanced. (Even so, a late eighteenth-century composer would not have hesitated to disturb listeners by defying their expectations just a little – but not too much! Anything really outrageous would simply sound wrong, but a very slight bending of the grammar could present a fresh point of view.)

It is, nevertheless, part of every artist's task to open up new formal possibilities; new ways of defining a novel, a poem, a piece of music. To do that you can't go on using grammatical functions devised for procedures that are well established and accepted without question. You have to re-invent the grammar. In effect this is what every truly innovative composer has always done.

'To a westerner the continuous repetition of a simple, short melody is monotonous. To an African it is electrifying, gratifying and pleasant. The European hears music as an independent art, whose beauty lies in the amount of scientific engineering used to shape the raw impulses of emotion producing it. The African hears music as an incidental and symbolic art whose beauty lies in the religious and social order which it helps to control.' (T. Vidal, 'Oriki in traditional Yoruba music', in *African Arts* vol. 3, no. 1, UCLA, 1969, p. 59)

'It is the duration of time that a drummer plays a particular rhythm, the amount of repetition and the way the rhythms change, to which the drummer pays attention, and not so much any particular rhythmic invention. The aesthetic decision which constitutes excellence will be the timing of the change and the choice of a new pattern.' (Chernoff, p. 100)

Getting into the right frame of mind

A useful entry point for this way of thinking about musical ideas is to observe how other (i.e. non-musical) structures work. Therefore, in this project students are asked to concentrate on the functioning of the parts, not upon the structure itself. If, from close observation of a physical structure, conclusions can be drawn about how the parts function in relation to one another to create the whole, then certain features of that control mechanism can be adopted to make sounds work together in new or unusual ways.

Assignment 1

Possibly for a large group of players or singers. This might produce music of 'monolithic' character, not because the starting-point is a pyramid but because the function of the elements (the building blocks) is to interlock and remain fixed, layer by layer; the highest layers revealing more of the individual character of the 'blocks' because there are fewer of them, and the whole piece displaying just four more-or-less identical 'sides'. The structure is, then, the outcome of deciding to use the elements in a particular way; and the elements have to be what they are because of their predetermined function.

Assignment 4

One possibility is that the delta model would suggest the onward flow of a strongly characteristic musical motif – perhaps a fairly substantial melodic or rhythmic idea – which changes unexpectedly. Just as a big river establishes its character and direction, so to begin with we might expect the main musical material to be established by repetition to the point where it is accepted as the habitual form (i.e. listeners will expect it to continue like that throughout). Very soon after this, however, the material would surprise by starting to diversify (the 'delta'). Going off in its various strands it might change only slightly, so that the relationship with the 'habitual form' would still be obvious, *or* it could change dramatically. Either way, in composing the piece, the decision to be made is how this change shall be brought about; and here we might borrow from behavioural psychology:

> The simplest rule for breaking a habit is to find the cues which initiate the action and practise another response to those cues.[2]

[2] J. Wolpe and A. A. Lazarus, *Behaviour therapy techniques* (New York, Pergamon, 1968), p. 4.

Examine the musical material closely. If it is a melodic idea, what kind of melody is it? Is it, for the most part, gently flowing, moving stepwise? Or does it have a jagged, leaping progress? If it consists largely of sustained notes, is the melody line simple and without embellishment, or are many of the notes decorated in some way? If there is an accompanying line or instrumental texture, what is its character and how is that maintained? In each of these examples the 'cue which initiates the action' is whatever is most characteristic in the starting of the idea. The way a melody (or any other kind of musical idea) begins normally conditions the way it continues. At the 'delta' point, 'practise another response to the cue'.

So, perhaps we have this as the start of a flowing, stepwise melody ▷

and we may expect that cue to trigger the next phrase ▷

but instead we deliberately break the habit by doing something unexpected:

Now we can practise that response by continuing, perhaps, like this:

– while at the same time an accompanying instrument goes off along another strand of the delta, practising its own different response to what had become the accepted and expected way forward:

Assignment 5

The situation of the person alone in the car, protected from the hurly-burly outside, might suggest a solo instrumentalist or singer whose music is 'enclosed' (i.e. reflective, quiet, restrained). This music persists, unwavering in spite of a great diversity of contrasting music from other players (or groups?) which surround the soloist. The surrounding music may occasionally drown out the persistent line of the solo, but that continues, eventually emerging still in the same manner and mood as at the start.

This could lead to a discussion on the idea of 'a concerto', comparing traditional (Classical/Romantic) concerto forms with more recent developments.

Assignment 6

Perhaps a 'moto perpetuo'. For example:

'100 *mph*' – *Perpetuum mobile*

Repeat ad infinitum

Assignment 7

Ideas about musical grammar can come from within music itself just as easily as from some literary or visual model. Here the grammatical model is the combination of two independent sets of notes, one to be used exclusively by a prominent solo instrument, the other used only by a group making an accompaniment for the soloist. The result will be another concerto-like piece which might usefully follow on from Assignment 5.

Again, the most pressing question is how it can be made to sound coherent. The two sets of notes are apparently unrelated (even, it might be said, in violent contrast with one another). The problem is how to exploit that contrast so that it makes an appropriate relationship between the solo and its accompaniment and gives the finished piece a feeling of wholeness.

The first thing will be to accept the inevitable dissonance; then to decide whether this will be used (a) powerfully (to produce, perhaps, a serious and aggressive style):

or (b) lightly, even delicately, to create a piquant or witty mood:

Some reference to bitonality could be useful as follow-up to this assignment. For example, Stravinsky's *Petrushka* motif, simultaneously in F♯ major and C major (quoted in Project 4, page 61). Also in Mozart's *Musical joke* for two horns and strings (K 522), and in works of Ives, Prokofiev, Hindemith, Poulenc and Milhaud.

Assignment 8

We return to a literary stimulus, but still with the aim of drawing from it a novel musical grammar. This should be reinforced by the theory of haiku, in which the aphoristic style of the poetry relates directly to the restriction on the number of syllables (normally seventeen) and the concentration upon a single train of thought. Haiku originally meant 'jest'; therefore you may wish to relate the pithy style to the musical notion of *scherzo*.

In the example given (page 102), the theory drawn from the poetic idea turns out to be a canon by augmentation. For students with suitable musical skills and sufficient composing experience, it could be appropriate to draw attention to that, and to show how such canons can be composed. They could play the following canon by Yehezkel Braun.

Grasshopper and snail

Yehezkel Braun

Look too at interesting examples such as the first of the four canons in Bach's *Art of fugue*, which works both by augmentation and contrary motion – another fascinating grammatical limitation.

On the other hand, the theory of two parts sharing similar musical material, and arriving together in spite of one going faster than the other, could be worked into a short piece of music (comparable with the succinct nature of the haiku) without any mention whatsoever of canon, let alone canon by augmentation! It might be done using indeterminate pitches as suggested in the first example on page 102. 'Indeterminate' interpretations (all for un-accompanied voices) of ideas arising from the other haiku might be as follows:

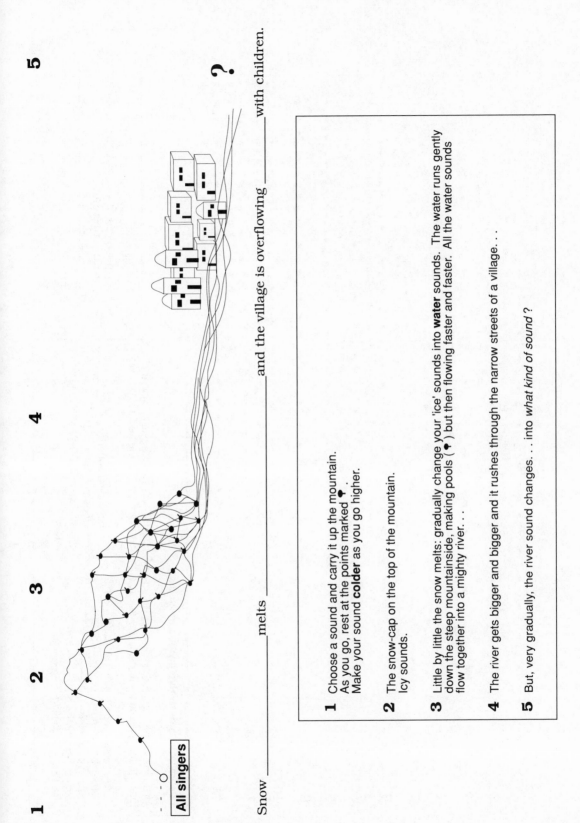

1 2 3 4 5

All singers

Snow _____ melts _____ and the village is overflowing _____ with children.

?

1 Choose a sound and carry it up the mountain.
As you go, rest at the points marked ♦.
Make your sound **colder** as you go higher.

2 The snow-cap on the top of the mountain.
Icy sounds.

3 Little by little the snow melts: gradually change your 'ice' sounds into **water** sounds. The water runs gently down the steep mountainside, making pools (♦) but then flowing faster and faster. All the water sounds flow together into a mighty river. . .

4 The river gets bigger and bigger and it rushes through the narrow streets of a village. . .

5 But, very gradually, the river sound changes. . . into *what kind of sound?*

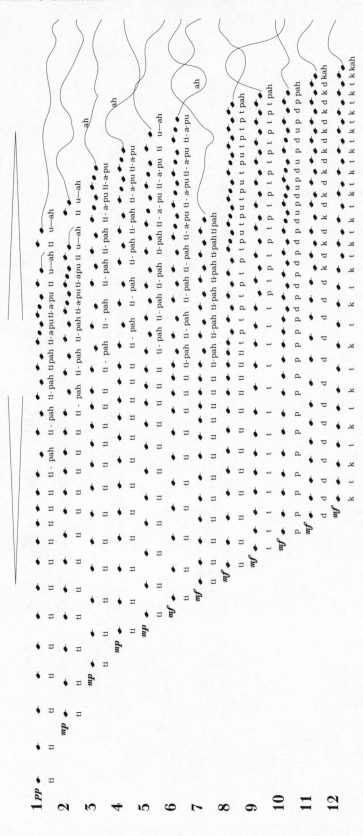

Rain drums on the pane
and runs down, wavering the world
into a dream.

Twelve voices or twelve groups of singers.

All sounds are *sung*. Each voice (or group) chooses its own starting pitch. Sing the tones in the notated patterns to any suitable 'raindrop' sound. Suggested sounds are:

ti - becoming ti-pah, ti-a-pu, ti-u-ah
t - becoming t p ——pah
p - becoming p d ——pah
d - becoming d k ——kah
k t k t - becoming ——kah

Let the ending sounds trail off gently into a 'dream'-like texture. Fade.

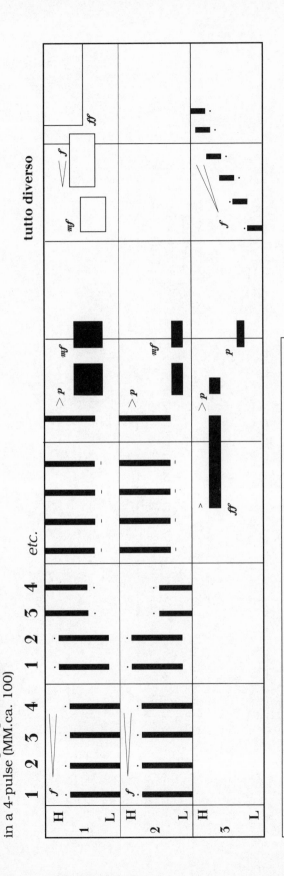

Moderato e pomposamente
in a 4-pulse (MM.ca. 100)

tutto diverso

In my new clothing
I feel so different
I must look like someone else.

Three groups of singers: agree upon suitable vowel sounds for the note clusters.
Note clusters should be pitched in accordance with the positions of the signs within each box (H=high, L=low).
Note clusters should also be expanded or contracted as indicated by the form of the signs.
The 'open' cluster signs in the last two bars of group 1 should be of a *completely different texture* ('I must look like someone else').
What kind of sound will be most suitable here?

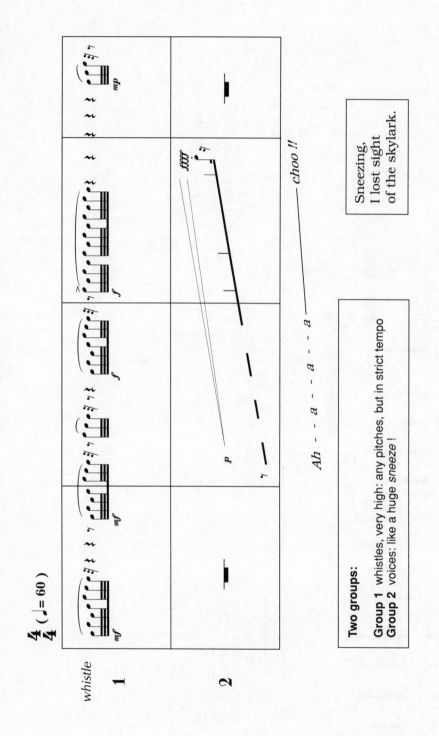

Two groups:

Group 1 whistles, very high: any pitches, but in strict tempo
Group 2 voices: like a huge *sneeze* !

Sneezing,
I lost sight
of the skylark.

Part III

Thinking and making

Project 9

New ears

Tradition can be something of a liability. So much that is valuable and stimulating has been received from the past that just to be aware of those achievements can be daunting, and may hinder new ways of thinking about things. Then again, familiarity can breed contempt, but it also tends to confirm assumptions. We have all heard so many good tunes that we may take it for granted that music, to be called music at all, has to be tuneful – or, at least, melodic.

Similarly, it is very easy to associate particular instruments with certain kinds of music, and that strengthens our convictions about what is or is not 'beautiful' and 'musical' sound. It is easy to imagine a harpist playing calm, unruffled music with lots of gentle sweeps across the strings; even when harp music is fast and energetic it still has that same 'beautiful' quality. Could this instrument ever produce an ugly sound?

Yet, if we had never heard the familiar instruments being played – if we came upon them unexpectedly and with no preconceptions – we might discover many unusual ways of playing them; and we'd listen to their sounds with new ears.

Student assignments

Assignment 1

For individual players using their own musical instruments. Think of ways of making musical sounds as different as possible from those normally expected from the instrument. Make a piece of music using only those unexpected sounds.

Assignment 2

For four string players (preferably the conventional string quartet). Listen to a number of Classical and early Romantic string quartets (e.g. by Haydn, Mozart, Schubert, Mendelssohn). Make a note of features that are characteristic of the string quartet sound. Think of ways in which those features could deliberately be avoided (i.e. ways of playing the instruments that would prevent the players from making the conventional sounds). Using these controls, make a piece which has an overall *new* 'string quartet sound', unlike anything that could have been composed in the eighteenth or nineteenth century.

Assignment 3

Make up the most unlikely combination you can think of with any three instruments available to you. Improvise together (to discover the musical possibilities), and then compose a piece of music for this unusual sound.

Assignment 4

Make up a melody that is not 'tuneful'.

Assignment 5

Make up a piece of music for drums that is not 'rhythmic'.

Assignment 6

Make a piece for any combination of strings, wind and keyboards in which every instrument is treated as a percussion instrument.

Assignment 7

Make a piece for singers in which the voices are always used like percussion instruments – except at one point only, where they produce the kind of sound usually expected of them.

Teaching points

Decisions, decisions . . .

The previous section was concerned with the nature and generation of musical ideas, and led to a point where we considered the possibility of an idea being an all-embracing proposition about the way the music should 'go'; a theory or a mechanism for that particular piece. Having taken those decisions, the theory must be put into practice by inventing the materials (the detailed elements; melodies, motifs, rhythmic figures, etc.) with which to compose the music.

To continue from there with the process of composition, further decisions have to be taken, principally on matters of control; that is to say, the way in which every minute element and nuance will be harnessed to ensure that the forward progress of the music is felt, that the development of ideas makes sense, and that the artistic conception as a whole is realised.[1] If that conception points in a somewhat different direction from most familiar forms of music, then the controls will also have to help maintain the newness of the sound; in effect holding off any tendency for the music to fall back into well-trodden paths.

Artifice and discipline

Fundamentally it is this, the control of the medium, relating all the elements in a unique working structure, that characterises compositional skill. To acquire that skill we have to cultivate inventiveness (seeing things in a new light) and imagination (presenting them in new ways); in other words, the artistry which produces the artifice – the illusion – of art as opposed to a mere copy of nature. That requires discipline and perseverance – a point worth making to students embarking on the assignments in this project. It must be understood that making a piece of music using 'unexpected sounds', or a string quartet movement that is 'unlike anything that could have been composed in the eighteenth or nineteenth century', or a melody that is 'not tuneful', or music for drums that is 'not rhythmic', does not mean 'anything goes'! These tasks are not incitements to musical lawlessness. On the contrary, because they involve deliberate avoidance of the familiar and the obvious, they call for extreme care in working out the possibilities, forming the ideas and carrying them through into interesting and coherent pieces of music, which must then either be written down or remembered in precise detail. Unusual sounds require more than usual care.

---

[1] This is rather like the device film-makers call a plot trigger. It is not the plot itself but a subtle and completely crucial element that gives all the characters in the story a believable excuse for being there at all, as well as making it possible for them to move through the story relating in various ways to each other's thoughts and actions. Alfred Hitchcock wanted a single, powerful word to express all of this, and since he couldn't find one he invented the term 'maguffin'.

A musical structure also needs a maguffin: an essential and aurally convincing reason why certain sound formations (ideas) are presented together in that particular piece and are made to relate to one another in various transformations as the music proceeds. The listener does not have to know what the maguffin is, but it will quickly be apparent if the music does not have such a rationale underpinning it. Indeed, this is a significant factor in distinguishing between successful and 'unsuccessful' music.

A maguffin may appear as some kind of complete overview of the music's shape and direction. Hindemith wrote that, for him, the conception of a work was frequently sudden and dramatic: like a landscape illuminated in a split second by a flash of lightning, the principal landmarks standing out but the detail only glimpsed.

Heritage

The music we have inherited from the past displays this artistic integrity, ingenuity and insight at many levels. We should aspire to those standards. At the same time, reverence for what is old simply because it is old would be misplaced.[2] We are not betraying our musical heritage if we recognise that to some extent it can hamper our own artistic adventurousness. Unquestionably we must know the great works of musical history, and go on improving our knowledge of them. Yet the more we know of them, the harder it may become to open up new musical ground. Not because they have said all that is to be said, nor because we cannot hope to measure up to those achievements, but principally because of the assumptions we take from them – such as the widely accepted notion that an expressive style is an appropriate goal for all music. In the string quartet repertoire, for instance, this view is so deeply ingrained that it is now very difficult for anyone to compose a string quartet that does not sound as though it is part of the accepted tradition. The only way out of this trap would be to side-step the tradition and require instrumentalists to play in a way that made the anticipated 'expressive' style impossible.

[2] Macaulay, in his essay on Milton, praised the poet for attacking 'those deeply seated errors on which almost all abuses are founded: the servile worship of eminent men and the irrational dread of innovation'.

Breaking the mould

This is exactly what the Dutch composer Guus Janssen does in his work *Streepjes* ('stripes' or 'lines') for string quartet. Starting from the argument outlined above, and 'reluctant to add yet another "classical" piece to the repertoire', he requires the players to use natural harmonics almost exclusively. These notes cannot, of course, be played with the traditional expressive vibrato; their thinner tone will automatically sound remote and 'inexpressive'.[3]

That decision severely limits the notes available. Therefore one string on each instrument is tuned to a non-standard pitch, so that by taking the four harmonics on each string the composer is able to produce a substantial chromatic scale over the four instruments (see opposite). It could be said that in doing this, Janssen was devising a new 'harmonics' instrument. His concept is of a single instrument with a sound quite unlike that of the classical string quartet, but with separate parts and needing four players! To emphasise this new view of 'string-quartetness' the composer plants occasional references to the conventional sound: a few carefully placed chords, played normally and *molto vibrato*!

Streepjes was composed in 1981. Thirty-one years before that, John Cage composed his *String quartet in four parts*, which in its own way also turns its back on the European tradition. The quiet, dispassionate – almost forlorn – non-vibrato chords seem to have come from nowhere and to be going nowhere. It is a string quartet in a trance; the swinging of a pendulum that has almost stopped but somehow just manages to move. (Extracts from both these works can be heard on the accompanying tape, track 8.)

[3] 'Inexpressive' in the stylistic sense only. Obviously all art is expressive in the broader sense of 'putting out' a particular view of reality.

'Streepjes': the complete range of harmonics used, from low to high

The project assignments

Students should work at these tasks before any comparisons are made with other music. While it may be helpful to know how Guus Janssen and John Cage have tackled the question of the string quartet's traditional sound, it is better that students should first think the question through for themselves; they may come up with some very surprising and interesting answers.

The intention in these assignments is to focus on controls as the first principle of musical artistry. Here and in the following project it is taken to a particular extreme – devising methods for managing the music coherently which also ensure that new sound-worlds are fully exploited. Later projects will examine the same question from different angles.

Students frequently need to be reminded that self-imposed restrictions on the way musical ideas are used are important, not only because limitations cause us to work at ideas and to draw out possibilities that might otherwise be missed, but also because they keep the composition process on course. Without such controls it would be difficult to make the music hang together, because it would lack a sense of direction and there would be the danger of wandering aimlessly in a kind of musical desert.

However, with this project we must also begin to emphasise other kinds of control: the checks and balances that have to be imposed on the development of musical ideas to make the music progress satisfactorily to a 'correct' conclusion.

Setting the limits

The first step is to create the framework. What kind of sound-world are we thinking of? It could be anything: pentatonic scales, the random sounds of found objects, a range of different sized drums or – as in Guus Janssen's string quartet – the environment of string harmonics.

There will, no doubt, be close links between this decision and the devising of the main musical ideas; both in the large-scale, overall concept of the piece and also in the more detailed matters of motifs, figures, melodies and rhythm patterns. This will also make clear just what can be used (and what cannot) to control the vital progressions and recessions that create musical interest, direction and form: timbres, melodic figures, rhythmic figures, range of pitches and dynamics, harmonic possibilities, and so on. Elements of surprise and the potential for dramatic increase in dynamic or tempo can be used to drive the music on (to create progression); features that can be repeated, coupled with decrease in dynamic or tempo, will be useful to restrain the progress (i.e. to create recession).

There is, of course, virtually no end to the ways in which these details can be arranged and re-arranged to make musical structures work. Repetition can be recessive if the ear tires of it and wants something new (new = more excitement = progression). On the other hand, a repeated figure that is getting louder all the time is clearly progressive. It all depends on how much progression or recession is needed at any particular point, having in mind the nature of the musical ideas and the likely duration of the piece.

Then again, if the musical environment has been deliberately and severely restricted, the opportunities for creating powerfully progressive moments are also likely to be limited. If progression is what seems to be needed, the resources will either have to be increased (e.g. this could be one reason for introducing a foreign mode of producing the sounds, as in Assignment 7) or the composer(s) must decide what, within the limitations already accepted, could produce an increase in tension. (Wide melodic leaps? Many different things happening at the same time? Increased density – i.e. pitches very close to one another, forced, as it were, into a small space?)

This is not something that can be explained, except in the most general terms by way of introduction. Precisely what will need to be done in particular circumstances can only be discovered by creative experiment.[4] When an assignment is completed the teacher must comment carefully on the music produced, drawing attention to the various ways in which the music has been made to progress and recess.

Style

Work from this project could also provide a basis for discussion of musical style and taste. Changes do not occur simply because people become bored with familiar styles and want something different; after all, many people are convinced that they don't want something different! Stylistic change is a necessary renewal of musical language to give it the power to match new perceptions of reality. The new directions composers take are marks of cultural change. They may look like denials of past values, but generally they are simply attempts to overcome the effects of tradition and to deal adequately with the present environment of ideas. Whether or not those attempts produce lastingly worthwhile music, if composers did not try to do something about it we should not be able to live musically in our own time; we should be tied to modes of perception and expression that, interesting and important though they were in so many respects, could not wholly reflect current thought.[5]

Renewing the language places upon composers – especially those who go to new stylistic extremes – the responsibility of making the

[4] Formal education, from first school to university, still assumes that most learning will be achieved by listening to explanations. Creative experiment in music, on the other hand, is comparable with the mental processes of learning to program on a computer: '. . . the process of learning is transformed. It becomes more active and self-directed. In particular, the knowledge is acquired for a recognisable personal purpose . . . The new knowledge is a source of power and is experienced as such from the moment it begins to form . . .' (Seymour Pappert, *Mindstorms: children, computers and powerful ideas*, Brighton, The Harvester Press, 1980, pp. 20–21).

[5] 'With scientific discovery and invention proceeding, we are told, at a geometric rate of progression, a generally passive and culture-bound people cannot cope with the multiplying issues and problems. Unless individuals, groups and nations can imagine, construct, and creatively revise new ways of relating to these complex changes, the lights will go out. Unless man can make new and original adaptations to his environment as rapidly as his science can change the environment, our culture will perish. Not only individual maladjustment and group tensions but international annihilation will be the price we pay for a lack of creativity.' (Carl R. Rogers, 'Towards a theory of creativity' in H.H. Anderson (ed), *Creativity and its cultivation*, New York, Harper & Row, 1959, p. 70).
Also, see again note 5 (p. 13).

significance of their ways of composing absolutely clear. This can only be done within the music itself (i.e. not by explanatory programme notes), and is dependent entirely upon the composer's artistry. Of course, the composer is entitled to expect that anyone who is prepared to accept the challenge of new ideas will, at the very least, listen to them attentively. But the music must make clear the limitations the composer has accepted, and the conditions under which the ideas are being developed. If it doesn't sound like anything we've heard before, then we should be able to discover, *from the music*, why that is so. If it seems to have links with other music we know, then again it should be possible to understand the extent of that relationship and why and how this new music builds upon the other.

There can be no guarantee of communication; we cannot argue that every piece of music must communicate to everyone. But if the composer has worked in a careful and disciplined way to ensure that the composition has wholeness and consistency of style, that no unnecessary material intrudes, and that the argument makes itself apparent, then there should be a good chance that the music will be meaningful and appealing in some degree to those prepared to give it their attention.

Alexander Goehr has said, 'I write music so that people can follow, from bar to bar; and know that some notes follow and others don't'; a view comparable with that of the American painter Jackson Pollock: 'Technique is just a way of arriving at a statement.' Statements are made to be received; and for anyone encountering a new musical statement it should, above all, be an adventure that captures the imagination.[6]

Perhaps, then, the most important thing to learn about listening to a new work – or indeed to any music in an unfamiliar style – is that it must be accepted on its own terms, and it must be accepted complete. A work of art is not a work in bits. It is more than the sum of its parts, and therefore we must engage with its whole argument – with its complete structure and all the interplay of features that contribute to that wholeness.[7] It is the purpose of this project to discover the artistic significance of these things because they are vital clues to understanding any musical style.

No one should be ashamed of having preferences; music appeals to us individually and for a multitude of different reasons. But 'I know what I like', used as support for refusing even to contemplate the possibility that something unfamiliar might be interesting, should probably arouse suspicion. How many people who make that claim really do know what they like? Not infrequently judgements are based on extra-musical associations, regard for particular performers, and second-hand critical opinion. If music education does nothing else it should make all of us aware of the breadth of artistic possibility, and the fact that we must *actually have heard the music* before we make any kind of judgement.[8]

[6] Cf. Merce Cunningham: 'I'm not expressing anything; I'm presenting dance in such a way that the experience for the audience can itself become an adventure.'

[7] Cf. Susanne Langer: 'The art symbol . . . is always the entire work.' And, 'A work of art is a single symbol, not a system of significant elements which may be variously compounded. Its elements have no symbolic values in isolation. They take their expressive character from their functions in the perceptual whole.'

And Robert Witkin: '. . . in and through the changes that constitute the work we sense a continuity, a relatedness or invariance . . . the relatedness of the whole is thus present at each instant'.

And Leonard B. Meyer: 'The entire meaning of a work . . . includes both the meanings of the several parts and the meaning of the work as a single sound term or gesture.'

[8] Many who use the 'I know what I like' defence would doubtless be horrified if judgements were made about them on hearsay evidence, yet so-called critical judgement about art is often no more than second-hand opinion. Cf. D.W. Harding's observations on criticism fifty-six years ago, in the first volume of *Scrutiny*: 'With people who assert that they know what they like, the one hope is to demonstrate to them that in point of fact they don't, that according to standards they themselves recognise elsewhere their judgement here is mistaken. As these inconsistencies are faced and abandoned, the possibility of agreement with other people grows greater.'

Project 10

Unity and variety: from twelve bar to twelve note

We have to get our bearings in a piece of music; to remember and recognise the landmarks, just as we should if we were visiting an unfamiliar place. With music it's particularly difficult because it depends so much on being able to remember what we hear as the music goes on. From the composer's point of view this is yet another important reason why there must be limitations set on the way the music proceeds, and why there must be careful controls to keep it moving within those limits. Even the most surprising parts of a composition still have to make sense; they must clearly 'belong', and every piece of music must have its own identity.

Student assignments

Assignment 1

a. Experiment with ways of making this idea go on. You could repeat it – but how many times? Two? Three? And what then? What do you think are the most easily remembered features of this opening phrase? Can you think of ways of using them so that they become the characteristic features of a long melody? How do you prevent the whole thing from becoming boring? Is there a recognisable climax, and when is the best point in the melody for it? (Try various possibilities.) What can be done to give the melody a satisfactory overall shape?

b. Invent other beginnings with strong and characteristic features which can be developed into long melodies.

Assignment 2

a. Use this phrase as an ostinato. That is to say, play it over and over many times without varying it in any way, while another player (on another instrument) improvises a long and developing melody that fits with the repeating phrase. Establish the ostinato first – two, three or four repetitions before the second player starts to improvise. The ostinato provides the *unity*, holding the whole piece together; the other instrument provides the variety – although that part too will have to have some unifying features. Develop the improvisation into a fixed composition.

b. Using the same ostinato, make another two-part composition (i.e. ostinato plus melody), but this time create even more variety by, at some point in the composition, moving the ostinato to a different pitch. Experiment to find the most suitable point to make this change. It will be more powerful if, to begin with, the original pitch is well established, i.e. if it sounds as though it will never change! But, having changed, how long should it then continue at the new pitch? To the end of the piece? Or should it move to another pitch? Or return to the original? With the ostinato changing position in this way, will it be necessary to limit the amount of variety in the other part?

c. Invent ostinato phrases and compose further pieces with added parts both above and below the ostinato. Make a piece that has two ostinato patterns: use the first for as long as possible, then change to the other. Can the music end there? Should it return to the first ostinato? (With the same music as at the start? Or with something new?) How long is 'as long as possible'? (Until it becomes boring? What can be done to keep it interesting?) Perhaps at the end the two ostinato ideas could be combined (used simultaneously)?

Assignment 3

a. Compose a piece which is made entirely from the idea of alternating chords like this:

Make the piece as long as possible. (Again, how long is 'possible'? What will you have to do to sustain the music's interest?) Do not introduce any other musical ideas.

b. Treat the two chords given in Assignment 3(a) as an ostinato to accompany a line of melody. You may move the ostinato up or down in pitch if you wish.

Assignment 4

A chord is any number of notes played simultaneously. Concords, such as major or minor triads ▷

produce less tension than discords – like these, in which the
notes are closer to one another ▷

Concords can be used to create points of rest, and discords can
add tension to music. Also, widely spaced chords (including
discords) ▷

create less tension than very dense clusters of notes ▷

a. Compose a piece made up entirely of slow-moving chords.
Begin in a relaxed way with concords, increase the tension very
gradually to a climax point which is very discordant, then
gradually release tension by making the chords less and less
discordant, ending where you started, with a simple concord.
How can the spacing of each chord help to control the very
gradual increase and decrease of tension? And will dynamics
(loud and soft) play any part?

b. Make another piece like the one in assignment 3(b), but using
two discords rather than two concords for the ostinato.

c. One way of uniting a melody and its accompaniment is to
make up chords that use some or all of the same notes as the first
phrase of the tune. For example ▷

Then the chords can either be repeated (like an ostinato) or,
keeping the same chord shapes, they can be moved to different
pitches. It is the chord shape which we recognise and remember,
and which gives the particular character to the accompaniment:

melody: 'E l'uccelino del bo'' (folksong from Lazio, Italy)

Invent chords based on the opening notes of the following melody and develop them into an accompaniment for the whole tune.

'Quand'è il tempo delle ciliegie' (folksong from Tuscany, Italy)

Assignment 5

On a keyboard make a group of three chords that are very close to one another (i.e. fall readily under the hand so that you can change from chord to chord easily and smoothly), but at the same time have as much variety as possible between them. For example:

Using your three chords as accompaniment, make up a melody. Start by inventing a pattern for the chords. Play them in that pattern and, as you play, improvise the tune. For example:

Assignment 6

Perhaps the most famous of all chord patterns is the 12-bar blues. In its basic form this uses just three simple chords – in the key of C, for instance:

A blues singer might strum these harmonies on a guitar and make up the song as he or she goes along. The pattern of the words is also traditional. Each verse has three lines, the second a repeat of the first:

I got up this mornin', heard ole train whistle blow,
I got up this mornin', hear the train whistle blow,
Lord I thought about my baby, I sure did want to go.

(Tape track 9)

Usually the basic chord pattern is elaborated by making each one a 7th chord (adding the flat 7th above the root of each triad):

a. Memorise this standard 12-bar sequence on keyboard or guitar, then make up blues tunes over it.

Two small but subtle changes(*) to the standard pattern give added scope for musical interest:

b. The form of the 12-bar blues is:
4/4 time: first four bars the same chord
        bars 5–6 a different chord
        bars 7–8 the same chord as bars 1–4
        bars 9–10 another different chord
        bars 11–12 the same chord as bars 1–4

Using this form, invent a completely new set of chords, quite unlike those in the 12-bar blues, and then use them to accompany improvised melodies. You can use any combination of notes that sounds interesting, provides suitable contrast, and flows easily from one chord to the next. For example:

What kind of melody does such a series of chords suggest? Think of a title for a piece, and then compose the piece using the musical possibilities you've been exploring in this assignment.

Assignment 7

For four players using the same kind of instruments (e.g. 4 violins or 4 clarinets or 4 keyboards – or 2 keyboards with two players each). Compose a piece to be called *Welcoming the sunrise*. Having thought about the possible musical implications of that title, start by selecting a chromatic range of between 15 and 20 notes, for example:

Allocate groups of these notes to each player (this could be an unequal division or it could be, say, five notes each). Invent a short but distinctive rhythm pattern to be played by the whole group together, for example:

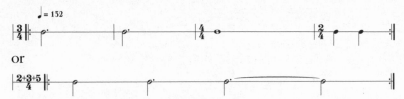

or

Your composition should now be based on the continuous repetition of the rhythm pattern, the players using only the notes allocated to them. It's up to each player to decide how his or her notes will be used within the agreed pattern – for example in a continuously repeating cycle, or in a different order for each repetition of the rhythm pattern, or introducing silences/gaps in the sequence of notes. The group must decide together how long the piece will last (i.e. how many repetitions of the pattern there will be).

Assignment 8

For groups of four players, two with high pitched instruments and two with low pitched instruments. (Those in the middle range will have to decide whether their instruments are predominantly on the high or the low side.) Compose three short pieces:

a. called 'Islands' – in which the high instruments play always in parallel 3rds, the low instruments in parallel 4ths or 7ths;

b. called 'Pathways' – in which the high instruments are restricted to parallel 5ths, the low instruments to alternate tones and semitones;

c. called 'Reflections' – like (b) (i.e. 5ths and alternating tones/semitones) but with the further restriction that the two pairs of instruments work always in contrary motion.

Assignment 9

For any 2 or 4 instruments. Compose a piece called 'Dance' that features the interval of an augmented 4th. Decide first how many different augmented 4ths you want to use on each instrument, for example:

Assignment 10

a. Make up a melody that includes all of these notes but uses each of them once only. Write it down. Are there any points in your melody where three consecutive notes form a triad? For example:

b. Make more 12-note melodies, as far as possible avoiding groups of consecutive notes that, sounded together, would form triads or other familiar patterns. Try to make the melody sound as unusual as possible.

c. From the melodies you have composed for (b), choose one you consider to be the most unusual. Write out its notes as a series – or row – of semibreves. For example:

As well as being a series of notes, this is a series of *intervals*:

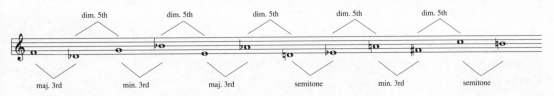

Name each of the intervals in your own series. It is the intervals that give special character to a series – and to any melodies you make with it.

d. Make a long melody by repeating the series as many times as you need to – keep going round the series with the notes always in that order, but vary the rhythm patterns so that the melody develops interestingly. Use contrasts of loud and soft to add further variety. How could you make the melody begin calmly but increase in excitement and tension as it went on? How could you calm it again at the end? Use these controls carefully so that the progression from calm to excited and the recession (easing of tension) to the end is very gradual in both instances.

Assignment 11

Now invert all the intervals in your series. Start on the same note as the original version, but where there is an upward movement, step or leap, make a downward movement by the same amount, and vice versa (i.e. an upward leap of an augmented 4th becomes a downward leap of an augmented 4th; a semitone going down becomes a semitone going up, and so on). As long as the *intervals* are the same and keep their original order in the series, the identity of the row will remain.

When a row is inverted in this way, the original row is called 'O' and the inversion is called 'I':

Two players (any instruments) improvise together on the two versions of the row (the same note row as before or make up a new one), one player taking the 'O', the other its inversion, 'I'. When you've got the feel of working with these notes and keeping the order, compose a piece called *Dreamtime*.

Assignment 12

Compose more pieces using this 12-note method, gradually expanding your resources:

a. Use notes of the same name in any octave (this won't alter the character of the intervals between the notes). For example, the note D could be any D ▷

depending on the range of your instrument. So, a 12-note row that began ▷

might be used to make any of the following melody ideas:

b. Transpose the note row on to any of the other eleven notes. This makes possible a further slight change in the 'flavour' of the music. For example, a melody that starts with the 'O' version of the row might use that twice and then change to, say, 'O₁₀' (the tenth transposition of 'O' – the one starting on B♭, the 10th semitone if you count C as 0, C♯ as 1, D as 2, and so on):

c. 'R' stands for 'retrograde' (= backwards). What would you expect 'RO' and 'RI' to be? Make melodies with these versions of the row.

d. Create chords as well as melody lines with the series (again, making sure that the notes are used always in the same order, so that the character of the intervals remains the same):

Teaching points

Significant detail

The aim is to examine the idea that, in musical composition, it is the smallest details that give us the greatest control.

The project could extend over a number of weeks, or even more than one term, depending upon how you deal with its topics. On the one hand it could be a fairly general exploration, ranging over melody, chords and accompaniment, the use of ostinato patterns, 12-bar blues, adding chromatic spice to chords, using the full chromatic range, and on to the broad outlines of, first, atonal and then '12 note' music. The work on ostinato might take off in the direction of jazz/rock riffs, and link up again with the blues (which itself could be a whole term's course). On the other hand, for students with the appropriate technical background the project could move quickly through the preliminary stages to concentrate on a substantial study of serial music.

In this project you should expect to see greater refinement and discrimination in students' compositions, and a more developed sense of identity in individual pieces. Similar development is evident in the history of music worldwide; simple rhythmic cells giving way to longer and more elaborate patterns; shouts and gestures becoming melody and polyphony. Always it is a process of extension, elaboration and, above all, refinement by working ever more closely with points of detail.

Melody and harmony are the most artificial features; that is to say, they are the areas of greatest artifice. All the other elements – timbre, texture, dynamics, rhythm – can subtly influence the progress of music, but it is in working with pitch that we find the greatest scope for precise distinctions. The movement of just one semitone can mark the most dramatic change of harmonic or contrapuntal direction. Possibly the most important feature in all the world's music has been the unfolding of forms in which notes and intervals are the principal agents of 'intensification through expansion', the musical ideas in sangita, gamelan, gagaku, fugue and sonata spinning out in more and more subtle nuances of pitch relationships.

The assignments

Assignment 1 a. This should not be like an examination exercise in melody-writing (four-bar phrases, 'question and answer', etc.). Avoid any suggestion of working to a formula. Ideas should be explored by using musical instruments and focusing on the 'identity' of the materials, so that students can discover for themselves how to make sense of melody by working with those characteristic features.

However, as a broad guideline, it could be useful to point out that, in making sense of melody, we are concerned with what is memorable. Music based on just one or two ideas and a lot of repetition is easy to follow because it is not difficult to remember what happens and when. Patterns repeated many times with very little variation force themselves upon the mind. That could be rather dull.

On the other hand, music doesn't have to be complicated to be interesting. A lot can be done with simple ideas, provided there is a reasonable balance between what listeners will find familiar (because it uses well-established 'vocabulary' or easily recognisable features) and what will surprise and, we hope, delight (because it is new and unexpected). Too much repetition may be boring, but if there is too much diversity there is nothing to hang on to; memory can't cope with all the new things happening, and so we lose the thread.

The main features of the idea given are

i. its overall shape:

a downward leap, then running up by step

ii. the syncopation:

One possibility, featuring the outline shape of the first phrase and the syncopation, would be:

Working first from the examples the students produce, draw attention particularly to the details that create progression and recession. This might be strengthened by seeing how such things work in a notably memorable melody, for example one of those dealt with in Project 16. You could make a digression at this point, or return later to some of the melodies made here in order to lead into the work of Project 16.

Assignment 2 a. Again, focus on the detail of the controls needed to maintain musical interest. The ostinato unifies the piece, but it is also generally recessive in effect: its continuous repetition restricts variety and is unlikely to increase interest. The responsibility for maintaining interest must then lie mainly with the melodic line above the ostinato, perhaps beginning like this:

or like this:

Even so, various things can be done with the ostinato to offset its recessive effects; for example, making it a gradual crescendo. Likewise, if the other part is too varied it will not easily make sense. In order to produce a successful and satisfying piece, very careful judgement is needed to balance the things that most obviously make for progression or recession in the two parts working together.[1]

In **Assignment 2 b**, changing the pitch of the ostinato might work like this:

It is a useful rule of thumb for a composition to start by firmly establishing an idea (motif, figure, key, timbre, etc.), and then, when it seems that this is the status quo for the piece, to do something different; if possible, something that takes listeners by surprise; something they would never have thought possible.

But the emphasis should still be on weighing up the interplay of progressive and recessive effects; checks and balances which here will be compromised by the varying degrees of repetition and novelty in each part.

Assignment 2 c. An important point is the relationship between the overall duration and the capacity to sustain interest by careful handling of progressive and recessive elements.

Assignment 3 a. The two given chords are 'the idea' in this piece; therefore it will be necessary to focus attention on them by repeating them. But for how long? – that must be left to students' judgement. Once the idea is established, interest could be maintained by keeping the chord shapes and moving them up and down to other notes. For example:

---

[1] Experience with ostinati might prompt us to ask whether variety is essential to music. Can monotony be interesting? Erik Satie's *Vexations* for piano, composed in 1893, consists of a short phrase repeated 840 times! Satie also produced (1920) *Furniture Music*, in which an ensemble of piano, three clarinets and trombone plays a short passage over and over until it becomes like the furniture (or the wallpaper): accepted without being noticed. Is that a justifiable function for music? If it is, what does a composer have to do to achieve it? Is there anything more to it than mere repetition?

For **Assignment 3 b**, the result might be something like this:

Assignment 4. A general point for this assignment: discords are normally progressive because they avoid the feeling of rest and finality that is characteristic of concords. Discords suggest there is more to come.[2] But if the constituent intervals of a discord have a

---

[2] At some point it may be useful to talk about the harmonic series, from which the principle of musical concord seems to be derived. This is nature's music, drawing everything back to the starting-point. The greatest diversity and instability is in the higher pitches which seem always to want to revert to the stability of the lowest (i.e. the first six harmonics), and most of all to the fundamental from which every other pitch is generated (as the leaves cannot exist without the branches which cannot exist without the trunk of the tree which cannot exist without the root).

A single tone played on a musical instrument is never a pure tone (unless the instrument is electronic and designed to produce a sine wave). What appears to be a single tone is in fact a complicated arrangement of overtones: the upper partials of the harmonic series; some more prominent than others, depending upon the instrument. It is the presence of particular harmonics of varying strength that gives each instrument its unique timbre and makes it immediately recognisable.

The harmonic series can easily be heard by striking the lowest C on a piano. This produces a particularly full-bodied sound, not only because the string is thicker than those of the higher notes but also because of the harmonics which sound with the fundamental note C. We may not be conscious of these overtones but we'd miss them if they were not there.

As an experiment, have four people at one piano hold down, without sounding, the notes numbered 2–16 in the example of the harmonic series given above. A fifth person then strikes the low C (numbered 1) once, sharply. The strings of the held-down notes will vibrate in sympathy with the harmonics which are present in the make-up of the low C and give it its unique sound.

Concords are made from the first six pitches of the harmonic series with their strong feeling of rest and completeness. This is why common triads may seem to suggest stability – and to some extent finality. But what is stable may also be regarded as static. Music is a time art and needs to move through time. Discords, which have more in common with the unstable upper levels of the series, can be used to drive the music onwards to the expected concords:

strong identity of their own, repetition of that chord or chords of similar shape will make those interval relationships familiar, so that the discordant quality takes on a kind of stability, giving the music unity but with the added piquancy of dissonant harmony.

Assignment 4 c. The tune 'Quand'e il tempo delle ciliegie' uses a very limited range of notes (mainly G, E, D and F), and the notes of the opening phrase, played together instead of consecutively, form two chords of a similar kind. Various arrangements of these notes are possible to make chords that can be used as an accompaniment for the whole melody:

This technique of taking notes from the opening phrase of a melody to create harmonic intervals which then define the shape of the accompanying chords was used frequently by Bartók to make new accompaniments for old Hungarian and Slovakian folk tunes. In the following two examples, from the collection of piano pieces *For children*, we can see how this was done:

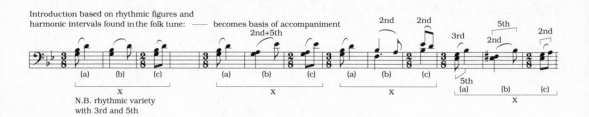

Assignment 6 a. In the history of the blues, harmonic adventure has been more prominent than experiment with the form. Even so, and in spite of the harmony having developed mostly by way of minor alterations to the chords, plus the occasional introduction of a 'new' chord, the advances have been quite striking in their subtlety.

The standard 12-bar sequence given at the bottom of page 128 is unlikely to be used today except in the most straightforward rock 'n' roll numbers. An early variant used the subdominant in bars 2 and 10 (see page 129), and other interesting changes were made by introducing the submediant 7th and supertonic 7th chords at the structurally important points, bars 8–9 and 12:

Bar 12 (with the lead-in of bar 11) forms the 'turnaround' – a particular characteristic of the blues. The final bar in the simplest form has tonic harmony, but since every chord includes the 7th it feels unresolved and joins easily with the same chord at the start of another cycle. In more elaborate blues sequences the turnaround is refined, generally making an imperfect cadence and often with faster changes of harmony (i.e. at the half bar):

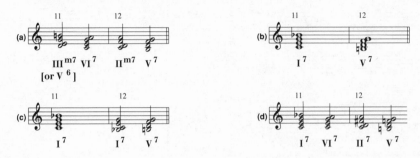

Bars 8/9 are significant in the overall form because they mark a point that is crucial in any 'classic' musical structure, approximately two-thirds of the way through, when the ear expects to be surprised.[3]

What do we learn from this? That, in a folk form, little by little, improvising musicians have expanded the expressive possibilities by being 'busy with notes'. They have generated variety by subtle harmonic variation within the form; by modifying the chords at those points which they recognise intuitively as the most telling moments of the structure.

Before leaving **Assignment 6 a** it might be useful to look at other developments of blues harmony.[4]

[4] Two excellent and very useful books are
Lionel Grigson, *Practical jazz* (London, Stainer & Bell, 1988).
Graham Collier, *Jazz workshop* (London, Universal Edition, 1988).

[3] This experience in music is directly comparable with what visual aesthetics knows as the Golden Section: a theory of proportion which finds its greatest expression in architecture. It can be summarised as the relationship of two parts, of which the smaller is to the larger as the larger is to the whole.

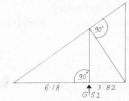

The ancient Greeks discovered this by geometry, but it can be found in nature (e.g. in the forms of fir cones and some shells). Mathematically it is expressed in the numerical series we call the Fibonacci Sequence (1, 2, 3, 5, 8, 13 etc.); and it would seem that this highly satisfying proportion is also perceptible in defined periods of time, such as musical works, which frequently take off in new and unexpected directions somewhere around 0.6 or 0.7 of the overall duration.

In the 12-bar blues the main Golden Section point (GS1) should be half-way through bar 8. In fact this is the very point at which we prepare for the really interesting subtleties of harmony in bar 9. Similarly, the other important chord change occurs across bars 4 and 5, and that turns out to be GS2 (the Golden Section of the duration from the start to the GS1 point at bars 8/9).

Assignment 6 b leads on from there, although it must be stressed that the aim is to encourage further intuitive exploration of harmony, not to develop a kind of atonal blues! Here the chords can be any combinations of notes that appeal to the student's ear. Encourage free improvisation of melodies over these chords, perhaps confirming the best ideas as fixed compositions.

The style of that '12-bar' sounds something like Bartók – and about as far away as possible from a traditional Afro-American blues!

Assignment 7 expands further the harmonic possibilities in a free use of the total chromatic range of notes. Students are no longer working within a conventional frame such as the 12-bar blues, but must devise their own unified forms on the basis of the musical content.

A successful composition diversifies a unity. As we have seen, the skill lies in first defining that unity as the concept of the whole piece and then devising a theory to make the idea work out. Here, a title is suggested as a starting-point for the overall *musical* idea. (If that title is not suitable, you or the students could think of another.) Precisely how the resulting musical idea will be fully realised is up to the students, but a theory for the piece is proposed to help channel their thinking into the use of all the available chromatic notes.

It is probably easiest to think of the suggested rhythm pattern as a series of durations ▷

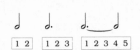

The players should first practise clapping the pattern together, over and over, until they can be sure of keeping an absolutely steady pulse:

When this is secure they can experiment individually with ways of using the allocated notes within this pattern.

One group's working out of this assignment is shown opposite.

In this case the instruments were chime bars, the players choosing
more or less at random from a mixed collection. Players 1 and 2
selected mostly 'black' notes, while 3 and 4 confined themselves to
'white' notes. The number of notes chosen was also random: 1 and 4
had six notes each, 2 had five, and 3 had four. And of those notes,
some were doubled: the note G with players 1 and 3, and B in the
notes chosen by 2 and 3.

Each member of the group approached differently the ordering
and musical use of the notes. Player 1 arranged them in two
three-note sets which alternate throughout the piece. Player 2 also
arranged the notes in two sets: (i) F and F♯, (ii) B, B♭ and G♯ – but
these were not alternated systematically. Player 3 seemed to
be trying to permutate her four notes as much as possible: C A G,
A B C, G A C, C B A, C A G, A B G. Player 4 clearly wanted a
two-bar ostinato (E D G E F A) but interrupted it in bars 5 and 6
with an oddly random arrangement which gives middle C its only
appearance in the piece!

Having experimented briefly with the ordering of the notes, the
players worked together to compose directly from the instruments.
That is to say, nothing was written down at this stage but, as they
went along, the group evaluated the varying combinations of the
notes and the 'necessary' duration of the piece. In this way it was

thought out and remembered, to be notated later by two members of the group.

The harmonies are, of course, largely accidental; and they are dependent upon what each player had decided to do with the notes she had chosen. There is, nevertheless, an attractive harmonic style (reminiscent of early Messiaen?) arising from the semitone relationships in this total chromatic soundscape. Clearly, the players responded to that, distinguishing significant points by a careful use of dynamic changes.

Assignments 8 and 9. Intervals are the point of focus here, together with the notion of complementary musical materials that are equal but different.[5] The intervals proposed for the various pieces may be used melodically or harmonically, and these tasks (along with those in Assignment 7) prepare the way for Assignments 10–12.

These provide an introduction to serial composition, a large and influential area of twentieth-century music that can only be dealt with here in a very general way.[6] Even so, experience of working with these tasks could offer students a useful background for listening to and discussing music by Schoenberg, Webern, Berg and their successors.

Those unfamiliar with serial techniques may tend to regard the whole process as more mathematical than musical. In point of fact the serial approach is no more mathematical than many techniques practised within tonal music over some 500 years. And a system of 7 unequal notes arrayed in 24 major and minor scales is just as 'artificial' as a system of 12 equal notes in a matrix of 48 possibilities. In both cases the composer must make musical judgements on the basis of what is heard. The only real difference is that the 7-note major/minor system evolved over a long period of time, largely by intuition rather than rational thought, whereas the 12-note 'method' was invented to deal with a particular aesthetic problem.

Just as tonal music in the major/minor system is made principally by exploiting the varying degrees of tension and influence between intervals (e.g. the fundamental 'attraction' of the tonic; the downward/upward pull of dominant to tonic; the upward-moving tendency of the leading note, and so on), so, broadly speaking, serial music is about what can be done with 11 intervals – rather than 12 notes. The method is designed to fend off any tendency in the music to revert to the functional assumptions of major/minor tonality. In this way it frees the composer to work with the characteristics of the 11 intervals; a new soundscape which can be designed afresh for each composition.

Students should be encouraged to try to forget the assumptions they are used to making with tonal music; for example, that melody can be driven by the functional relationships of tonic, dominant, leading note, or whatever, and that the same features, applied to harmonic rhythm, control the use of chords. In serial composition those functions don't exist, because – unlike the major scale which is divided unequally and has some steps of a tone and others of a

[5] As in nature, so in art: things do not have to be the same in order to be equal; the most effective combinations are made by the linking of *complementary* forces.

[6] If you want to develop a more thoroughgoing course in serial composition you are recommended to consult: Reginald Smith Brindle, *Musical composition* (London, Oxford University Press, 1986), pp. 111–47. Reginald Smith Brindle, *Serial composition* (London, Oxford University Press), 1966. David Cope, *New music composition* (New York, Schirmer, 1977), pp. 14–25.

semitone – the 12 note scale has only *semitone* steps. Therefore some other way must be found of giving the music progressive features (forward impetus, increased tension, excitement) and controlled recession (relaxing tension, etc.). One obvious possibility is to vary the note durations and rhythmic figures:

Inverting the intervals widens the scope of the music without destroying the character of a particular series. It is important that the inversions are made with the greatest care, and checked afterwards to see that each of the twelve notes still appears only once.

Similar care must be taken with the transposition of the row. Probably the easiest way to see all the available notes displayed is to make a 'row box' – a 12 × 12 matrix. Using note letter-names, write out the row in its original form across the top of the matrix:

'O'→

F	D♭	G	B♭	E	A♭	D	E♭	A	F♯	C	B

Then, from the starting note in the top left-hand box, write the notes of the *inversion* of the row down the left-hand side (and check that this contains all twelve notes):

‘O’→

	F	D♭	G	B♭	E	A♭	D	E♭	A	F♯	C	B
A												
E♭												
C												
F♯												
D												
A♭												
G												
C♯												
E												
B♭												
B												

'I' ↓ (left side label)

Now, because the original row starts with F, find first in the left-hand column the note a semitone higher – F♯. From there, write in the other eleven note-names of the series, across from left to right, in each case one semitone higher than the corresponding note of the original row (the top line of the box).

That is the first transposition of the row. Next, find G in the left-hand column and complete that line, one semitone higher again than the notes in the F♯ line you have just written. Then find G♯ (or

‘O’→   ←‘R’

	F	D♭	G	B♭	E	A♭	D	E♭	A	F♯	C	B
A	F	B	D	G♯	C	F♯	G	C♯	B♭	E	E♭
E♭	B	F	G♯	D	F♯	C	C♯	G	E	B♭	A
C	G♯	D	F	B	E♭	A	B♭	E	C♯	G	F♯
F♯	D	G♯	B	F	A	D♯	E	B♭	G	C♯	C
D	B♭	E	G	C♯	F	B	C	F♯	E♭	A	G♯
A♭	E	B♭	C♯	G	B	F	F♯	C	A	E♭	D
G	E♭	A	C	F♯	B♭	E	F	B	G♯	D	C♯
C♯	A	E♭	F♯	C	E	B♭	B	F	D	G♯	G
E	C	F♯	A	E♭	G	C♯	D	G♯	F	B	B♭
B♭	F♯	C	E♭	A	C♯	G	G♯	D	B	F	E
B	G	C♯	E	B♭	D	G♯	A	E♭	C	F♯	F

‘I’ ↓ (left label); ‘RI’ ↑ (bottom-left label)

Ab) and fill in that line one semitone higher than the G line. And so on, to complete the remaining notes in the 144 squares.

From such a layout it is very easy to choose transpositions of the series – in its 'O' (original) form, its 'I' (inverted) form, or in the 'R' (retrograde) of either 'O' or 'I'. These can be combined in two or more contrapuntal parts or to make chords, but care must be taken to avoid the same note appearing in both versions at more or less the same place. The series does not have to be used in its entirety; and it can start anywhere (because all the notes are of equal importance, and as long as they are kept in serial order the essential quality of the intervals will remain).

A useful way of expanding the range of available notes within a particular system of intervals is to work with 'sets' (drawn from 'O', 'I', 'R' and 'RI' as necessary) that have no notes in common and so can be used to form chords as well as melodies. (N.B. repetitions of individual notes are possible before moving to the next note of the series, so long as the note order is not changed.)

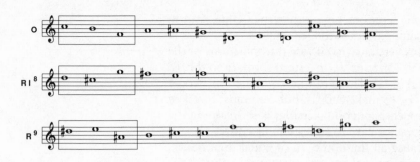

As a way of composing music, serial technique offers an exceptionally wide range of expressive possibility because it gives added emphasis to the levels of tension and relaxation in music.

Project 11

Starting and stopping

The beginning and the end of a piece of music are obviously crucial moments. The start raises our expectations and gives us an idea of what the composer has in mind; the end tells us whether the piece has fulfilled those expectations. What happens in between is important, of course, but it could be argued that it is only in the very last moment that we truly 'have' the music, because it is only then, when we have experienced the piece of music as a whole, that we can know whether it made sense as it was going on.

One of the most important skills in composition is the ability to *transform* motifs, figures, gestures and textures so that listeners gradually come to understand the direction the music is taking, and where it might end – even though they don't know how. It is like being led through an elaborate garden to experience an amazing view that can only be seen by looking back from the end of the path. As you go on, the changing combination of flowers, shrubs and trees give you a foretaste of what you will see when you reach the viewpoint; but only in the final moment is the full effect achieved and the expectation fulfilled.

Student assignments

Assignment 1   Transformations

Assemble several musical instruments with strongly contrasting qualities (e.g. a tambourine, a triangle, maracas, a violin, a trumpet, and a flute) to make a piece that consists of a series of linked solos, each one leading into the next, but all in some way pointing to a revelation at the end – something like a game of Chinese Whispers:

i. an idea is announced on the first instrument, played with for a short time, and then:

ii. taken up by the other players, one by one in turn, and extended and modified so that it gradually changes its character as it passes around the group to reach:

iii. a surprising conclusion.

This process makes the whole piece of music. It develops continuously from instrument to instrument without a break, and subtly transforms the original idea. Whatever is played by the first instrumentalist must be able to be copied as closely as possible by the second player. But the second instrument will have its own special characteristics; so even though the idea is copied it will begin to sound different, and some features will have to be changed.

These changes can be exploited and exaggerated by successive players. For example, the second player passes on to the third a transformed but still recognisable version of the first player's idea; some of the original characteristics must remain so that the connection will be apparent. The third player takes this over, copies it as closely as possible and then expands it in ways that will make the best use of that instrument's unique qualities. Transformed still further, the material is now passed to the fourth instrument, and so on to the last player. It could stop there or go round again, either by starting from the original idea and developing differently, or by the first member of the group continuing the transformation process.

Important features of this idea are:

a. the continuous flow of music for solo instruments, the players interacting carefully with each other as the developing musical material is passed from one to another; and

b. the very gradual and controlled transformation of an idea initiated by the first player.

The musical interest must be maintained, and particular care taken of the points where one player hands over to the next, perhaps momentarily dovetailing the two instruments' lines. Everyone should try to think of ways in which this 'handing on' can be made a special feature of the piece.

Assignment 2

What does it all add up to?

At first glance this may look like a mathematical formula! In fact it is part of an abstract design made by an artist; an arrangement of numbers separated (or linked, perhaps?) by two crossed lines. Set out in this way, the lines and figures could mean almost anything. No clue is given; and there is certainly no suggestion that it could be a piece of music. But, for the purposes of this assignment, we shall assume that it *is* a piece of music. You must decide what the various parts indicate; what kinds of sounds will be used; how they will be used; and where it is all leading. Two of what? Five of what? Three of what? Rhythmic patterns? Instruments? Different ways of producing the sounds? And why minus one?

The crossed lines seem to be significant. Do they indicate four separate but related events? Is it a huge multiplication sign? Does it suggest anything about the way the music will go on and, in particular, about how it should end? Try to think of a way in which all the musical ideas you derive from this figure could work together to lead to a surprising conclusion.

Assignment 3

Here are four motifs, two emphasising melodic features and two rhythmic:

With these make four pieces of music (each piece using all four motifs) that develop and end in contrasting ways:

i. Starting gently, gradually becoming excited, then calming and drawing to a peaceful conclusion.

ii. Starting slowly but strongly unified, quickly gathering momentum and then diversifying: the ideas going off in different directions, becoming increasingly frantic, and ending suddenly and dramatically.

iii. Starting loudly and disjointedly, gradually calming and becoming more clearly unified, and ending quietly.

iv. Quiet and restrained throughout. How can this be made to lead the music to a satisfying conclusion?

Teaching points

With the end in view

Every work of art strives towards its unique completeness, the point at which it is received and understood as a whole.[1] This is very clearly the case with painting and sculpture. We may admire particular features, but it is obviously the work as a whole that matters. Moreover, a painting or a piece of sculpture is likely to be seen in its entirety right from the start. Even if you subsequently decide you don't like it, perhaps objecting to just one small part of it, it would be difficult not to have had at least an impression of the whole thing.

A work of music, dance, drama or film, on the other hand, has to take its time. We know it can't be fully appreciated until it has run its course, but that may not stop some people from walking out before the end if the piece is offending or boring them. This is in part because, unlike the experience of painting or sculpture, it is not possible to get a quick impression of a piece of music or a play; we must hear it or see it through to the end or not 'have' the work at all. In those circumstances there is an understandable tendency for details that sustain the structure to take on an independent existence. So that, for instance, we may remember – and have a lot of pleasure from remembering – a particularly good tune from a symphony even though we can't recall anything else about the work.

However, there is also the danger that those features – memorable tunes, fascinating rhythms, subtle combinations of instruments that stir the imagination and help us to identify with the work because they draw us into it emotionally – will be thought of as 'the music'.[2] But 'the music' is, of course, the whole thing; the continuous, seamless form created by careful transformations of its elements and designed to carry the listener to that crucial moment when the last sounds die away. It is when that works well – when the 'that's how' of the ending confirms the expectations that have been growing within us all along – that we feel especially satisfied by a piece of music because we know why everything else led in that direction. Paradoxically, it may be the very satisfaction with the wholeness of a piece that sends us away recalling the great moments; but we should try to understand those moments in context, not as highlights but as significant steps in the making of the whole structure.

Naturally, the onus is on the composer (as on the playwright, choreographer or film director) to transform and develop the ideas in such a way that they warrant attention and make people want to

[1] It can never be too strongly asserted that every piece of music is unique and projects something greater than the sum of its parts. It has an essential wholeness, both in conception and presentation. Cf. Susanne Langer: 'A work of art is a unit originally, not by synthesis of independent factors. Analysis reveals elements in it, and can go on indefinitely, yielding more and more understanding; but it will never yield a recipe.' (*Feeling and form*, p. 105)

We must help students to understand the dynamic relationship between ideas and form. Form cannot have independent existence; it is content; it is what happens to the invented ideas. The important thing about the 'sonata principle' is not the extent to which classical sonatas conform to a pattern of exposition–development –recapitulation, but the quality, nature and potential of individual musical ideas that have been unfolded in so many amazing and satisfying ways under the umbrella of that principle.

[2] Although it is clear that the music is only being used as a framework for the chat show, it is unfortunate that popular radio programmes such as 'Desert Island Discs' appear to support the fallacy that an excerpt has a valid artistic life of its own.

hear the work through to its end.[3] The artistry needed to do that well is largely instinctive – and, at the highest levels, possibly a matter of genius – but that is not to say that the techniques cannot be explored by those with far less experience.

Just how a piece of music can be brought to a meaningful conclusion is a particularly important question. Although you can practise various strategies for starting a piece and for developing individual ideas, it is not possible to practise ending something until you know with reasonable certainty what it is you are trying to end; in other words, not until most of the detail of development and transformation is clear. Quite apart from the expectations that will have been set up by the ideas and what happens to them, there are the purely technical matters of how to form the ending.

For example, if the music has gone as far as it seems to want to go, and has developed to a point of great diversity with many different things happening simultaneously, the music could simply stop, leaving all the disconnected fragments as loose ends. But unless that is done with great panache (which probably means continuing to increase the excitement and tension right up to the very last moment, and with no relaxation of the pace) it will sound unconvincing – as though the composer really had no idea how to end the piece. The alternative might be gradually to draw the apparently disparate threads together until they are at least rhythmically in line with one another, and then to calm the dynamic (and perhaps the tempo) in order to conclude the piece with some semblance of agreement between the parts.

Obviously, everything depends upon the nature and quality of the ideas. Nobody can lay down rules about this kind of thing. But, in the same way that earlier projects have drawn attention to techniques which are progressive – driving the music on, increasing the excitement and the tension – so, in this project, the aim should be to focus also on the recessive possibilities and, in particular, on different ways of making the music stop with recognisable finality.

The assignments

The players may want to start Assignment 1 as an improvisation, inventing a simple musical idea which can be copied and improvised on by each in turn around the group. Ultimately, though, the progress of the idea from instrument to instrument will have to be thought out with great care, leaving nothing to chance. In other words, to work properly, it must be *composed*. A lot of experiment will be necessary, not least to invent a suitable starting idea; one that is memorable but which also can be subtly transformed.

The order in which decisions are taken will depend upon what comes out of the initial exploration. It may not be clear at the outset which lines will be the best to follow, and some will almost certainly lead to dead-ends. This is in the nature of creative experiment; it calls for perseverance and the courage to go on trying various possibilities until the 'right' procedure is revealed.

[3] A composition is an unqualified statement – an opinion. The composer is not entering into a discussion with us; we must take the music or leave it. The verb 'to compose' describes the process of 'posing' – setting before other people ideas that the composer would like them to contemplate in the form in which they are 'placed together':

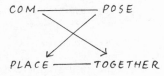

We may often be surprised by the ideas composers choose to juxtapose (as, for example, with the first and second subjects of Beethoven's 3rd symphony), but a composer's main task is to reveal the potential of these connections, and to do so in a form which is coherent and convincing. Dukas advised Messiaen to aim for 'complexity without complication'.

For example, the first experiments may suggest that the instruments chosen are not the most suitable. Or it may become clear that there are too many instruments in the group, making it difficult to sustain the piece purposefully.

Five players will normally be about the right number. The more instruments there are, the longer the piece. It would be better to have several short five-instrument pieces than one lengthy (and possibly incoherent) piece for twenty instruments. A large group makes it difficult to resolve the many questions that arise in the course of constructing a piece on this plan.

Even when you've talked through these preliminary questions, it may still not be possible to take a decision until there has been more exploration of the potential of the main musical idea. The group will have to bear in mind that

- important characteristics of the starting idea will depend upon which instrument is chosen to begin the piece, and also that

- the music invented for that instrument must contain features which can somehow be transferred to other instruments.

Various possibilities should be tried out on all the instruments in different orderings. With the selection suggested here, if the decision was to start with the violin the player would probably invent a melodic idea. But although that sounded well on the violin, if the next player had the maracas how could the violin's melody be taken over? Obviously that would be impossible. The maracas could play the rhythmic pattern of the melody, but the essentially melodic features of the idea would disappear as soon as the violin handed over to the second player. For a piece which raises expectations of a smooth flow and a very gradual transformation of the principal motifs, that would weaken the structure by making too abrupt a change so near to the start.

Various strategies then suggest themselves:

i. Don't think of the first idea in isolation, but consider carefully where it is going to and what is most likely to happen at the end. Given the instruments already selected and the order determined so far, ignore the most obvious melodic qualities of the violin and try something different. Perhaps, instead of a melody, the violinist could play a shimmering pianissimo tremolando on various notes, gradually making the sound as much as possible like a thin, 'breathy', rustling sound of the maracas (e.g. by gradually changing from normal bowing to *sul tasto* or *sul ponticello*).

At an agreed point (to be worked out by experiment but then firmly established – i.e. composed into the piece) the maracas player starts, overlapping with the sound of the violin which by now is almost identical with that of the maracas. Little by little the maracas player transforms the continuous rustling into (say) an articulated rhythmic pattern. This will still be limited by the timbral characteristics of the maracas, but it could be matched by a very breathy sound on the flute (not yet playing clearly pitched notes). The flute player could then continue the piece, moving gradually from the misty, breathy quality towards clear tones (though, perhaps, at first maintaining the rhythmic pattern which was the principal new contribution of the maracas). Now it is the turn of the flautist to transform the material further, adding something of significance before handing over to . . .

How could this go on? How could it finish?

ii. Rather than abandon the violin's melody, change the other instruments. Instead of the maracas, have the flute follow on from the violin. Now, perhaps, the violinist develops the melody, playing it in different registers, little by little moving it higher and making it flute-like so that, when the flute does take over, the quality of both instruments is matched as closely as possible.

The flautist can then extend or change the melody in some other way – e.g. playing staccatissimo and percussively in order to hand on to (say) a glockenspiel. The glockenspiel player could damp the bars as they are struck and so make an even shorter and more percussive sound, which would also lose much of its pitch characteristic, thereby transforming the material so that it could easily be handed on to a non-pitched percussion instrument on which the *rhythmic* features could be taken up and developed.

iii. The piece could begin with a rhythm pattern on the maracas which is then taken up on a drum, first by scratching the drum skin lightly with the fingers (to imitate the maracas) and then gradually transforming that sound into a more sharply defined pattern, perhaps with a hint of pitched sound if the player has three or four different-sized drums. This material could be handed on to a xylophone (the bars at first dampened to sound something like the drum), the player finding a way of transforming that to bring it close to something playable on flute or violin . . . Are there ways of making a flute or violin sound like a xylophone?

Assignment 2. The figure is wide open to interpretation: it could suggest virtually any style of music – melodic, harmonic, rhythmic, timbral. But whatever musical ideas are evolved, they should take into account every aspect of the figure and anything else that can be deduced from its elements. The main question to be answered is 'Where is the piece going?' What does it all add up to?

Almost any 'sign' like this could be similarly intriguing, and might provoke imaginative glimpses of potential musical structures. The train of thought is rather like that of an archeologist faced with an unidentified object from a dig and trying to guess what it might have been used for – even though the truth may never be established precisely. A possible solution to the problem can be deduced by putting together whatever evidence is available: knowledge of the location where the object was found; inscriptions or other references that could link it with religious, military or domestic functions; and so on. The archeologist's solution may never be verifiable, but if it is the result of carefully collating all the evidence it is likely to be as good a guess as any.

In this assignment, students may find it helpful to think of the figure as an inscription, discovered some time in the distant future.

They must imagine that it can no longer be interpreted with any certainty because the tradition has been lost. However, as it has been discovered on a card which also bears the names of known composers of the time, it could be reasonable to guess that the sign had something to do with music.[4] It may even be a complete musical score. This conjecture could be right or it could be very wrong! Nevertheless, working on the assumption that it *is* musical notation of some kind, it is possible to go on from there and make deductions; but only on the basis of the internal evidence – the figure itself, how it might work and how the music might have sounded.[5]

Presentation

Every piece of music made in the classroom should be heard, and the teacher should comment on it. Those observations ultimately point towards assessing the achievement of each piece; in detail, the way in which it moves successfully (or otherwise) to its end.[6] In this respect, the relationship between ideas and duration is vital because asking 'What direction do these ideas want to take, and where are they going to end up?' very soon leads to the rather more difficult question, 'How long should it all last?'

[4] This design, by Vera Vasarhelyi, was reproduced on an invitation to an exhibition of her work mounted jointly, in February 1977, by the Departments of Fine Art and Music in the University of Nottingham. The exhibition was inaugurated with a concert of music by Stravinsky, Smalley, Sculthorpe and Britten. The association of graphics and music may prompt us to imagine the figure in the top left-hand corner, as well as the overall design – numbers, two coloured squares, an oddly hatched letter 'R' – as some kind of musical score.

[5] This is similar to Tom Phillips' fantasy that, in picture postcard 'views', the people we see are actually performing a piece of music! All you have to do is work out, from what you can see on the card, how the music is being made; then you too can perform it.

The idea has a scholarly aspect: the performing traditions of much medieval music are uncertain, and are a matter of conjecture on which scholars are not agreed.

[6] Music only truly exists when it is performed. Musicians *present* music – make it present, make it happen. Because performance is so vital to music it must never be allowed to become casual or lacking in commitment. Every sound must be made with the greatest care.

Project 12

Letting go

There is no end to the ways in which musical ideas can be controlled, but possibly one of the more interesting is to see what happens when the ideas control themselves. In this project we explore ways in which chance can play a major part in the development of a piece of music.

Student assignments

Assignment 1

Instruments like this have been made in Japan for many centuries. The small bamboo sticks are hung in a circle so that they strike one another when the wind blows them.

Make wind chimes – perhaps several sets using a different material for each set. Hang them where they will move in the wind. Tape record the music the chimes make. Listen critically to the tape. Do you think the sounds are beautiful? Are some more attractive than others? Why?

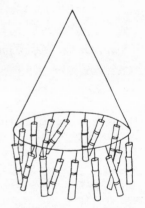

Bamboo wind chimes

Assignment 2

Make a group improvisation with four contrasting sets of hand-held chimes (wood, glass, metal). In this case the rule is that players can set the chimes moving but mustn't do anything to stop them (i.e. the dying away of the sound is an important feature of this improvisation). Apart from choosing appropriate moments to make the chimes sound (by listening carefully to the other chimes; to the way in which their sounds are dying away or overlapping with one another), the only other control you have is to hold the chimes absolutely still so that every sound dies away and the improvisation comes to an end.

Assignment 3

Discover as many things as possible that make sounds which you can set going but thereafter cannot control (or can control only to a very limited extent). For example:

i. Pouring water. You can pour water into vessels of different sizes (to produce different pitches?), and you can stop the pouring whenever you wish. You can pour into containers made of different things (wood, plastic, glass, metal – how does that change the sound?). But you can't affect the sound very much in other ways (e.g. its loudness – unless, of course, you have some pourers at a distance from others). Compose (i.e. not an improvisation) various pieces for poured water. Design some pieces especially for recording, perhaps using a large number of performers and having them positioned at various distances from the microphones.

ii. Sounding objects (such as lengths of wood or metal) can be suspended to cover a wide area (like a downward growing forest!). Walking among them makes them swing and strike each other. You have no other control over these sounds.

Assignment 4   Open forms

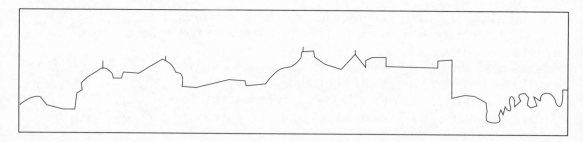

i. Draw the shape of the skyline you can see from the room where you are. Assign notes to the various levels. Find suitable instruments and perform this 'score'. For example:

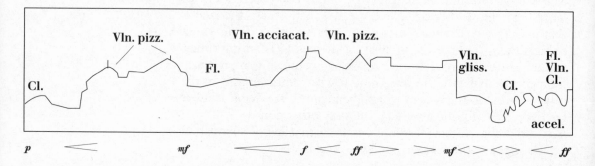

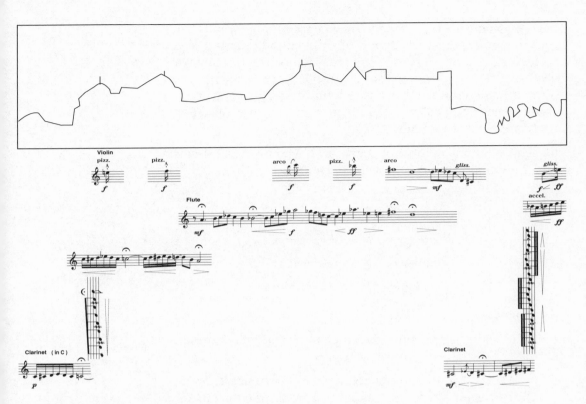

ii. Twelve singers perform the following open form score:

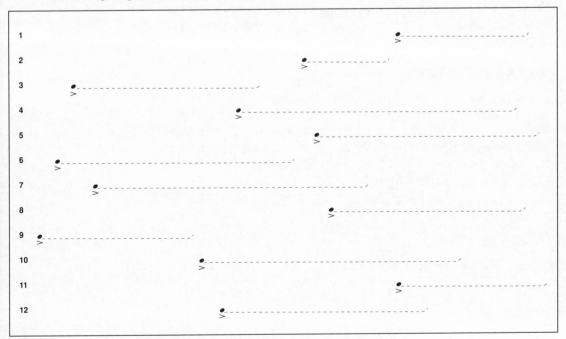

The voices enter strictly in the order indicated. The overall duration is free and the choice of pitches is free; but, having started on a particular note, each singer must hold that note steadily and quietly for as long as the line seems to indicate. Each entry must be judged in relation to those already singing (e.g. voice number 4 cannot enter until after number 10, but number 10 cannot start until number 9 has stopped). Experiment with ways of adding interest to the sound-texture but without changing any of the rules of performance. Invent a way of adding twelve instrumental sounds.

iii. This is for any number of performers, who must first decide on the meaning of the numbers and the lines:

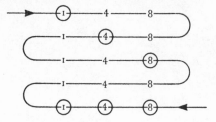

Assignment 5

i. Invent and design a musical card game. Get different groups to play it. Tape record their performances.

ii. Invent and design a musical board game. For example, one in which the sounds made are determined by instructions in the squares the players land on. (What other possibilities can you think of?) Get other groups to play it, and tape record the game in progress. Make sure that no sounds are heard other than those indicated by the game itself.

Assignment 6   Aleatory compositions

i. Choose four instruments of contrasting timbres and select one note on each instrument (giving you four different notes in all). Represent two of these notes by the head and the tail of a large coin, and the other two by the head and tail of a small coin. Toss the coins alternately and write down, in order, the notes they select. You may get something like this:

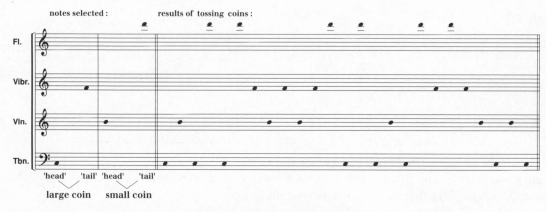

The group can now perform this in various ways:

a. The notes, just as they are, form a complete piece of music. They are played in the given order but the instrumentalists decide the durations, for example:

b. As in **(a)** but played all on one instrument:

c. As in **(a)** but with two players using instruments that encompass the complete series of notes. Begin together, but thereafter each player is free to choose how long each note shall last. Agree upon a general tempo (e.g. 'fast' or 'very slow'). On two pianos the result might be something like this:

ii. Choose at random six notes on the keyboard. Number the notes 1–6 from lowest to highest. By throwing a dice, make a long succession of these notes from the chance numbers appearing at each throw. For instance:

Original selection of notes :

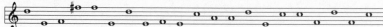

Series 'dictated' by the dice :

Using a different chance operation (i.e. not dice), determine

(a) how long each note should last, and

(b) which notes should sound by themselves and which should be sounded together.

Write this out as a piece for keyboard. You can take the notes in any octave (i.e. if the dice selects 'C' this could be any C on the keyboard – but you must decide which). The result could be something like this:

iii. Collect together as many different pitched instruments as possible. Having discovered the range of notes available (i.e. from the lowest playable note on the lowest pitched instrument to the highest playable note on the highest pitched instrument), decide how, by throwing dice, you can select notes from across the whole range. For example, you could divide it into areas and throw once to determine the area and a second time to determine the precise note within that area. How will the numbers thrown indicate which note is chosen? Keep a careful record of all the notes chosen by the dice in the order in which they are selected.

Next decide how to determine the length (duration) of each note by throwing the dice. For example, throwing a certain number could indicate a semiquaver, another number a quaver, another a crotchet, and so on. Do this for each one of the notes already selected. Think of a way of including different amounts of silence between some of the notes.

Now write out the composition exactly as it has been 'dictated' to you by the dice. You can insert bar lines (e.g. in 4/4 time) to make it easier to read.

Finally, decide what each instrument shall play. You have absolute control over this! Try to use all the instruments you've got, not all at once all of the time, but at various points in the piece; some as solos, others playing together in twos and threes, and just occasionally all together.

Another possibility would be to go through the whole procedure (selecting notes with the dice, writing them out, and so on) for each instrument in turn, and then to think of a way of letting the dice decide which instruments play together. That would introduce another element of chance – how will they sound together? You will not know precisely until you have completed the whole composition and can perform it.

Make other aleatory compositions, varying the number of things controlled by you and those controlled by the dice. Try to make at least one piece in which as much as possible is determined by the dice, e.g. choice of instruments, the order in which they play, tempo, dynamic changes (*pp, p, f, ff*, crescendo, diminuendo), etc.

Assignment 7

For a group of between seven and ten wind and stringed instruments. All play the following series of notes ▷

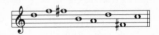

Start together on the first note, but from there on the players individually sustain each note for as long as they can (or as long as they wish). Everyone will move from note to note at different times, producing accidental harmonies. Throughout, play as quietly as possible so that you can hear the different harmonic effects as they come and go and merge into one another. The piece ends when the last player finishes the last note.

Compose a piece of your own like this. Every performance will be different; but is there perhaps a way in which you could choose particular notes for the series so that, in spite of being produced by the accidental coming together of the instruments, the harmonies will have a particular character?

Assignment 8

For between six and ten players using mallet instruments (xylophones, glockenspiels, etc.), with one player designated 'leader'.

i. One player keeps a quaver pulse going on a xylophone throughout the whole of this piece, absolutely steadily and never varying in speed ▷

When this pulse is firmly established, the leader – keeping time exactly with the xylophone pulse – plays any two 'white' notes followed by two silent quaver beats, and continues to repeat this pattern of two notes and two rests. For example ▷

The other players copy this (in any octave) and play along with it, joining in when they feel sure they can remember the pattern. When everyone is playing this, and while they keep it going, the leader changes the pattern by adding a third quaver note (or perhaps two semiquavers) and altering the number of rests (perhaps reducing it to a single quaver beat rest or increasing it to three rests), for example:

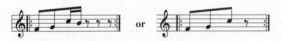

Everyone else keeps the first pattern going and at the same time listens to the new pattern the leader is playing. They should each join in with the new pattern as soon as they feel they can.

The two patterns will go along side by side, the first gradually fading away as more of the players join in with the extended pattern.

When everyone is playing the second pattern, the leader again extends it by adding one further 'white' note quaver (or its equivalent, e.g. two semiquavers) and altering the number of rests ▷

Once again, the other players keep the second pattern going but at the same time listen to the new pattern, joining in with it when they can.

The piece continues like this for as long as the leader wants to extend the pattern of notes and rests. Obviously, there will be a limit to what everyone else can remember; and the longer the piece goes on the more there is to remember, and the more difficult it becomes to keep playing a long pattern (and counting the correct number of silent beats) while taking in whatever the leader does next. Much also depends upon the ability of the first player to keep the pulse going steadily on the xylophone! If that proves too difficult, you could use a synthesizer keyboard set to repeat. The piece finishes when the last player joins the final version of the pattern and everyone is playing it together. The leader must think of a way to signal the last repetition of the pattern.

ii. Experiment with this form. A piece like this should not last too long. On the other hand, it will take some time to establish what is happening (the very gradual changes and the textures of overlapping lines as the players move individually from one figure to the next). Try a different procedure. For example, instead of having a leader, everyone in turn adds new material.

Can you keep three patterns going at the same time (i.e. change to the third before everyone has joined in with the second)? Or more? Everyone must play all the patterns. How can you use changes of dynamic to vary the textures?

iii. Instead of having a xylophone to keep the quaver pulse going throughout, use maracas. Increase the speed of the pulse. This time compose the piece fully, inventing a series of, say, ten short figures – often of a contrasting nature – each of which is repeated as many times as each player wishes. As long as the steady pulse is maintained, the notes can be of any value. Occasional long notes help to clear the texture; or, alternatively, use more rests in a pattern:

iv. Make up a short phrase of notes and silences. For example:

Everyone in the group plays this together and repeats it until it is accurately memorised. Beginning all together, play the phrase over and over several times at the agreed tempo. Then, while everyone else keeps going at that speed, one player gradually increases the speed, getting out of phase with the rest. Others follow until everyone is playing at the faster tempo. This should be done very gradually so that the sounds overlap in various ways and form interesting textures. Now reverse the process; the leader starting to slow down and then other players following one by one until everybody is again playing at the original tempo.

v. For two groups. Clap these patterns:

Group 1

Group 2

Both groups start together and keep an absolutely steady quaver pulse. What happens to the clapped patterns? How many times does group 1 have to repeat their 8-beat pattern before group 2 is once again clapping with them exactly as at the start – i.e. with the accented beat coming together in both parts? How many times does group 2 have to repeat the 7-beat phrase?

Teaching points

At the drop of a hat and the toss of a coin

Musical action involves feeling, responding, thinking and making, and – at least until the early years of the twentieth century – the mainstreams of European music took that to mean that composers should have overall control of their musical ideas in order to express the consciousness of being. For the composers' part, they clearly wanted to be able to exercise that control over ever-larger works – large both in the number of performers and in duration; and in the operas of Wagner and the symphonies of Bruckner and Mahler we find the high point of the expression of consciousness on a grand scale. It led directly to the intense and ultra-emotional 'expression-ism' of Schoenberg, which in turn became the springboard for more and more minutely controlled compositions.

However, not every composer wanted to follow that path. Some, like Debussy and Satie, were attracted by much simpler harmonic ideas, modal and pentatonic, with trance-like repetitions that dissipated tension and removed the 'burden of consciousness'. This music was both new (in the way in which it broke with routine harmonic and rhythmic practice) and old (in its association with ritual and magical uses of music, not unlike those found in some ancient oriental cultures).

Subsequently it provided a basis for exploring ways of creating music which, if possible, would be divorced from the will and the taste of the composer – the very opposite of the traditional expressing and communicating objective. For John Cage and many of his contemporaries, composing became no longer a matter of putting together all the details of a carefully calculated and evaluated structure, but rather of setting up opportunities for 'sound events' to happen. All sounds and any sounds could come in and find a place in the music; and the accidental structures they created could be as delightful in their own way as the random sounds of nature – which we can enjoy without their having been 'composed'.

Random the sound-patterns might be, but they still produced musical works; and formal principles could be defined. These are now usually grouped together under the umbrella of 'aleatory music'; although, strictly speaking, that term should be applied only to works in which every detail has been determined through a chance process operated by the composer (i.e. not left to the performers). 'Aleator' is the Latin word for a gambler: more precisely, a 'dice-player'. To make aleatory music you must first define the rules of the game (e.g. if you throw dice, what will the resulting numbers indicate – instruments? pitches? durations?), and then apply those rules strictly. In other words, we have no choice in what happens; the details of the music are produced by the game of chance; we notate what the dice 'dictate' as precisely as possible, and perform it exactly.

Cage used dice, and marked sticks, and the elaborate processes of an ancient Chinese manual of divination known as *I-Ching* (literally 'Book of Changes') to produce chance numbers that could then be related to musical notes. He also took the accidental arrangements of ink marks on blotting paper and, by setting them under a grid marked on a transparent sheet, allowed the ink-blots to represent sounds. Today, with advanced computer systems, it is even easier to produce random numbers which can then be associated with all the parameters of music – pitch, duration, timbre, dynamic, articulation, and so on.[1]

Another and more widely used 'chance music' technique is indeterminacy. Here the composer retains control of the overall shape and direction of the music, and to a greater or lesser extent invents the musical material, but the performers play a larger than usual part in the creation of the musical form by elaborating or improvising upon figures and motifs which they select from options provided by the composer.

In some works of this kind the indeterminate elements are intended to be worked out in detail by the performers and more or less fixed for given performances. In such cases, the composer's framework ensures that, although there may be marked differences between one performer's interpretation and another's, repeat performances of any one interpretation are unlikely to vary all that much. But in the style known as 'open form' there is often a great deal more freedom for performers, and the expectation may well be that every performance, even by the same musicians, will be very different.

Certain musical instruments are designed to produce a particular type and range of sounds that cannot be precisely controlled. Wind chimes and aeolian harps make an indeterminate music that has fascinated people for many centuries – especially in China and

[1] At some stage in this project it would be useful to get the students' views on whether they think what is produced in this way can truly be called music. If it is music, what, if anything, does it express or communicate? Is there any reason why it should do either? But then, doesn't communication depend on what each listener makes of it anyway? Might it be said that, by its very existence – in a performance – any music makes some kind of 'comment'? Perhaps the very fact that the composer has decided to allow the music to be organised by chance is itself the expression of something important? What might that be?

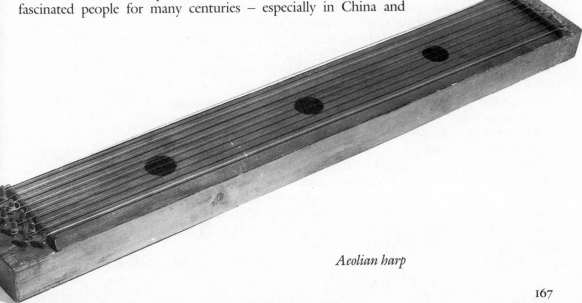

Aeolian harp

Japan. Hung in a window or from a tree, the bamboo sticks of wind chimes strike one another randomly when the wind blows. In the same way the wind gently vibrates the strings of the aeolian harp to produce mysterious chords.

Chimes of bamboo, metal and glass can be used in musical compositions so long as we accept that the performers' control of these instruments will be limited. They can be stroked quickly or slowly to produce different effects but it is not always easy to damp them. Therefore they must generally be left vibrating until their sounds die away naturally. In this project we make positive musical use of that characteristic.

An indeterminate composition is rather like a game of cards; there is an understood framework within which the players must operate. There are also fixed elements – like the playing cards themselves – but these are re-ordered and re-directed by the choices and skills of the players. The overall structure and the outcome will always be broadly the same (i.e. the game of cards has its rules and a recognised way of ending), but the internal details of the form will change every time the game is played.

Are we still in with a chance?

Aleatory, indeterminate and open form techniques had an important place in the New Music of the 1960s. With hindsight some people are inclined to think that a lot of that music led us nowhere; that it was, artistically, a dead-end. The present day avant-garde is certainly moving in very different directions. Nevertheless, the 'free' procedures of the 1960s did provoke fresh thinking about music and its possibilities, and encouraged widespread and uninhibited inventiveness. Composers felt able to use a much wider range of sounds than had formerly been accepted as 'musical'; and for many the concept of composing changed radically.

This was understandable at the time. The late 1940s and early 1950s were years of austerity; the constraints of the war period were not entirely cast off, but people were looking for some kind of renaissance. It arrived with the 1960s. This was not a time to go on doing what had 'always been done'; it was a time for something completely different.

In any case, the problem with all well-established ways of doing things (especially in the arts) is that once they have become familiar and widely accepted, they may easily degenerate into mere formulae and become artistically empty.[2] In normal circumstances it is quite difficult to break away from formulae because they provide the attraction of security; and that tends to inhibit imagination. However, the post-war musical avant-garde had a very good reason for wanting to break with tradition, echoing feelings that were then becoming fairly general in Britain, Europe and America. At that point the 'swinging sixties' swung.[3]

Free forms may look like an excuse for lack of musical discipline;

[2] Hilaire Belloc's observation – on ointment that he'd hoped would ease his feet, sore from walking (*The path to Rome* p. 105) – could be apposite here: 'As always happens to miraculous things, the virtue had gone out of it with the lapse of time.'

A very similar thought, applied to education (and to art?), is characterised by Ezra Pound as a process in which:
i. A master invents a gadget, or procedure to perform a particular function, or a limited set of functions. Pupils adopt the gadget. Most of them use it less skilfully than the master. The next genius may improve it, or he may cast it aside for something more suited to his own aims.
ii. Then comes the paste-headed pedagogue or theorist and proclaims the gadget a law, or rule.
iii. Then a bureaucracy is endowed, and the pin-headed secretariat attacks every new genius and every form of inventiveness for not obeying the law, and for perceiving something the secretariat does not. (*The ABC of reading*, London, Faber & Faber, 1951, p. 200).

[3] 'When things are hopping . . . definition: the BIG WORLD, complex in excitement, simple in rules, no analysis. When things are not hopping . . . definition: the little world, simple in excitement, complex in rules, utter analysis.' (Harry Partch, *A somewhat spoof*, 1972).

but that is not so. Freedom has its own discipline – a point, incidentally, that can usefully be made through classroom composing projects in which new conventions (or rules of the game) have to be defined; and also through performances of open-form scores in which performers must first determine and agree upon an interpretation of the signs. The musical language of the 1960s is no longer current, but it does have offspring; and many of its ideals – not least the notion of allowing chance to play a part in generating and ordering musical material – are still, collectively, a powerful stimulus for innovative thinking.

The assignments

1, 2 and **3**. These activities could link with or follow on from the projects and assignments in Section I.

3 ii. was undertaken as a visual arts project following a visit by a class of school students to a museum of modern art. They had seen just such a 'maze' or 'hanging forest' filling a whole room. Walking through it, they discovered that it made attractive sounds. With their teacher, they decided to re-create it (or something very like it) in their school art room.

Obviously, a project like this takes time (and space!). The first step is to choose the materials. (Lengths of metal or wood or a mixture of both?) The separate pieces then have to be suspended from the ceiling or from a frame; and at that stage experiment will be needed to find out how best to hang them so that they will be secure and will sound well. The suspended bars (or whatever) must not be too close together, but there must be enough of them to give the impression of something substantial. Finally, it should be possible to move among them so that they swing gently and make a variety of sounds as they strike each other.

Assignment 4 focuses again upon notation; in this case open form scores which the performers have to flesh out by deciding what kind of sounds and sound events the signs could indicate.

In **4 ii**. individual singers choose *any* note and whatever vowel sound they think appropriate. The overall effect is better if the start of each note is strongly articulated (i.e. *sfpp*), and if singers then hold each note until the breath runs out (although that rule might be compromised by the need to observe the order of entries). It is important to produce good singing tone and to sing quietly all the time, so that the resulting texture, with its shifting tonality and more or less random articulations of notes, can be appreciated.

4 iii. can be performed by any number of players. Between them they should evolve as many ways as possible of interpreting the pattern musically. For example:

a. On the circled numbers, everyone plays sounds lasting for that number of beats. The numbers not circled count as rests. The series is played forwards and then reversed (as the arrows suggest), ending where it started. Entries are staggered, either following on as soon as the first player (or group of players) reaches the second number, or line by line (like a round).

b. Tuned instruments play on the circled numbers; untuned percussion play on the uncircled numbers. Each note is a single sound sustained for however many beats are indicated by the number.

c. As in (b) but tuned and un-tuned instruments change places when the series is reversed.

d. In a very slow pulse, melodic instruments play on the circled figures; but instead of sustaining a single note for that number of beats, improvise freely on any notes within the period of the number. Non-pitched percussion play on the uncircled figures, single sounds as in (b). The instruments do not change places when the series is reversed.

e. As in any of the above, but with the added rule that the higher the number the louder the sound. Have three sharply differentiated 'terraces' of dynamics, e.g. *ppp, mf, fff* rather than *p, mf, f.*

f. The continuous line, forward and reverse, is a flowing, improvised melody on a prominent solo instrument (e.g. oboe). The figures represent various kinds of related sound events played by large groups of instruments. Each number indicates several things about the way the instrumental groups should produce their sounds.

Assignment 5 ii. It is essential that the performers understand that they are making a piece of music, and that the only sounds heard should be those that fall within the intended frame of the piece. What about the sound of the dice?[4]

Assignment 6. The distinction between 'aleatory' and 'indeterminate' is significant. Even though it is not widely observed it does assume very different approaches in the methods of composition.[5]

In **6 iii.** the suggested addition of bar lines is principally to provide guides for the eye. Since the dice 'decide' durations and not accent or pulse, it would be reasonable to bar the whole piece in either 3/4 or 4/4.

Assignment 7 is a kind of 'inverted race' in which the winner is the last one in![6]

Assignment 8. These assignments are all within that area now generally known as minimal music (but sometimes called 'systems' or 'process' music because the listener cannot avoid being aware of the system, i.e. the process by which the structure is made; in much the same way that Modernist architects have featured the things that make buildings function – plumbing, girders, etc.).

Minimal music offers no dramatic (in the sense of sudden or unexpected) transformations and developments. Instead its wave-

[4] Cf. David Bedford's *An exciting new game for children of all ages* (Universal Edition 15333), and the same composer's *Fun for all the family* (Oxford University Press). Trevor Wishart's two books of musical games, *Sounds Fun* and *Sounds Fun 2* will also provide you with ideas about pieces like this.

[5] *Music of Changes* by John Cage is a work for piano solo in which the pitches, durations and silences were all determined by I-Ching. Cage writes about I-Ching, *Music of Changes* and indeterminacy in his book *Silence* (Wesleyan University Press, 1961; M.I.T. Press, 1967) in the section 'Composition as process'. Other composers of indeterminate music whose works it would be useful for students to hear in connection with this project are Christian Wolff, Morton Feldman and Earle Brown. There is a good account of aleatory music, with descriptions of works by these composers, in Eric Salzman, *Twentieth century music: an introduction* (Prentice Hall, 1967).

[6] Morton Feldman's *Durations* would be a useful follow-up to this assignment. See also *Autumn, Fog* and *First star* by John Paynter (Universal Edition) – three short pieces for voices and instruments which use this technique.

like forms change only gradually and very subtly over long periods of time in which 'minimal' rhythmic and melodic figures are repeated over and over, with occasional minute alterations to the patterns.

Although this music is precisely composed, certain aspects have strong associations with the indeterminacy of the 1960s. In the first place, the static, trance-like effects have a lot in common with African drumming, with Indonesian gamelan music and – via the gamelan – with the music of Debussy and Satie which, as we've seen, led to the simplicity (or 'accidental complexity'?) of ideas such as the one explored in Assignment 7.

Secondly, many of the commonest forms of minimal music rely upon chance *phasing* to bring about the harmonic and textural changes. You can observe phasing very easily when you are sitting in a queue of cars with windscreen wipers going: there will be a point at which the wipers of the car in front coincide with your own, from which point, because they are moving at slightly different speeds, the two sets of wipers move gradually out of phase until they are at opposite sides of the windscreen; then gradually back into phase again, and so on.

Minimal music uses both indeterminate and aleatory phasing. For example, in Assignments 8 i–iv of this project, the subtle overlapping of figures is indeterminate; dependent upon the moments when individual players choose to move on, speed up or slow down. Assignment 8 v, on the other hand, exploits the effect of aleatory phasing. Precisely how the two parts move out of phase and back into phase again is pre-determined by the way the repeating figure is designed:

Clapping piece

Once that has been set in motion it cannot be altered. What happens then is as much dependent upon the system as strict aleatory music is dependent upon the throw of a dice. The will or preference of the composer is no longer part of the action; the system has, as it were, been put onto automatic pilot, and must work itself out.

The process works in this case by maintaining the same short rhythm pattern in both parts, except that part 2 loses the quaver rest at the end of the first bar, putting it out of phase with part 1. This controlled time difference shifts the phasing by one quaver at each bar until, at bar 7, the start of the pattern in part 1 coincides with the end of the pattern in part 2. One further repetition brings the parts into phase, and then the process begins all over again.

More complicated patterns could be constructed requiring more repetitions before the parts came back into phase. Having more than two parts would also extend the process. Entries could be staggered, patterns could be gradually extended (rather than losing beats), and each bar could be repeated several times.[7]

The best known composers in this field are currently Terry Riley, Steve Reich, Philip Glass, and John Adams. Riley's *In C* (1964) is now regarded as a classic of early minimal music, and Philip Glass has extended the techniques into the realm of opera (*Einstein on the beach*, 1976; *Akhnaten*, 1984). The highly amplified minimal music of the Dutch composer Louis Andriessen is also of considerable interest and influence.

Apart from its connections with African, Indonesian and oriental music, minimalism has other European antecedents. For example, the repetitive systems of medieval isorhythm and hocket; and, in the music of J. S. Bach, frequent extensive passages of fast-moving semiquavers in which the harmony changes subtly and slowly in a manner very close to the style of some present-day minimalists (cf. the long harpsichord cadenza in the 5th Brandenburg Concerto, Preludes 1, 2, 5 and 10 of book 1 of the '48', and numerous similar examples in the suites/sonatas/partitas for keyboard, unaccompanied cello and unaccompanied violin).

[7] Cf. Steve Reich, *Music for pieces of wood* (Universal Edition). You can also read more about the principle of phasing in Reich's *Writings about music* (Universal Edition, 1974). Other works by this composer which would be useful as models for classroom creative experiment are *Clapping music, Pendulum music, Four organs, Phase patterns* and *Piano phase* (all published by Universal Edition).

Part IV

Models of time

Project 13

A classic structure

The flow of musical time is controlled by progression (moving towards moments of tension or excitement) and recession (drawing away from tension). There are many different ways in which this can be done, but one model in particular has found widespread acceptance. This project examines that 'classic' way of structuring a piece of music.

Student assignments

For a group of between 20 and 30.

Assignment 1 Resources for music

Tear up some newspapers and give everyone a piece with plenty of words on it. Each person selects a block of words on their piece of paper – i.e. a long sentence or a short paragraph – and then, with someone to 'conduct' the group's starting and stopping, everybody reads aloud in a normal voice. Do this first all together, and then divided so that each half of the group in turn can listen to the effect. This is the raw material from which four short sound-patterns will eventually be made.

Music normally requires sounds that can be very precisely controlled; and musicians practise continually in order to keep up their mastery of instrumental technique, and to be able to play with precision. Speech is made up of a large and very varied group of sounds which most people use daily with the greatest possible precision in every tiny detail. The smallest inflexion of the voice, or an unusual emphasis on just one letter, can change the meaning of a word in the most subtle way. And we do this without thinking about it because we've been able to practise the technique so continuously from an early age. Although it's not usual to think of these carefully controlled sounds in the same category as music, they can be used in all the ways that other sounds are used to make music.

You can easily appreciate the richness and musical potential of this material when you hear a lot of people speaking together, but, because they are all saying different things and at slightly different speeds, you can't distinguish the words. Once the individual meanings are obscured, you can concentrate on the sounds as sounds.

Assignment 2

Using the block of words you have already selected, go on to explore the sounds in greater detail. Experiment first with differences in dynamics: how loud can you read the words? How soft? Let the whole group, directed by the conductor, start as loud as possible and then very gradually get quieter, making a carefully controlled diminuendo without any one voice standing out above the rest. Concentrate on creating an even texture of sound. Individual words should not be distinguishable.

Assignment 3

As you try to control the quietest level, you cross the boundary between voiced sounds (i.e. normal speech, using the vocal cords) and unvoiced sounds (whispering). There is an appreciable dynamic range in the unvoiced area. The group should now read the words in whispered sounds only, starting as quietly as possible and getting louder and then soft again on signals from the conductor (i.e. so that all make the crescendo and diminuendo together) but never using the vocal cords. The effect will be quite surprising.

Assignment 4

So far the reading has all been at normal reading speed, even though that varies from person to person. But what happens if you read (in a normal voice) very fast or very slow?

Try this with everybody reading as fast as possible (still all together), then as slowly as possible, with the words (especially the vowels) stretched out as though they were elastic.

Do you notice anything about the pitch of the sounds?

Try the same thing again but this time reading fast in as high a voice as possible, and then reading very slowly in the extreme low register of the voice.

The contrast between these two sound textures will be dramatic; the overall effect of the high pitched texture busy and bright, and the low sounds dark, sinister, and gloomy. As before, you should not be able to distinguish any of the words, but the word-patterns coming together in this random way will produce many subtle shifts of sound-colour.

Assignment 5

From here you can begin to explore particular sounds as they occur within the words you have used so far. For example:

a. A word such as 'used' combines 'y', 'oo', 'sssss', and 'd', and these elements can be articulated in various ways. Normally we stress the 'oo'; but the 'd' is so short that it is hardly a sound at all. 'Used' can be given different emphases simply by lengthening or shortening the 'oo' and the hiss of the 's':

'u------sed'   or   'usssssss'd

Any part of the word could be expanded, contracted or modified with loud or soft, crescendo or diminuendo to produce effects which work like musical sounds:

b. Clearly even the shortest and apparently most insignificant sound in a word has great power.

In the passage you've been reading, underline all the letters that sound hard in the words where they occur:

d, m, t, g, n, k, o, b, p,   and 'hard' sound combinations, such as xt

It is the sound within the word that matters; so 't' in 'cat' is hard but 't' in 'the' is soft (and so it is not underlined for this experiment).

When everyone has completed underlining these letters, read all together, as before, at normal reading speed but this time hearing the words silently, in the head, and sounding out loud only the letters that have been underlined. This is quite difficult to do, and needs a lot of concentration.

The effect is unusual: a texture of random point sounds spread out across the whole group of voices. Every sound – however small – is important in its contribution to the total sound-pattern, which may appear to be almost tangible and plastic; as though it could be moulded in various ways by changing pitches and dynamics.

c. Experiment with the point sounds texture:

i. using the different timbres and registers of male and female voices in various ways;

ii. exaggerating the way each sound is produced, e.g. with individual voices using a wide range of pitches, changing from one extreme to the other at each new sound, or giving added emphasis to each sound as though it were being forced out with maximum power.

d. As **b.** but this time putting circles round all the letters that sound with some kind of hiss or slight buzz:

(z)　(s)　(sh)　(ch)

Read the passage silently in the head, sounding only the letters/sounds that have been circled. This will produce a texture of a quite different character. What does it suggest to you: sleepy, airy, light . . .?

Try combining this texture with the aggressive, explosive point sounds of the hard letters. Perhaps half the group starts with the gentle, hissing sounds and then, when they are established, the other half enters with the louder, more varied and more powerful point sounds, and the combined texture is developed into a semi-composition/improvisation. (Controlled by a conductor – or not?)

Assignment 6　Word-sound compositions

The group divides into four to make short compositions based on the sound materials explored earlier, in each case working to a specified duration which must be strictly observed:

Group A　– a piece lasting 10 seconds
Group B　– a piece lasting 15 seconds
Group C　– a piece lasting 5 seconds
Group D　– a piece lasting 30 seconds

Each of these pieces should be a texture which has a distinct character of its own. Don't try to do too many different things. In fact, having decided on the style of the sound texture, maintain that (with suitable development) throughout the piece.

You'll find all the sounds you need in the words of the passage you've been reading. (But remember, whole words are not allowed; and you should avoid any suggestion of sound-effects!) Concentrate on making interesting and complete sound patterns that work within the specified timings.

The time limitations present a challenge for all four groups, but there are, perhaps, special problems for those who are making the 5-second piece and the 30-second piece. In the former, a lot must happen in a very short space of time; it needs a distinctive and memorable idea that can be made to 'go some-where' in just 5 seconds! With the longer piece the problem is to invent a not-too-complicated idea with a strong forward momentum, yet capable of being sustained for 30 seconds (i.e. it must not 'arrive' too soon).

Teaching points

The overall aim of the project is to observe the working of a structural process that underpins a great deal of music, past and present. This will be achieved by performing and commenting on a particular work – no. 3 of a group of four *Sound Patterns* by Bernard Rands.

The composer calls this work 'a project for voices', and has designed it for both school and professional use. He regards the creative experiment using word sounds as an important preliminary to understanding the musical material – and hence the nature of this piece; and certainly, it makes a very appropriate start to this workshop-style project.

In addition to presenting what is notated in the printed score, the performers have to make up four short pieces of their own to fit timed spaces left blank in the score. These are the pieces called for in Assignment 6.

In rehearsal and performance, the voices are arranged in four equal groups: A, B, C and D. It will be useful to have some idea beforehand of how this division will be made – and, indeed, these could be the groups for Assignment 6. If they are self-selecting there will probably be a mixture of high and low voices in each, with perhaps the added interest of the different timbres of male and female voices. Otherwise the performers can be arranged in various ways to provide contrasting timbres. A, B, C, D could be the usual choral S.A.T.B. Or any two parts could be given to high voices while the other two parts are taken by low voices. Or again, the whole work could be performed by either high voices or low voices, perhaps using the extreme registers (including the high falsetto voice) to emphasise the high–low contrast. Other arrangements would be acceptable for either the whole or for various parts of the work.

Preliminary experiment

This should be done with everybody together. As we have seen, it leads easily to the division into the four groups and the making of the texture pieces; but at that stage there is no need to mention *Sound Patterns 3*. In fact, it is best not to produce the score until the four short pieces have been heard and discussed. At that point, to reveal that the experiment with word sounds has been preparation for the rehearsal of a larger work, and that the idea of the performers making their own pieces is part of the composer's overall design, can give added impetus to the rehearsal of the notated sections.

All the ideas in the notated score relate to word sounds (i.e. not the sounds of whole words but of individual component sounds as they function in words). Therefore it will be most suitable if the pieces made by the groups use similar resources. In spoken language many tiny sounds are combined in hundreds of different ways. Independently of sung sounds, speech provides a very rich resource for musical expression but one which, surprisingly, has only come to be used extensively during the second half of the present century. Perhaps this is because, in song, words have traditionally been an adjunct to musical pitches, telling a story or giving some other kind of description. The sounds *of* the words have been used, but not the sounds *within* the words.

The tasks suggested for this project should be sufficient to demonstrate the expressive possibilities; but if you want to extend that experiment, in addition to the hard letters and the hissing/buzzing letters explored in Assignments **5b**, **c**, and **d**, students could explore the effects of other letter sounds (e.g. 'l', 'w' and 'wh' sounds).

It is important to stress that you are dealing with these sounds as a musical resource. Like other musical sounds, they can be precisely controlled:

fast or slow
high or low
grouped together or presented as isolated timbres and pitches
modified by dynamics, instantly or in crescendo and diminuendo
affected by varied articulation

When it is suggested that the group should read slowly, drawing out the vowel sounds, that will almost certainly produce a lower pitch – even though nothing will have been said about pitch. It is better that way; when the low sounds appear naturally you can draw attention to what has happened, and then suggest that the group should capitalise on this discovery by deliberately exaggerating the pitch levels.

Likewise, as the different sound textures begin to emerge from the experiment, you can allot them to small groups and try superimposing them to demonstrate how contrasting dramatic or emotional impressions can be evoked by equally strongly contrasted texture (tape track 10).

The point sounds texture will benefit by being worked at. It is, of course, produced by everybody reading different material at their own speeds; but they must be sure to hear all the words they read at normal speed, in their heads, even though they are sounding aloud only the underlined letters. The random patterns are dependent upon this, and the effect will not be the same if the underlined letters are sounded at regular intervals, one after another as if in a list. Correctly done, this is a fascinating sound that exploits the full range of the voices (tape track 11). When you are sure that everyone knows how to do this, extend it as suggested in Assignment 5 (c) (tape track 12).

Composing

The next stage is to divide the voices into four groups and to assign to each one of the four timed blocks left blank in the score. Precisely how these pieces will be made is up to the members of the groups, but, as we shall see, the given timings are crucial to the work's structure.

It should be sufficient to say 'group A makes a piece lasting 10 seconds'. But if time is limited or if you are working with younger students, it can be helpful to suggest literary or pictorial ideas as starting-points for the imagination – nothing more. For example, 'make an angry piece lasting 10 seconds'; 'make a sleepy piece lasting 15 seconds'; 'make a piece lasting only 5 seconds suggesting light (either light in weight or light and bright like the sun)'; and 'make a piece lasting 30 seconds that feels like moving through a long, dark tunnel'.

Either way, it is important for the groups to understand that they have to create characteristic textures from the same kind of sound material as they have been exploring. Time will be wasted if they go off in new directions; and sound-effects must be strictly forbidden! It would be worth explaining that you don't want snoring sounds in a 'sleepy' piece, but rather a sound texture that, of itself as a whole, evokes a sensation of 'sleepiness'.

Far better, though, to do without such literary references if at all possible, and to concentrate upon what can be done with vocal sound-patterns that sustain interest for their own sake within the durations specified.[1]

After about twenty minutes or so (during which you should visit the groups and, with appropriate questions, encourage them and help them to develop their ideas) the pieces should be ready for performance. Notice how very different these short sound-patterns are from one another, even though they have been made from similar materials. The sounds themselves offer a wide range of expression, and the given durations stimulate the imagination to use the resources in particular and concentrated ways.

[1] 'Music is pre-eminently non-representative even in its classical production, its highest attainments. It exhibits pure form, not as an embellishment but as its very essence. We can take it in its flower.' (Susanne K. Langer, *Philosophy in a new key*, p. 209).

Sound Patterns 3
by Bernard Rands

Now is the time to turn to the notated music of *Sound Patterns 3*.[2] It will be much easier to learn what the various signs mean as the rehearsal proceeds, section by section, rather than by trying to memorise all the signs first.

[2] Universal Edition 15348.

Have the four groups seated in a semicircle in front of the conductor:

B C

A   D

[C]

Other arrangements are possible,[3] but the members of each group must be able to see each other because they will have to start their own short pieces without any hesitation at precisely the right moments in the score.

[3] For example, given sufficient time in which to do it, the whole work could be memorised and performed as a music-theatre piece; perhaps with the performers positioned in various parts of the room at the start and coming together in a circular formation towards the end.

Rehearsing Sound Patterns 3

The conductor gives a down-beat at each of the vertical lines numbered 1–21 on the score (approximately every five seconds). This is not measured music: that is to say, there are not five 'beats' in each 'bar'. Between the down-beats the performers individually make the sounds indicated, taking their own time and not attempting to synchronise with each other except where a sign has an arrow above it ▷

These arrowed signs are indicated by a signal from the conductor's left hand.

The first section

Draw attention to the general appearance of the notation between down-beats 1 and 7. The dominant feature is the wide black line indicating a cluster: a tight, dense chord of sustained sounds, everyone taking a different pitch and using the vowel-sound shown below the cluster sign. Spend a few minutes practising a cluster with the whole group. Concentrate on producing a quiet and completely homogenous texture with a very carefully controlled but minimal crescendo/diminuendo from *pp* to *p* and back to *pp*.

The horizontal line through each of the four parts can be taken to represent approximately the middle pitch of each person's voice. So group A's starting cluster is very quiet and above middle pitch (on 'm' – a *ppp* hum). The intensity of the cluster is increased very slightly (from *ppp* to *p*; no further!) through the five seconds or so of the first 'bar'.

Meanwhile, the voices in group D enter after approximately 3 seconds, but each in his or her own time, without waiting for a signal from the conductor. This is a middle pitch cluster on 'l'.

On down-beat 2, group C enters with a quiet, high cluster on 'ar'. (And, since this occurs on a numbered down-beat, all start precisely together.) At the same time the voices in group A slide their cluster down to below middle pitch and change the vowel to 'ee'; while group B comes in with a middle-pitch cluster on 'oo' approximately 3 seconds after down-beat 2. (As before, individual performers take the initiative and enter in their own time.)

At 3 group D slides the cluster upwards and changes the sound to 'm' (i.e. a hum like A's opening sound – indeed the whole of what is given to group D here is in effect an inversion of A's material thus far). The other groups have sustained their clusters across down-beat 3; group A making a diminuendo to *pp* and stopping independently just after 3 – but starting again, with a middle-pitch cluster, after a gap of about 3 seconds. (If possible A should try to be aware of what C is doing so that A's 'z' cluster starts very soon after C's cluster has stopped.) The members of group B all stop together precisely on down-beat 4.

It is helpful to rehearse group A first as far as the point where they stop (in their own time) just after 3. Then spend a few minutes explaining how the other parts fit together, before rehearsing the whole ensemble from the beginning to down-beat 4.

Next rehearse the arrow-synchronised sounds:

- First, group B's low-pitched 'ee', a fraction over half-way between 4 and 5, followed by a similar short 'l' on down-beat 5 itself.
- Then the exchange between groups C and D (6–7): each of these sounds is made by the whole group, precisely synchronised with the conductor's left-hand signal.
- Notice too that group D has two short voiced sounds – 'm' and 't', the former slightly lower in pitch and a little louder than the latter – but that group C has a loud 's' marked with a cross (**X**) indicating an un-voiced sound; in other words, a short, sharp 'sss' hiss.

Now the whole of the first section can be rehearsed together, paying particular attention to the dynamics and producing every sound as carefully as possible to create the texture as notated.

The second section

Go straight on to the next section of the composer's notation (i.e. ignoring, for the moment, the gap where group A's 10-second piece will be performed – that, and the other short pieces, will come later when the complete work is put together).

Continue to rehearse by gradually building up the section 8–13. The only new sign here is the unvoiced 'p', extended by breathing out strongly through loosely closed lips, so that the lips vibrate rapidly. Group A has this figure, all starting together at 10, followed closely by the members of group D, entering ad lib approximately 1 second after 10.

The third section

The third block of the score introduces the sound of popped lips or tongue-clucks *🖋* – the choice is left to the performers – plus two sounds made with the hands: a finger snap ⊕ (all precisely together on down-beat 15, like a well-rehearsed orchestral string pizzicato!) and a hand clap ⊠ (not the flat-hand clapping of applause, but rounded to produce a sound that matches the tongue-cluck).

This short section – just ten seconds long – is quite difficult to perform, and even more difficult to conduct! You must make sure that everyone has time enough to deal with all the sounds. The texture is very active at this point, and in the complete performance it has to lead directly into the third group composition – the shortest and most tightly compressed of the four pieces.

The fourth section

From 17 to 19 there are no new signs; so it should be possible to sight-read this section all together, and then to spend a little time working on the arrowed sounds for groups B, C and D to see that they are accurately placed and given the correct dynamics.

Group B's rattling fade at the end of this section ▷ must also begin precisely. (It may be helpful to give it a sforzando start.)

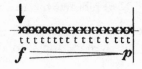

The last section

Finally, 20 to the end. You will find that it's easiest to explain quickly what happens here and then rehearse it all together. It is difficult to work at it group by group because the significant features are:

i. Swiftly following entries (group A precisely on 20, C about one second later, D immediately after C and then group B);

ii. A co-ordinated shout (high pitch for groups B and D, middle pitch for group C) coinciding exactly with the conductor's down-beat on 21 but followed a split second later by group A;

iii. A profound silence for approximately 3 seconds immediately following the fortissimo shout – nobody must move a muscle or rustle paper – and then the 'cadence': a gentle unvoiced exhalation of breath on 'ha', dying away to nothing.

Performance

When all the notated sections have been rehearsed, the work should be performed complete with the four group compositions.

A paradigm of classical form

Bernard Rands' *Sound Patterns 3* is a spectacular vocal work, attractive to professionals as well as to student/amateur performers, and as effective in a classroom workshop as it is in the concert hall.[4] (Tape track 13 is a complete performance.)

As a workshop project, rehearsing and presenting *Sound Patterns 3* is self-sufficient; it needs no further discussion or explanation. However, since it is constructed so brilliantly and with such care it will repay detailed study. There is a great deal to be learned from it about the development of musical material and, because the notation used brings out the various timbral characteristics to an extent that would be impossible with staff notation, it is particularly easy to see how the progressions and recessions control the time structure.

Internal cadences are among the most crucial structural features of any music, appearing to relax the onward drive and yet, at the same time, sustaining the flow.[5] Therefore, as important as a cadence itself is the manner in which it is approached and quitted. In a sense, as soon as any music starts it raises expectations of how and when it will come to rest. So the ear is always alert to the slightest hint that the forward impetus may be about to give way. It is just this anticipation that provides much of the excitement and satisfaction in music, and whets the appetite for the assured appearance of the final cadence; the point which seems to sum up all that has been heard throughout the work and to provide the ultimate satisfaction, a sensation of 'possessing' the music in its entirety.[6]

The character and formation of opening ideas will subtly suggest to a listener's mind the way in which those ideas will be continued. The composer must therefore try to structure the music so that those expectations are not disappointed. A start that suggested great things to come but relaxed the tension too soon would obviously be unsatisfactory. The classic formula for avoiding that hazard is to make the texture build up to its maximum density part by part. Adding new voices, each of which carries forward the same material, creates a strongly progressive sensation and avoids the risk of the musical tension dipping. We can see this technique at work in the opening of *Sound Patterns 3* (see top of next page).

This first section is unified by a particularly strong idea: very quiet, dense clusters which span a texture space from high to low-middle pitch and, in effect, encompass all the materials subsequently to be explored in detail by the composition.

The entries of the four voice parts are staggered, and alternate between the upper and middle registers. The hints of crescendo, together with group D's extended and inverted version of group A's opening, provide just the right amount of progressive variety within

[4] The idea of 'educational music' ('watered down real music') is unacceptable to Bernard Rands. He believes that it is important for composers today to provide, for school students and amateurs, music that is in essence no different from what is produced for professional performers.

[5] The notation of *Sound Patterns 3* helps to put the idea of discord into perspective. Discord is not just an unpleasant distortion of harmony for effect, but a fundamental feature of musical process, applicable to any type of musical material (i.e. it is not exclusive to pitched or harmonic sounds). Cadences highlight this function. 'Discord is an incident, a momentary interruption of concord (i.e. 'agreement') . . . discord is merely a method of preparing a fresh concord . . . to obtain a variety of texture and . . . rhythmic independence . . .' (R. O. Morris, *Contrapuntal technique in the sixteenth century*, p. 33). Cf. Langer's definition of rhythm as 'the setting up of new tensions by the resolution of former ones.' (*Feeling and form*, p. 127).

[6] Again, Susanne Langer: 'There are certain aspects of the so-called inner life – physical and mental – which have formal properties similar to those of music – patterns of motion, rest, tension, release, agreement and disagreement, fulfilment and preparation, etc.' (*Philosophy in a new key*, p. 228).

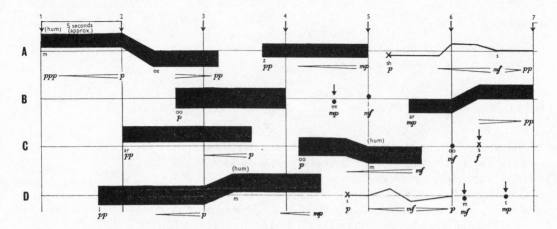

the well unified texture. The stopping and starting of the clusters (parts A and C at 3 and 4), with the resulting gaps which momentarily thin out the texture, instead of producing the recessive effect one might expect, actually helps to progress the music. This is because the gaps in those parts are never long enough for the impetus to be lost; they work rather as tiny silences that give extra prominence to the re-starting of the voices on different sounds ('z' and 'oo').

This is indeed a classical beginning such as can be found in hundreds of polyphonic and fugal works throughout several centuries of European music. And, as in all well-ordered classic structures, there is a skilful mix of the checks and balances which so precisely manage the progressions and recessions. Not least among these controls are some very subtle differences of dynamics. For example, at 4 and 5 the clusters appear to gravitate towards the middle and lower pitches – a feature which could easily suggest an approaching cadence. A collapse of tension so soon into the piece would be disastrous. But this is neatly avoided and the forward movement maintained; firstly by a slightly more pronounced crescendo (part A to *mp* and, a few seconds later, part C to *mf*), and then by the judicious introduction of some new ideas: point-sounds within a restricted pitch range characterised by carefully placed dynamic variety and supported by the crescendo and diminuendo of gently hissing line-sounds.

Even so, the new ideas appear to be firmly rooted in what has been heard so far; they offer us now a hint of a more detailed exploration of what was heard first, in the clusters. And clusters are still an important feature, moving downwards and upwards in pitch, first in one part and then in another, imitated by inversion. The whole texture thins out and quietens to what is now very clearly an appropriate cadence point from which the first of the small group compositions must take off.

The notation of this first section shows at a glance the firm establishment of the principal idea, gradually and imaginatively disturbed by limited but related ideas which maintain the music's forward drive and yet allow it to recess to exactly the right extent at 7.

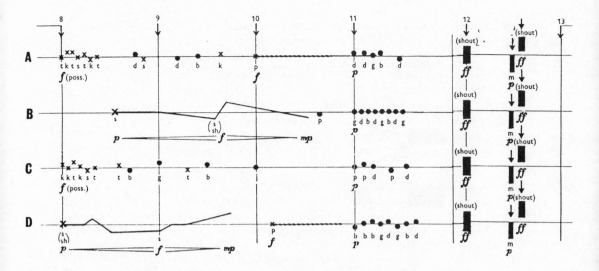

The second section develops the new features that started to emerge between **4** and **7**; and although only five seconds shorter than the opening section, the increased diversity of the material here gives the impression of time passing more quickly. There are greater contrasts of loud and soft; an elaborated mixture of voiced and unvoiced sounds, point-sounds and line-sounds, hard and smooth articulation; and voices, working together quietly in a restricted middle-pitch range, then suddenly leaping from low to high in *ff* shouts. All this drama and vitality ensures the continuous progression of the structure. By down-beat **13** the piece has quite clearly reached a point of climax.

From here the composer might have decided to begin reducing the tension in order to signal a move towards the conclusion of the piece. But he does not – and eventually we shall see why. Instead he maintains the progressive quality by means of a short but extremely dramatic burst of completely new invention (**14–18**):

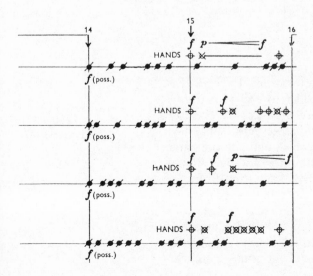

Fresh as these ideas appear, they are not entirely unrelated to what has gone before. The as-loud-as-possible tongue-clucks are a further development of the point-sounds of the earlier sections; and they are reinforced here by the cupped-hand clapping. Similarly, the 'pizzicato' of the finger snaps is a sharpening of the hard, unvoiced 'tktkst's at **8**. The introduction of the hand sounds is totally unexpected, and therefore very strongly progressive.

This episode is brief, but a lot happens, carrying us forward on a crescendo and an illusion of increased speed to topple over into the shortest of the group compositions. And that is over so quickly that there is no risk at all of losing the impetus of **14–16**.

However, at **17** familiar ideas return: the clusters, point-sounds and hissing of the opening, with a dramatic *f* to *p* diminuendo on 'ttttttttt' – a fleeting reminder of what happened at **8**.

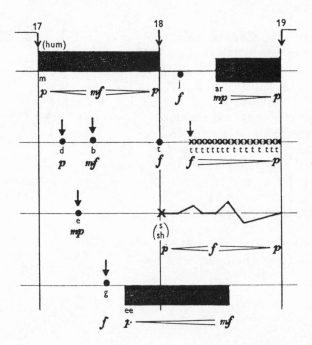

We are now, as it were, on the descent path towards the end. It is important for listeners and performers alike to feel that this is happening at the right moment. Therefore the recessive effect of bringing back material that has been heard before must be handled with care. Too big or abrupt a recession at this point, so soon after the climax of **14–16**, would be disappointing (and we should almost certainly feel it to be so in the way it detracted from the power of the final bar when that arrived). The sensation of forward movement has to be reduced, but that must be done at a satisfactory rate. This is achieved by balancing the clusters (which, because they are now familiar, help to diminish the textural vitality) against the short duration of the section, the diversity of the sounds, and the variety of dynamics (all of which, combined, contradict the recession and so sustain – i.e. 'hold up' – the form).

Somewhat surprisingly, you may feel, further impetus is injected at **20**:

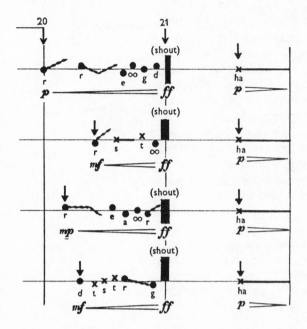

What could be more progressive than staggered entries with point-sounds on 'r' elongated into fast upward and downward moving trills mixed with unvoiced sounds, the whole rising in pitch in a brief but very powerful crescendo to conclude with a fortissimo shout at **21**? The sensation of quickening pace would appear to be self-defeating if the work is here approaching its final cadence. Yet once again the composer is using an old and well-established technique. Compare, for example, the last two bars of Bach's C major fugue in the first book of the '48':

At first the parts move towards each other; an accepted way of preparing for a cadence. Then – utterly surprising because it is unlike anything else that has happened previously in this fugue – Bach enlivens the texture with a rising flourish of demisemiquavers which quickly dissolves into the high and gently rocking figuration of the cadence itself. The unexpected increase in activity here heightens the sense of finality.

In *Sound Patterns 3*, the composite trill on 'r' is like Bach's demisemiquaver flourish; and the cut-off to silence after the shout, followed by the ensemble's quiet and co-ordinated exhalation, is as elegant as any classical cadence.

To his composed score Bernard Rands adds the adventure of the performers' own creativity. How much of a risk is he taking? Could the unpredictability of these four short pieces destroy the structure he has so carefully put together? There is a risk, of course; and that adds to the challenge and excitement of the piece. At the same time, the composer has built in certain features which should safeguard the integrity of his work and also strengthen the structure.

In the first place the instructions for performance contain his detailed suggestions for the experimental part of the project, showing how textures to match those he has composed can be evolved from the rich but commonplace sounds of speech.

Secondly, the positioning of the group compositions and the timing given for each one relates to the form and duration of the work overall. None of these short pieces will be long enough to overbalance the composer's material. The first and second fit comfortably in proportion with the first two notated sections; and because they are of moderate length they do not disturb the general progression towards the climax points. The third piece is very short, effectively ensuring that, whatever ideas the performers come up with at that point, having to compress them into five seconds will increase the tension already generated in **14–16**.

Now we begin to see why the composer goes beyond the climax of the fortissimo shouts at **12** to produce an even more telling climax at **16**. Once again, this is classical strategy. The overall duration of any musical work is to a large extent determined by the character of the ideas and the amount of time they need to expand fully and make themselves understood. In this work, as we should expect, the principal characteristics are contained within the opening section. These ideas are gradually opened up and elaborated to reach the first peak at **13**. Just as visual artists and architects have, for many centuries, recognised the dramatic significance of the so-called Golden Section, composers too have understood intuitively that the most effective point for the principal climax is somewhere in the region of two-thirds of the way through a work.[7]

[7] See note 3 on page 141.

Precisely where that point will be depends upon the nature of the ideas and their development in the first stages of a piece. In *Sound Patterns 3* it is apparent by the time we reach **13** that the slow unfolding of the opening section will seem pretentious if the overall duration is too short. Instinctively we feel this material needs more time to make its impact; therefore it is necessary to maintain the progression of the music and build towards a further climax somewhere beyond **13**.

The mathematical expression of the Golden Section is the ratio 1:0.618, and this can be applied to durations. Given the sensitivity of composers to the way music operates in the time dimension, it is not surprising that climax-points frequently coincide with the

Golden Section (G.S.) points of the total duration. The overall duration of *Sound Patterns 3* is approximately 145 seconds. 145 × 0.618 = 89.61 seconds, and down-beat **16** will occur at about 90 seconds into the work. The composer's intuition that this is the real climax is obviously correct: not calculated but felt. Constructively he reinforces intuition by deliberately placing the performers' most compressed invention at this point. From **17** the controlled recession can begin.

But what about the last of the performers' compositions, 30 seconds long? Isn't it running an enormous risk to place such a protracted piece at this point? Will it not either re-excite the work too much (by focusing interest upon its own new ideas) or kill it off completely before the carefully composed final section is reached? Possibly; but it's a risk work taking because, whatever is inserted here, even if it should turn out to be a busy (and therefore potentially progressive) texture, the sheer length of it (30 seconds) should have a recessive effect. Equally, should the inserted composition emphasise the drawn-out feeling of the 30-second block, by comparison with the earlier shorter pieces, any suggestion of anticipating the essential recession of the final cadence will be foiled by the brief reawakening at **20**. One way or the other, it is likely that performers and listeners will feel that the work as a whole reaches its close within a duration appropriate to its ideas and their development.

The musical significance of the ideas in *Sound Patterns 3* is revealed through this classical structure controlled by the progression and recession of the vocal textures. The resources (sounds derived from words) may be unusual but the structure created with them is virtually a paradigm of some of the greatest musical forms:

- An idea is established at some length.

- It is disturbed, ever so slightly, by something new.

- Development follows, materials move on with greater vigour in a series of short episodes to a high point of climax.

- This is followed by recapitulation of earlier material, modified to keep the progression alive.

- Then an extended, controlled relaxing of the tension;

- And finally a brief 'reawakening' to emphasise and add strength to the final cadence.

Project 14

Figures in a soundscape

It is not always necessary for ideas to develop – in the conventional sense of being extended and transformed. Instead, motifs might take on an almost 'monolithic' nature, like sculptured figures standing in a landscape, yet still functioning as part of a structure that goes on in time. This project explores a form which works in that way.

Student assignments

Assignment 1

Listen to the music on the tape (track 14).

Music needs no explanation or justification. All you have to do is to listen to it – although you should be prepared to hear it through from start to finish.

At this stage it is not even necessary to know what this piece is called or who composed it. What matters more is the impression you have of the music as it goes on, and at the moment when it is completed.

There are several reasons why you might find it interesting. Perhaps it makes you think of people and places, or incidents – dramatic, sinister, sad or happy; or gives you the impressions of something grand, broad, immense, powerful. Or again – more directly – you may think of the instruments being played: flutes, clarinets, bassoons, trumpets, trombones or large gongs.

Everyone has their own way of listening to music, and it doesn't matter what that is as long as it draws you into the world of sounds the composer has created. To enjoy music you must find something exciting or moving in the music itself.

Assignment 2

Listen to the whole piece again. We tend to like music that sounds familiar; and anything unusual may take time to get used to. On the other hand, the surprise of unfamiliar music can stimulate the imagination and make a very big impression on first hearing. It should at least make us want to find out more about what happens.

Assignment 3

Listen to the recording for a third time – and this time try to remember as much as possible of the detail.

First, three short phrases, spiky and jagged in character: the woodwinds jumping and growling. Then silence. Two groups of four bell-strokes echo and die away. Silence again. A sudden blare of brass: a brief fanfare of trumpets and trombones, followed by four powerful low tones, like an immense procession, out of which grows the steady roar of gongs and tam tam; a long, resonating roll which reaches a climax and is allowed to fade away, emphasising the intensity of the silence which follows. Then it all happens again: the jumping, growling woodwinds; the bells; the fanfare; the gongs – but this time very slightly different. (Can you spot any of the differences the second time round?)

There are just three ideas; four if you count the 'idea' of the intervening silences, which are as much part of the music as the sounds.

Assignment 4

Now make a piece of your own using similar ideas and a similar form. Choose suitable instruments for a leaping, jittery motif; instruments that can produce short, spiky, 'dry' sounds. They don't need to be wind instruments: xylophones could have the right quality; or something suitable on a synthesizer. It's probably best to avoid glockenspiels and metallophones because they will be too much like the bell sounds needed for the second motif.

For that second idea collect various bell-like sounds, but make sure you have a range of different pitches. In the piece you have been listening to only one tuned percussion instrument is used – the tubular bells – but for your music you could use several things made of metal or pottery, large or small, which produce clear sounds that ring on after they have been struck.

Finally you will need something for the deep, 'processional' tones and the long crescendo. This must be as powerful as you can make it, and if you haven't got a tam tam or a large gong it may be best to use the lowest notes of the piano, perhaps with drums to add power to the crescendo.

Don't try to copy what you have heard on the tape. Use that as a pattern for your own music. The structure presents you with a problem: how to invent three quite distinct ideas and make them work together interestingly:

i. a short jerky pattern played simultaneously on several melody instruments, preferably not all playing the same notes (i.e. the rhythm pattern and melodic contour should be the same, but the choice of pitches can be free for each instrument). Try to make the overall sound as disjointed and 'jagged' as possible by using wide leaps in rhythm patterns that have very little repetition. For example:

The material developed for Project 2, Assignment 3 could be used again here.

ii. 'a bell-scape': like a landscape of bell sounds.

iii. something massive, simple, noble, leading to a long, powerful crescendo which is then allowed to die away to nothing.

In the model we are using, each of the three ideas makes a statement which is complete in itself and is not developed in any way. They relate to one another but do not grow; they are like huge blocks, standing in a landscape (soundscape?), each surrounded by its own silence. We move past them once; and then again, from a very slightly different angle.

There are, then, only the two opportunities for each idea to make its musical impact. Therefore it is vital that you invent really good ideas. Don't be content with the first thing that comes to mind: work on it and consider carefully all the possibilities so that what you choose in the end makes a truly strong musical statement. As you work on them, think of the three ideas in relation to one another. Together they must make a single group.

The 'silence ideas' must be thought about, too, and explored in the same way as the sound ideas. Perhaps it is the silences which really make this piece work. They may seem to be points of no action, but in fact they hold everything together.

The duration of each silence is critical, but it cannot be calculated. It must be felt by listening carefully to the sounds that have been made and thinking about the sounds that are to come next. If the pause is too long, the structure will collapse; if it is too short the power of the sound ideas will be lost. This is a problem of musical composition that cannot be solved by talking about it, but only by experimenting, listening, judging and deciding.

Teaching points

Unlike some of the earlier projects, where recorded music has been used as a follow-up to the creative experiment and composition assignments, this project begins with listening. In order that the music itself (one complete section of Messiaen's *Et exspecto resurrectionem mortuorum*) will be the focal point from the start, it is better to introduce it with as little information as possible.

Brought up, as most of us have been, on the idea that every concert needs its programme notes, we tend to assume that a preliminary input of background information always builds bridges between the listeners and the music. But that is not necessarily so. Oddly, perhaps, even titles and composers' names can be off-putting for some people. For the composer, a title can be a helpful link with whatever prompted the work in the first place; a kind of confirmation that those first thoughts have indeed been realised. But for a listener (and especially when the title is coupled with the name of a composer who is both famous and dead!) it may suggest some kind of Unavoidable Obligation to a Work of Art. When presenting music for listening, the 'innocent ear' approach is often a great deal more successful, especially in schools.[1]

Comments, after listening to the recording, should emphasise the nature of the musical ideas and the way they function in this form; and from there, lead into the creative work.

When the students have made their own pieces and performed them, this would be a suitable time to listen to the recorded music again: first as a reminder of how similar problems were tackled by the composer of this piece; and then (and only then) to say something about the composer, the history of the piece, and the background to its composition – if that seems an appropriate and useful thing to do.

---

[1] I have noticed exactly the same phenomenon with poetry in the classroom. If, with the minimum of preliminaries, I read a poem to a class, there would be attention and interest; but if I started by announcing the title and the poet's name, there was generally a very obvious 'switching off'. To a large extent, appreciation of the arts is compromised by popular assumptions about what we are expected to do when poetry, music, drama or dance is presented to us (or 'done at us'!). In the presentation of music and poetry these assumptions have an unfortunate way of getting between people and the artist.

The composer William Schuman once observed, in a pre-concert talk, that there are noticeable differences of attitude between audiences for concerts and plays. In the theatre, as the house lights go down, members of the audience sit up in their seats and look attentively at the stage, anxious to see what is going to happen, who will say what, and when. By contrast, in the concert hall, as the lights dim and the conductor raises the baton, people sink back in their seats and wait for the music to flow over them! Is this, perhaps, because in the concert hall convention suggests that all you need to know is to be found in the programme notes; and the music itself cannot tell you anything more?

The structure

All music creates the sensation of time passing. Most commonly this is achieved by repeating, extending and transforming thematic material – melodic/rhythmic/timbral figures and motifs – controlled by various progressive and recessive devices which produce a feeling of movement and direction.

In this piece Messiaen creates a rather different model of time. It does, of course, move forward; time passes – because that is the essence of the musical experience. So we must expect to find some progressive features (the vibrant, leaping woodwind figure; the brilliance of the brass, the powerful and relentless crescendo of gongs and tam tam). Yet, by making certain recessive elements prominent, Messiaen is able to create the illusion of a music which is virtually static. In spite of the dynamic within each of the motifs, the overall effect is massively 'sculptural'.[2]

[2] The third section of *Et exspecto resurrectionem mortuorum* ('And I wait for the resurrection of the dead') by Olivier Messiaen.

Born in 1908, Messiaen is considered by many to be the most important French composer since Debussy and Ravel, and indeed one of this century's most innovative musical minds. He is a devout Catholic, and much of his life has been spent as organist of the Church of the Holy Trinity in Paris. Religious themes on a grand scale have a prominent place in his compositions, and his orchestral works frequently display the 'monumental' style found in *Et exspecto*.

This work was composed in 1964 in response to a commission to commemorate the dead of the two World Wars. The orchestration is extensive and colourful but the overwhelming impression is of great grandeur and simplicity. It is music to match the awe and majesty of the universe: high mountains; the huge, silent depths of oceans; the inspiration of vast buildings; the immensity and eternity of space. While he was composing it, Messiaen lived in sight of the Alps and surrounded himself with pictures of pyramids, ancient Egyptian temples and Gothic cathedrals. Above all, he had in mind spacious acoustics; it has been said that this is music to be played on the tops of high hills! Its first performance was in private – in a church resplendent with colour, most particularly from the stained glass windows; a setting which fitted exactly with the intensity of 'colour' in the music. The first public performance was given in Chartres Cathedral in June 1965.

Et exspecto consists of five sections, each headed by a short biblical text. The orchestra is made up of three large groups of woodwind, brass, and metal percussion (gongs, tam tams, tubular bells, tuned cowbells). It is this – an ensemble without the more delicate suggestions of stringed instruments – that creates the solemn and 'monumental' sound-force the composer needs. Bells are also nature's instruments, with qualities that link us to eternity; there is not much that a player can do to control their sound: it takes its own time. (For more on this fascinating subject see Wilfrid Mellers, *Le Jardin retrouvé*, The Fairfax Press, 1989, pp. 36–41, and also Mellers' comments on Percival Price's book *Bells and Man*.)

Messiaen's melodic ideas are influenced by the plainsong of Gregorian chant and his other life-long interest, birdsong. In this third section of *Et exspecto* the jagged, leaping woodwind motif is made from a slowed-down version of the song of the *uirapuru*, a bird of the Amazon forests. Often, in other works, Messiaen uses the songs of many different birds together, counterpointing their melodies against one another throughout the orchestra. Here, however, the single song is in keeping with the majestic simplicity of the rest of the music in this section. At the same time, its agitated shrieking and growling makes an important contrast.

There is also a literary association which prompts the composer to choose the uirapuru song at this point. It is said that this is a bird that 'one hears on one's deathbed'; thus it symbolises the quotation set at the head of the music: 'The hour comes when the dead shall hear the voice of the Son of God.'

The recessive elements which Messiaen exploits are principally:

- the long decay of bell, gong and tam tam sounds
- the rich unison of low brass instruments and the descending diminished 5th at the end of that figure
- profound silence

Silence is, of course, the most recessive element of all – and an enormous hazard in any music; if it is not used with the utmost care it will stop the flow altogether! However, Messiaen needs just that power to counteract the progressive features in the other ideas. In his concept of this form, the music must indeed stop, but in such a way that it does not completely lose its vitality. It must be able to produce the next motif, not in a forced way but naturally; as though, with the minimum of physical effort, we had moved on to the next 'figure' or very slightly altered our viewpoint.[3]

Technically, the really clever thing is the subtle use of sound decay. The silences appear to be profound, but usually there is a hint of the bell sounds echoing on. So we have the impression that the silences belong to the other motifs which they 'surround'. This also presents the percussion, wind, and brass figures as statements, rather than as ideas we expect to hear developed.

One very important aspect of the form is the almost exact recapitulation of the material – with minor changes in scoring and a re-ordering of the bell notes. This simple device enhances the monolithic character of the three statements. Repetition can have a recessive effect (the mind is not as excited a second time by what it has already heard and accepted); but it can also be used to establish ideas. If the ideas themselves are as dynamic as they are here, exact – or more or less exact – repetition is heard as neither progression nor recession, but as affirmation.[4]

Finally, we should notice that all the ideas, including the 'active' silences, are conceived on a grand scale, simple and direct; and one – the four low notes for trombones, tuba, bass clarinet and bassoons plus the long tam tam and gong crescendo – is immense in quality and in the profundity of its musical image.

This is not complicated music: there are not very many different things happening. But the decisions that had to be taken to make it are complex. The listener must feel that each silence lasts exactly the right amount of time; and to achieve that, the composer has had to judge very carefully the relationship between the points of stillness and the kind of sound ideas he is working with.

Discuss similar structural points in the pieces made by the student groups (Assignment 4). Were their musical ideas 'massive' enough to stand alone as simple statements? Were their silences too long or too short for the kind of ideas invented? On the other hand, do they feel that, even with limited resources, they were able to make pieces that were suitably static, yet flowing musically? What part did repetition play?

[3] A similar, equally positive and profound use of silence has been observed in the traditional manner of performing folk-songs. Apparently the singers frequently interrupted the flow of the songs with silences of varying length, not merely to articulate the ends of lines and phrases, but as powerfully expressive 'decorations' in an otherwise detached, unemotional and static style of delivery. Bartók drew attention to this 'astonishing custom' in Serbo-Croatian and Bulgarian folk melodies. It was, he said, a feature that would 'invariably deceive the best trained musicians when they first listen to this kind of interruption. They will without fail interpret the rests erroneously, that is, as section caesuras.' (Béla Bartók and Albert B. Lord, *Serbo-Croatian folk songs*, New York, Columbia University Press, 1951, p. 74).

[4] Cf. the repetition of the exposition in first (normally allegro) movements of classical symphonies. Fast, dynamic ideas need the repetition to take some of the wind out of their sails and to affirm them before the very considerable progression of the development's new departures.

The background

Some outline information has been given (note 2, above). This could be a basis for further study of Messiaen's work, including, perhaps, some acquaintance with his own book about his methods of composition.[5]

However, if you have not already done so, with such powerful and self-contained music in mind this could be a good moment to explore with students the connection between historical and biographical information and the music itself. In Messiaen's case this has more than usual significance. It is clear that he sees strong symbolic links between his musical ideas and other kinds of ideas (e.g. the quotations from scripture and the legends associated with certain birds); and from one source or another there is a lot of information available about those links. Some people undoubtedly find that this helps to make the music more approachable. Even so, it is important to distinguish between understanding those facts and understanding the music itself. The music is not explained by information about the origins of the composer's ideas, however interesting that may be. Independently of such things, the complete piece of music speaks to us through its own form; and that – beyond anything words can do – is the only way it can speak.[6]

[5] *Technique de mon langage musical* (2 vols, Paris, 1944; English translation 1957). Other useful books are: Robert Sherlaw Johnson, *Messiaen*, 2nd edn (London, Dent, 1989) Paul Griffiths, *Olivier Messiaen and the Music of Time* (London, 1985) Roger Nichols, *Messiaen*, 2nd edn (Oxford University Press, 1986)

[6] On the subject of music's ability to speak for itself, it may be pertinent to recall the words of the critic William Mann, who described himself as 'one whose greatest stimulus in all music is the first impact of a new piece' (*The Times*, 17 May 1980).

Project 15

How time goes by somewhere over the rainbow

What makes a good tune 'good'? Like any other musical form, if it is to be successful, a self-contained tune, with or without an accompaniment and whether or not it has associated words, must fulfil the expectations raised by its main musical idea. This may be nothing more complicated than a rising or falling interval at the start; or a distinctive melodic or rhythmic figure in the opening phrase. Nevertheless, it is this which dictates how the tune shall go on, how it shall sustain itself throughout its course, and what its overall duration shall be (or – if the composer is working in a convention such as the 32-bar standard of so many popular ballads and show songs – how the ideas shall fulfil that duration satisfactorily). Assessing the correct treatment for the main motif is a vital part of the art of composing a tune.

Student assignments

Assignment 1

Continue these beginnings to make complete melodies. Start by assessing the musical characteristics of the given opening. What is there here that you can use? Bearing in mind all that has been said in earlier projects about controlling the onward flow of music by the interplay of progression and recession, make each of these beginnings grow into a complete musical form.

a.   (significant interval)

b.   (shape of opening figure)

c.   (strongly progressive start – high note, very loud)

Assignment 2

Play each of the following tunes, noting all the points of recession and progression and the interplay between them. How do these factors sustain each tune through to its end?

As time goes by   Herman Hupfield

Summertime   George Gershwin

Over the rainbow   Harold Arlen

Sweet William   traditional

It's ear - ly, ear - ly all in the Spring, My— love roved out for to serve the— king, with the

ra - ging seas and the winds blow - ing high, Which— par - ted— me from my sail - or boy.

Teaching points

This project looks at the forms of melodies which are complete in themselves, as opposed to those which are part of larger works – generally instrumental pieces – in which melodies are in various ways extended and developed.

Self-contained tunes of this kind are, perhaps, most frequently found as songs. Whether or not they have an instrumental accompaniment, they stand or fall on the merits of their own forms. It is therefore important that we understand those forms musically.[1]

The first and most obvious point is that the melody must fit the rhythmic pattern of the poem and can only be as long as the stanza it sets. But there is rather more to it than that. We expect the sentiments of the words to be reflected in the tune's style and motifs; but, having invented those motifs and decided how to

[1] 'Form' here does not just mean something to be 'filled out'. Even where there is a predetermined verse structure the composer must make a *musical* form, working with musical ideas which must fulfil themselves, musically, as well as fulfilling the time span of the verse structure. The interplay between progressive and recessive elements must work for both views of the melody's form.

begin, the composer must thereafter concentrate upon mainly musical decisions about how to create a complete melodic form that is capable of sustaining itself. This is entirely in addition to questions about the mood and meaning of the lyrics. That aspect must be satisfactory, of course; and it is conceivable that a tune could be completely wrong, stylistically, for certain words. But, given a style to suit the words, a melody will only work as a melody when the dynamic forces that drive it forward are appropriate to the characteristics of the main melodic motifs.

Generalised notions of melody writing – quasi-rules about balanced 2- and 4-bar phrases in 16-bar periods, ABA patterns, modulations to dominant, relative minor, subdominant, and so on – will only be helpful up to a point. Melodies can't be composed to formulae. It's more important to deal with specifics; and that means exploring a variety of melodic ideas and their most prominent features in order to decide how the structural implications of those features can best be fulfilled. A characteristic opening figure will generally be sufficient to start working out the possibilities for musical action that will determine a satisfying overall form. That may indeed turn out to be 16 bars or 32 bars; on the other hand, it may not! Everything depends upon the nature of the ideas.

Assignment 1

Students should be encouraged to try various possibilities with each of the openings given. Don't be too concerned about the number of bars in a completed tune. Let the point of focus be the ways in which the most obvious features can be exploited, paying particular attention to the effect that different strategies will have upon the rate of progression.

a. The dotted-quaver semiquaver figure could be either a strong beat or an anacrusis. The upward leap of the major 6th has a positive, aspiring quality which can be exploited to progress the melody. However, reaching upwards as it does, there is the danger that it will be too strongly progressive and will take the melody too high too soon, draining it of energy before other features, such as the dotted crochet, have had time to expand sufficiently. In that case, invention would either fizzle out, making a lame ending, or the tune would go on winding up and down, taking a long time to get nowhere!

b. The opening semiquaver figure is obviously characteristic and can therefore be made an important feature of the whole melody. However, it will be boring if the intervals within it are never varied. Better to maintain its shape but vary the intervals. It can also change direction (i.e. it can be inverted).

c. Beginning loud on a high note and moving on immediately to two faster notes gives the tune an energetic – and therefore strongly progressive – start. Is that energy going to be maintained throughout? If so, can the tune generate even more forward drive towards some kind of climax? Or will it require a carefully controlled relaxation of the tension before renewing the progressive elements?

Assignment 2

a. The song 'As time goes by' is probably best known through Dooley Wilson's singing and Max Steiner's arrangements in the Warner Brother's film *Casablanca*, where it was associated with that equally memorable line of dialogue, 'Play it again, Sam!' It is in fact much older than the film.

The deceptively simple form, and the ease with which the melody flows, hides (as indeed it should) a number of highly significant structural choices.

The opening 'turn' (rising one step then curling back on itself to rest momentarily a step lower than the starting pitch) provides a strong identity tag for this tune. Presumably it derives from the pattern of the opening line of the lyric ('You must remember this'); it fits those words with such ease that it quite rightly becomes the most prominent feature of the tune.[2] Even so, it is not laboured in any way. After the climax in bar 5 (which is, incidentally, G.S.1 of this 8-bar section), it is not used again, having done its work.

The progressions and recessions are subtle. The turn figure itself balances both: rising, falling, and rising again to pause on a dotted crotchet – which is long enough to keep the progression in check but not so recessive as to stop the flow altogether. Before that can

[2] It is possible that the tune was invented before the lyric. In the tradition of the stage show, it is not unknown for composers to produce the melodies and for lyric writers then to follow the composers' rhythm patterns. 'As time goes by' was composed by Herman Hupfield in 1931 for the show *Everybody's welcome*. More than ten years later it was imported into the film *Casablanca*.

happen the gradual upward direction of the line is renewed, beginning, as before, from the E but now lifting itself through a minor 3rd to the G at the start of bar 2 and presenting the turn again.

So far the progression has been restrained: enough to make itself felt but firmly under control, so that the climax is not anticipated. But now, between the final note of bar 2 and the start of bar 3, the progression is more pronounced. This time the melody leaps a 4th, but the strength of that upward movement is instantly countered by the tune coming to rest on a sustained A.

We may assume that, in the conception of this song, it was understood that the accompaniment would maintain the impetus under that long note; but the choice of note on which to land at this point is also crucial. Had it gone to the upper C or the lower E rather than the A; or had it not leapt the 4th (G-C) but had instead, in bar 3, made a progression of approximately the same 'weight' as that of bar 2, the effect of landing on, say a long G would have been considerably more recessive at this dangerous point.[3] As it is, the extra progressiveness of the rising 4th and the careful positioning of the sustained note on A preserves the flow remarkably well, even without an accompaniment to keep things going at that point.

The climax is exactly right. The line takes off again, but from a higher note, and reaches up to an even higher level – to the D where it hasn't been before. It could so easily have been a C again (marked * in the example below) – and all the excitement and originality of this tune would have been lost:

[3] Dangerous because, with or without an accompaniment, the form must be able to sustain itself; and to 'sit down' on a long note at the half-way point could so easily kill it off there and then. The choice of note on which to sit is a matter for careful judgement.

That is what might have happened had the composer been thinking merely of filling an 8-bar phrase. The sustained A could have been seen as a convenient rest point from which, after a modest lift to C, the tune could curl back down to a perfect cadence, perhaps continuing to feature the turn:

Obviously, that would have been far less successful as a melody; not merely because the 'turn' is overused and becomes tiresome, but principally because the progression from the half-way point is not sufficiently powerful to give the melody the impetus it needs as it goes into the concluding phrase. This part of the tune (the end of bar 5 through to the cadence) needs to be very carefully controlled to avoid anticipating the finality of the cadence. It must feel recessive (so that we know we are approaching the close) but, at the same time, it must avoid too strong a recession. To do that effectively in the space of 2½ bars requires a sensitivity to the combined effects of intervals, directions (rising, falling) and the progressive or recessive power they generate.

No doubt the structural factors that make this such a good tune were intuitive, but that does not diminish their importance. Such things cannot be learned as rules, but we can observe their effect, and we can try to be aware of similar forces at work in the melodies we compose. Beethoven's sketch books show him 'working' the important structural features of melodies which, in their final versions, the world now so greatly admires. But those admired melodies did not arrive without a great deal of thought.

b. 'Summertime' from Gershwin's *Porgy and Bess*. Unlike 'As time goes by', which makes its progress towards the climax very gradually, or 'Somewhere over the rainbow' with its strong upward octave leap moderated by the slow-moving minims, Gershwin's famous song, for all that it is a lullaby, opens with a tension born of nostalgia. In addition, the melody's tessitura literally heightens the emotion; so much so that the recessive controls (notably the falling 3rds and 4ths) must work all the harder, as it were, to maintain the balance and prevent the tune from bursting at the seams.

The 'seams' (i.e. the internal cadences) in any melody need careful handling because it is from these points that the impetus must drive the tune on.[4] It is interesting to see how Gershwin handles this problem:

[4] The sculptor Austin Wright speaks of the need to 'identify the points at which things legitimately stick together. They should show because they are the strength of the structure.' Similarly in music, we should be aware of the points from which the structure progresses to carry the ideas further. (Cf. also in architecture: the piers of a bridge and the pillars of a cathedral nave.)

c. Another wonderful melody from the world of cinema: the Rainbow Song from *The Wizard of Oz*. The composer is Harold Arlen with lyrics by E. Y. Harburg. This remarkably generous tune demonstrates so well how the forces released by intervallic and rhythmic tension can be integrated to produce a wholly satisfying form which fulfils the span of its duration (a very different thing from simply filling an 8-bar period).

The composer's imagination is supported by the kind of skill that clearly observes the many tiny but important structural points which sustain the flow of the music. His judgement is exactly right at every one of these points.

Here we are considering only the first part (the 'A' section) of the song. The 'B' section makes a dramatic departure from what has been established in 'A', the new material being strongly progressive and tempered only by its clear reference to the falling 3rd that ends the 'A' section. The reprise of the familiar 'A' melody is, of course, recessive after the powerfully new effect of the middle eight, but this is necessary in the 32-bar form to produce the sensation of fulfilled time. (See the analysis overleaf.)

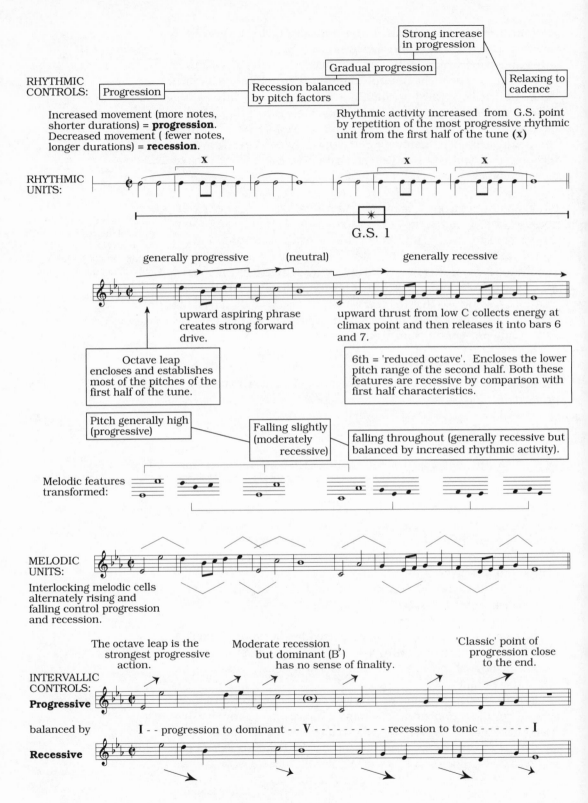

Functions and forces in the first section of 'Over the rainbow'

d. 'Sweet William', a folk-song from Newfoundland.[5] Although a folk melody never arrives at a fixed state, there is a sense in which the continuing process of honing and polishing must to some extent eliminate any serious structural weaknesses that may have been present in the melody's earliest forms. The tune has been preserved by oral tradition rather than notation, but features that can be seen to play an important part in the 'achievement' of this version must surely demonstrate an intuitive sensitivity to musical form on the part of singers who have nurtured and developed the melody across the centuries.

[5] See *Folk songs from Newfoundland*, collected and edited by Maud Karpeles (London, Faber & Faber, 1971), p. 159. 'Sweet William' is a sea song on the 'drowned lover' theme; a song 'widely distributed in the British Isles and in North America'.

This tune is modal (transposed mixolydian); solemn, hesitant and characterised by a tendency to draw back from such peaks as there are. Falling melodic lines are easier to sing than rising ones (and are often evident in children's songs), but their effect is also strongly recessive.

Thus, the first phrase of this song, descending through almost a full octave to the final of the mode, makes such a powerful recession that we might feel there was nothing more to be said: it could surely end there. Not only is the recession defined by the falling line but it is given added strength by the repeated and then sustained final D (on 'Spring').

Compare this with the opening phrase of Gershwin's 'Summertime'. That too dips steeply from high to low, featuring the falling intervals, but retaining the enormous energy of its start because the tessitura of the song is high.

What sustains the first phrase of 'Sweet William' and gives it the power to go on is the subtle way in which it avoids the obvious. Although it is a descending phrase, the surprises in it signal that there could just be more to come. Unexpected features produce tension and stimulate thought, and possibly the most unexpected thing here is the very first note: the 7th of the mode. We might have expected the tune to begin on D; and although the C immediately leads downwards to B, A and G, it has, by then – quite literally – raised our expectations. The repetition of the A also diverts attention from the recessive downward direction. When this phrase is used again at the very end of the tune, it is worth noting that the A is not repeated; it is allowed to move on without the intervention of anything that might dissipate the power of the recession to the final cadence.

Project 16

A passing phase

Debussy said 'There is no theory; you have merely to listen.'

Everything is in the music. It comes and it goes; it is just a passing phase. Yet, while we listen we inhabit a world of special time; a world where the landmarks are sounds. The sounds are interesting, exciting perhaps, and sometimes very surprising. But as important as *what* we hear is *when* we hear it. The unique skill of the composer is in being able to judge precisely when things should happen in the timescape. That can't be calculated; no one can lay down rules for it. Only your ears can tell you when it's right. Every composer must practise making those aural judgements about musical ideas, but it is also helpful to listen to other people's music, and to try to imagine how they reached their decisions.

Student assignments

In this project we listen to one piece of music; a piece made in an electronic music studio by working directly with the sounds on tape, and with a computer and a synthesizer.

The composer created and assembled the musical materials, devised a general plan for the piece, and then used his imagination and aural judgement to decide what should happen to the ideas: how they should be developed and transformed; and, most importantly, *when* those changes should occur.

Since no other musicians were involved, there was no need to provide a written score. So, you have no notation to look at; you can only use your ears. This piece is on track 15 of the accompanying tape. Listen to it very carefully, as many times as is necessary, and find out as much as you can about the way it is composed.

Make a chart of all the things you discover, plotting as precisely as possible the progress of the ideas. Try to discover the composer's plan for the piece, and how the structure works; what are its strongest features; what makes it hang together; and what tactics the composer has used to hold our interest throughout the duration of the piece.

Here are some of the things you will need to think about (perhaps you can add to this list?):

- How many different ideas are there?

- What are the detailed characteristics of each of the ideas?

- How does the composer make the ideas relate to one another?

- Are some ideas more important than others?

- Is there a real surprise anywhere? Is it a surprising idea or is it the way an idea is used?

- What 'classic' structural techniques are there in this piece?

- What are are the notes and rhythm pattern of the ostinato?

- Are the silences between the repetitions the same every time?

- Is there an identifiable pulse? If so, how can the pulse rate be precisely indicated?

- What is the overall duration of the piece?

- What is the relationship between the overall duration and the timing of those points where ideas are brought in or taken out, where changes occur in texture or dynamics, or where other important things happen?

- Does the piece have a climax? If so, how is it made and when does it occur?

- The piece is called *A passing phase*. Why do you think the composer gave it that title?

Teaching points

Aural analysis helps to educate creative listening, which is at the heart of all musical experience; it is especially important for anyone who wants to compose. Analysis of scores is essential too, and can show us a great many things about techniques of composition. But sometimes the visual concentration hinders our perception of music's time dimension. We can train ourselves to listen to the way time passes in a piece of music by analysing what we hear while it is in progress – i.e. solely from what we can learn by listening without the aid of a score.

Electro-acoustic music is particularly useful here because in most cases there are no scores – at least, not in the conventional sense. What we learn from careful listening is more or less what the composer also would have learned in the process of making the piece. We participate in those aural judgements and decisions. We consider the nature and the quality of the materials; how they have been developed, and how they might have been developed. Above all, we have to evaluate

- the pace of the musical events

in relation to

- the quality and characteristics of the ideas within
- the time the music appears to be taking

to fulfil

- its eventual duration.

It is upon these relationships more than anything else that the success or failure of music depends.[1]

How can we decide such things purely by what we hear? In fact there is no better way. When all is said and done, music is an aural art, and if it satisfies us at all it does so through our sense of hearing. It is, of course, an intellectual process. We have to do rather more than just let the sound wash over us!

As we listen to music our minds are receiving and processing the sensations of the musical ideas and what happens to them, relating those sensations to the timescape they seem to want to occupy. That is to say, the mind assesses the musical qualities of the ideas and computes the overall timespace needed to exploit those qualities. As the music comes to an end, those expectations will be confirmed if the timepace (i.e. the rate at which the mind's predictions have been fulfilled) was 'correct'. We shall probably then feel satisfaction with the music, and find we like it; not only because of the intrinsic interest of individual ideas or developments, but also because we recognise that those particular musical materials were managed in exactly the right way for that specific timescape. It goes without

[1] This has something in common with making judgements about the built environment. If a new building is being put up we may be anxious to see how it will work in the space available and in relation to other buildings around it. We assess the quality of the architect's ideas mainly in relation to the position and the imaginative use of space. In the end, it matters little that the ideas are exciting in themselves if they do not fulfil that space – which is rather more than merely fitting in with the other buildings. Relationships between the decorative features, the dynamic of the structural elements, the dimensions of the building, and the townscape in which it stands, are in parallel with the ideas, the time-pace, the time-space and the time-scape of a piece of music.

saying that we must have some sympathy with the musical ideas in the first place; or at very least be prepared to 'suspend disbelief' while we listen.

A passing phase
by Nye Parry

This piece was composed almost entirely by direct aural judgement, with very few pre-conceived ideas and no pre-compositional calculation. The composer recalls how he went into the studio and worked with the sound materials, exploring various possibilities 'until it came right'.

Getting it to 'come right' must have involved important qualitative judgements about the musical ideas, their relationships and developments; and strategic decisions about the timing of events relative to the overall conception of the piece. Those decisions would have been taken largely on the basis of subjective reactions informed by imagination and sensitivity. In retrospect, students can observe the results and, by working backwards, as it were, participate in the decisions.

In this assignment it is essential that students should be able to listen to the recording of *A passing phase* as many times as necessary. It should not be treated as an aural test but rather as creative detective work. They can do this individually or by way of small group discussion, but preferably not as a whole class group.

They should be expected to discover as much as they can about:

- the materials (i.e. the basis of the musical ideas)
- the ideas (i.e. what the composer makes of the materials)
- the structure (i.e. how the ideas are developed and how they are used structurally to create the form of the piece)

Musical materials

a. A 'click' (akin to a light stroke on a side drum). This develops into reverberating sounds (like things dropping and bouncing). It was produced by delay techniques on a drum machine.

b. A six-note melodic ostinato (synthesizer, computer controlled: i.e. not a tape loop)

c. A whisper (solo voice appearing to gather other voices)

d. A quiet electronic hum

e. A 'band' (organ, guitar and bass guitar): again, synthesized

f. A 'party in progress' (apparently lots of people enjoying themselves). This, like the 'whisper', was produced by one voice (the composer's), multi-tracked, delayed and shifted

g. An electric guitar (i.e. not synthesized).

Musical ideas

i. The ostinato. This is clearly the single most important idea. It quite literally marks time, but in a subtle and often surprising way.

The repetition of this unit of notes and rests gradually establishes a sensation of pulse (at about ♩ = 110). It has a habit of not always appearing precisely when we expect it, and although it raises our expectations, at a crucial point in its progress it 'misses' entirely. Interestingly, this does not have a recessive effect.[2] Instead, the unexpected asymmetry draws attention to that moment as one of those strategic points where 'things legitimately stick together';[3] a point of strength which holds up the structure and from which it is carried forward in an unmistakably significant manner.

ii. The Band. The ostinato stays with us from start to finish: an archetypal symbol of time passing. However, its temporary link with The Band is structurally very important. Like every other idea in this piece (except the ostinato), The Band appears as though from nowhere, but counterpointed against the ostinato and out of phase with it by just under half a beat. This crucial combination arrives, happens, and passes on: clearly the 'passing phase' of the title. (Although, as we shall see, that can be applied to many other features of this work.)

iii. The Party. The speech sounds are heard as a development of the opening whispering, and they act as a foil to the insistent melodiousness of the ostinato – lest it should cloy! The Party also appears only gradually; hinted at (as though behind closed doors) then disappearing, to return about 30 seconds later. By that time the phasing of the ostinato and The Band is well under way, so that The Band also appears in some way to be phased with the other ideas.

There is a sense, too, in which The Party could symbolise phasing and time passing; and indeed music itself. Its climax is also the climax of the piece as a whole. Its dramatic growth in intensity and excitement parallels the idea of a party as an emotional peak; a social event which we anticipate with pleasure, which has its moment and is gone. A party, like a piece of music, suspends the time of our workaday lives and offers us a substitute model of time.[4]

iv. The electronic hum. This grows alongside the whispering at the

[2] 'There is no excellent beauty that hath not some strangeness in the proportion.' (Francis Bacon, Lord Verulam, *Essays or counsels civil and moral*, no. 43).

[3] See note 4 on page 205.

[4] I can't resist quoting Susanne Langer just one more time! 'All music creates an order of virtual time, in which its sonorous forms move in relation to each other – always and only to each other, for nothing else exists there.' (Susanne K. Langer, *Feeling and form*, p. 109).

And 'Music suspends ordinary time and offers itself as an ideal substitute or equivalent.' (Basil de Selincourt, 'Music and duration' quoted in Langer, p. 110).

beginning of the piece, and is eventually integrated with and modifies the ostinato. Its effect is stabilising; at one and the same time a continuum and a timeless moment; 'time present and time past.'

v. The drum machine 'click'. This also 'marks time', but not as insistently as the ostinato. Its very gradual development is again structurally important. It is the first thing we hear; the merest hint of sound which initiates the ostinato and then begins to articulate the whispering and to create a sense of anticipation as The Band is heard, at first very distantly. Is the drum part of The Band or isn't it? We never really find out. It remains ambiguous, and only after The Band has gone does it come into its own as an essential element of the work's final section. There, the drum sounds, falling, bouncing, turning and changing, seem to guide the ostinato out into the silence.

vi. The guitar keeps a relatively low profile for the most part, except at one point where, in its typically restrained way, it plays a major role. At first it is part of The Band, but after the climax, when the rest of The Band has departed, the guitar sings on; a wistful, bell-like phrase, drooping through distorted pitches in the region of C Bb A. It is an emotionally charged moment which, for all its restraint, generates exactly the amount of progression needed at that point to carry the piece into its final section. Had the idea been more powerful (in the sense of being more clearly defined or louder) it would have overbalanced the texture and had an effect quite the opposite of what is needed here. As it is, we hear it just four times, becoming more distant with each repetition, over a period of about 30 seconds. It is perfectly judged and amazingly effective.

Structure

The duration of the complete work is 4'08". Its structure is broadly 'classic', in that it develops towards a clearly recognisable climax point about two-thirds of the way through, from where it winds down to the end. However, the classic procedures take place alongside the ostinato and the phasing – techniques associated with the very different structural assumptions of 'process' music. The resulting disorientation is both emotionally powerful and intellectually intriguing.

We don't quite know what we should believe about the way this piece works. On the one hand, the 'process' elements seem diametrically opposed to the 'classic' structure; while on the other, the ostinato and Band phasing, linked with the clearly developing texture of The Party, creates a classical climax for the work – and at exactly the right moment! Moreover, the elements themselves appear to carry extra-musical meanings – mysterious whispering voices, a rock band, a 'real' party in progress, 'things that bounce and echo'; meanings made more potent by the way in which the sounds come from nowhere and – very much in the pop music tradition – disappear at the end gradually, repetitively, *a niente*. The final cadence, which the classic structure leads us to expect, never arrives.

These ambiguities, so carefully and sensitively judged, give this music its peculiar charm. In the end we become aware that ideas such as The Band and The Party, apparently loaded with extra-musical references and meanings, are not what they seem to be. Like the two structural devices which simultaneously oppose and derive strength from each other, the quasi-referential characteristics cancel out. Individually they are stimulating, and retain their intrinsic fascination, but they function solely as powerful elements of the structure, independently of which they have no musical meaning.[5]

[5] Cf. Albert Roussel (1929): 'What I would like to achieve is music that is self-contained; music determined to free itself from any suggestion of the picturesque; completely non-descriptive and unassociated with any particular locality in space.' (quoted in A. Hoérée, *Albert Roussel*, p. 66).

The detailed scheme is as follows:

0′00″   drum click

0′02″   ostinato begins

0′18″   whisper begins; slight crescendo

0′37″   electronic hum begins (distant); whisper much louder and continuing its crescendo

0′52″   whisper fades; hum grows very slightly

1′10″   whisper gone

1′14″   drum click

1′20″   drum click

1′26″   organ and bass (very distant): phasing starts

1′32″   ostinato 'misses'

1′37″   drum click

1′50″   party starts – a hint only, then disappears; band and ostinato phasing continue, band growing louder

2′20″   band clear and prominent

2′25″   party starts again; crescendo

2′40″   party at its loudest

2′46″   party cuts off abruptly; ostinato alone, then plus hum

3′01″   guitar, distant

3′10″   fade starts

3′17″   drum click (reverb)

3′32″   drum click (reverb)

3′37″   drum loud and echoing

3′44″   drum click (distant) ostinato alone (fading)

4′08″   finish

Structural proportions

In some of the earlier projects reference has been made to the Golden Section and its application to music as well as to painting and architecture. It would be unwise to make too much of this, but it is interesting to notice how often a composer's intuitive sense of proportion in time-structures coincides with the Golden Section divisions.

Nye Parry did not for one moment consider this relationship while he was composing *A passing phase*. Even so, one is struck by the way in which important events in this piece occur at or very close to GS points:

- GS 3 The whisper disappears and the hum becomes more prominent. Progressive because it suggests that things are now about to develop.

- GS 2 The ostinato 'misses', disturbing the expectations that have been built up. This is a progressive event, heralding new material (the first appearance of The Party).

- GS 1 The Party at its height: the climax point of the whole piece.

And if we take the final section (from the first solo guitar entry after the climax – 'the beginning of the end' – to the point where the last distant sound disappears) we find:

- GS 3 the first of this final series of drum clicks (linking with the start of the piece – as it were, a recapitulation of 'first subject group' material).

- GS 2 The fourth and last of the 'cadential' guitar phrases.

- GS 1 A climax point in this end section: the echoing of the loudest of the 'bouncing' drum sounds. In a truly classic structure this would be that moment of revival that so often signals the arrival of the final cadence. In so far as this piece has a final cadence it must be the two quiet drum clicks that follow this and then allow the ostinato to fade completely into the distance.

It's all in the music

The composer may well feel that this sort of analysis reads far too much into what he has created. He never intended any such thing: all he wanted to do was to make an interesting piece of music!

Obviously, that's true; although it doesn't invalidate the analysis. It tells us simply that there is more than one way of looking at what is happening in a piece of music. The composer's view is a very special one because it is seen from the inside of work in progress: a view of a structure growing. There is, naturally, an emotional investment in the music that is taking shape. And much more than that; in its own way, composing is uncompromisingly analytical: putting ideas and fragments of ideas together; taking them apart again; weighing one possibility against another; selecting this option and rejecting that: a kind of forward analysis, predicting what should happen if it all 'comes right'. The difference between this and the aural analysis we've pursued in the project is that the person at the centre of the composing analysis can have no certain idea of what the outcome will be until the final sound is in place.

There is another, particularly fascinating, feature. During the process of composing, some things seem to come together as if by accident. This is presumably the result of the subconscious mind busily computing all possible relationships and transformations and coming up with the most appropriate solution; the intellect fully engaged with the problems but a lot of work going on behind the scenes. That is hardly surprising. Given the enormous complexity of the task, the sifting and evaluating of perhaps hundreds of different combinations and tiny nuances of sound, it would be impossible for all those operations to be kept at the front of the mind all of the time.

As for the meanings of other connections and correlations that appear as the work proceeds – links with ideas beyond the purely musical, or the potential for deeper significance in this or that aspect; these are unlikely to be apparent to a composer engaged on a piece, simply because full attention must be directed towards the immediate activity of working with the sounds and their transformations. There is literally no opportunity to consider anything else.[6]

And in the end it is the composer who must have sufficient confidence in the work to know when it is complete. Neither critics, nor performers, nor the general public, nor scholars and analysts, but only the composer can sanction a finished work. All technical mastery and all artistic sensibility is directed towards that end: the wholeness of the statement a piece of music makes.

The composer knows when it has come right; knows what the total structure means in its completeness – even without being aware of every possible nuance of the music's mechanism. The mind has done all the analysing necessary to create the music; there would be little point at this stage in going back to unravel the details of how it all came about. It is more likely now that the composer will want to go on to something else.

Why, then, bother to read all these other things into a piece of music; things the composer has no inkling of? Because they are there. The more fanciful interpretations may be open to question, but the structural relationships undeniably exist; even though, by now, they are probably of little importance to the composer, for whom the complete statement of the music is really all that matters. But by observing those connections at work we can learn so much about how the structure behaves and what it is in the music that can give us pleasure.

Composers may not be all that interested in analysis of their own works; after all, they are bound to feel that they have taken those particular musical ideas as far as they can. Artistic confidence in what they've achieved should be sufficient. But analysis of other people's

[6] ' . . . every composer begins with a musical idea – a MUSICAL idea, you understand, not a mental, literary, or extramusical idea . . .' (Aaron Copland, *What to listen for in music*, New York, McGraw-Hill, 1939, p. 23).

work is a different matter. There is not the same kind of emotional commitment to someone else's brainchild. Therefore it is possible to look at it more objectively.

That we must all do if we are in any way involved with composing. We must know a lot of music and we must know it in detail. And we must keep open minds, because the possibilities for making new musical forms are virtually endless.

Analysis won't provide a recipe; it won't enable anyone to make a perfect work of art or to avoid mistakes of judgement. Music is not like a mathematical problem; you can't produce results by calculation. Indeed, if you tried calculating, say, Golden Section points and other structural niceties, the outcome would almost certainly sound forced and banal. But detached observation does reveal important things about mechanisms; and it alerts us to forces that work beneath the surface, sharpening our sensitivity to the potential of our own ideas.

Postscript

Hawksmoor aimed at an indivisible unity, a geometrical pattern which would suffer neither addition nor subtraction and yet possess an intrinsically church-like form.
(John Summerson, *Georgian London*)

Man's quest for integration and unity seems to be an inescapable part of the human condition . . . music is the art which most aptly symbolises this quest.
(Anthony Storr, *Music in relation to Self*)

Contents of the cassette

Track

1. Cathy Berberian, *Stripsody* (extract)

2. Trevor Wishart, *Journey into Space* (two extracts)

3. Wind sounds

4. Birdsong: (a) at normal speed, (b) at half speed

5. Animal sounds: (a) elephant, (b) lioness, (c) chimpanzees

6. (a) Wilfrid Mellers, *Cloud canticle* (extract)
   (b) Harry Partch, *Windsong* (extract)
   (c) Henry Cowell, *The banshee* (extract)

7. Javenese gamelan music

8. (a) Guus Janssen, *Streepjes* (extract)
   (b) John Cage, *String Quartet in four parts* (extract)

9. Big Bill Broonzy, 'Mr Conductor Man' (extract)

10. 11. and 12. Bernard Rands, *Sound Patterns 3* (voice-sound compositions in rehearsal)

13. Bernard Rands, *Sound Patterns 3* (complete performance)

14. Messiaen, *Et exspecto resurrectionem mortuorum* (third section)

15. Nye Parry, *A passing phase*

Index of bibliographical references

General index

absolute music, 93n
abstract art, 17
accompaniments, composing of, 28, 78–9, 134, 138–9, 140–2, 204
Adams, John, 172
aeolian harp, 65, 167–8
affective education, 10
African music, 85, 104–5n, 171, 172
Afro-American, Afro-Caribbean and Asian musics, 28, 82, 85
Akhnaten (Philip Glass), 172
alarm clocks, composition for, 46
aleatory compositions, 160–3, 166–7, 168, 170
Allegro barbaro (Béla Bartók), 64
Alpha and Omega, 16n
ambient sounds, 49
An exciting new game for children of all ages (David Bedford), 170n
analysis, 152n; aural, educates creative listening, 210; cannot provide a recipe for composing, 152n, 217; as a feature of composing, 215–16; functional, 96n
Andriessen, Louis, 172
animal cries, 41, 42
anthropology, 52
appreciation of music, 5, 12, 13, 14; fundamentally subjective, 15; 'innocent ear' approach to, 195; passive, 20; teaching of, 92–3n
apprenti sorcier, L' (Paul Dukas), 18
architecture, 16, 17n, 205n; the built environment, 210n
Arlen, Harold, 201, 205
arranging music, 28
art and nature, relationship between, 36, 38
art objects, 17; artistry in, 124; feeling of obligation towards, 195
art of fugue, The (J.S. Bach), 110
articulation: contrasts of, 72; instrumental, 28, 64, 69; rhythmic, 52
artifice, 119
arts in education, 6, 9–11, 21–2
'As time goes by' (Herman Hupfield), 201, 203, 205
assessment, 6, 9
associative possibilities of art, 17
asymmetry, 212

atmosphere, sounds evoking, 35, 36
atonal music, 134
attack (start of a sound), 34, 71
attainment targets, in the National Curriculum, 22
attentive listening, 12, 19, 35, 85, 124, 210
audiences, attitudes of, 195n
aural analysis, 210, 216
aural awareness, 26
aural judgements, 208, 210, 211
Autumn, Fog and *First star* (John Paynter), 170n

Bach, J.S., 55, 94, 110, 172, 189
Bacon, Francis, Lord Verulam, 212
Bailey, Derek, 90–1, 96n
banshee, The (Henry Cowell), 42
Bartók, Béla, 56, 64, 80n, 82, 83, 84, 139–40, 142, 198n
Bartók (snap) pizzicato, 28
Baschet, François and Bernard (sculptors), 50
beauty, of musical sound, 45, 47, 53, 117, 212n
Bedford, David, 170n
Beethoven, Ludwig van, 42, 153n; sketch books, 205
behavioural psychology, 106
bells, gongs and tam tam, 193, 196, 198
Berberian, Cathy, 36–7
Berio, Luciano, 36, 82
birdsong, 18, 39, 40–1, 42–3, 196n
bitonality, 109
Blake, William, 5, 23
blues, 82, 134; form of, 129; harmonic adventure in, 140–1; 'turnaround', 141; twelve-bar chord pattern of, 128–9; words of, 129
Boulez, Pierre, 73n, 83
Brandenburg Concerto no. 5 (J.S. Bach), 172
Braun, Yehezkel, 110
bridge (of stringed instruments), playing on far side of, 60, 65
broken chords, 54, 56–7, 64
Brown, Earle, 170n
Bruckner, Anton, 166
Bulgarian folk melodies, features of, 198n

cadence(s), 105, 184, 204; final, approach to, 189–90, 191, 207, 214; internal, 185, 186, 205
Cage, John, 18, 49, 65n, 120, 122, 166, 167, 170n
canon by augmentation, 110
Carter, Elliot, 53
cell, melodic, 97
chance, 166–9
chant, 52; Gregorian, 196n
character: of opening figure of melodies, 202; of sounds, motifs, ideas, etc., 29, 39, 44, 69, 71–2, 75, 87, 88, 89, 90, 125, 134, 154, 181, 209, 210
chimes, of wood, metal, glass, 157, 167, 168
'Chopsticks', 62
chords: alternating, 126; as a basis for melodic improvisation, 128, 136–7, 142; derived from melody, 127; new pattern based on form of twelve-bar blues, 129, 142; twelve-note, 133
'Clair de lune' (Debussy), 93n
Clapping music (Steve Reich), 172n
'Clapping piece', 171, 172
Clarke, Edward, 12
climax, 190, 204, 205, 209, 212, 213
clusters, vocal, 182–3, 185, 186, 188
coherence, of composition, 109
collage of sounds, 42, 45, 48, 49
commerce, sounds of, 45
common language of music, 77, 80, 82–3
communication through music, 14–15, 85, 124, 166, 167n
complementary ideas, 144n
'complexity without complication', 153n
composers, strategies of, 216
composing, process of, 47, 136, 153, 178, 181, 185–91; simultaneously analytic and synthetic, 91
composing/performing/listening, in school curriculum, 7, 11–13, 26
composition: analytical, 215–16; aural judgements in, 144, 208, 211; as the basis of musical art, 91n; through chance operations, 167, 169; empirical, 21, 211; in groups, 21; in the school music curriculum, 5, 7, 10, 26, 91

220